JAMES

B. Dale Ellenburg
&
Christopher W. Morgan

I recommend Chris Morgan's and Dale Ellenburg's *James: Wisdom for the Community* to serious students of the Word of God, especially pastors, for five reasons. First, the commentary is closely tied to the text of Scripture. It majors on what a commentary ought to major on – the exposition of Holy Scripture. Second, the writing is clear and accessible. Readers will not be put off by technical nomenclature. Third, unlike many biblical commentaries, this one is theological. It does not skirt the hard issues. It reverberates with the themes of wisdom for the community and the necessity of consistency in the lives of God's people, themes needed to be heard today, as much as by James' original audience. Fourth, it is full of illustrations from Scripture and life that help readers grasp the truth. Fifth, the biblical exposition is applied to life, in a way that James would have approved. All in all, this is a solid and useful commentary written by two pastor-scholars to help the church be the church as God intended.

Robert A. Peterson,
Professor of Systematic Theology,
Covenant Theological Seminary, St Louis, Missouri

The book of James is a book about practical Christian living. James, the half brother of our Lord Jesus, was the pastor of the church in Jerusalem in the First Century. He was a wonderful theologian, but he also was involved in people's lives in a practical way on a daily basis. His writing comes from the heart of a man who understood that Christianity was supposed to produce good works.

Dr. Dale Ellenburg and Dr. Chris Morgan are a lot like James. They are wonderful theologians and serve as pastors. They do not merely study in a cloistered setting, but also are involved in the lives of church members and the people in the communities where they serve. Both are godly men, excellent scholars, and genuine 'shoe-leather Christians.' They live what they believe. That's what James is calling all of us to do. You will learn that as you study the book of James, verse by verse, in this wonderful commentary written by my dear friends."

Steve Gaines
Bellevue Baptist Church, Memphis, Tennessee

JAMES

Wisdom for the Community

B. Dale Ellenburg
and
Christopher W. Morgan

B. Dale Ellenburg was associate pastor at Kirby Woods Baptist Church and Vice-President of Academics at Mid-America Baptist Seminary and is now pastor of Dotson Memorial Baptist Church in Maryville Tennessee

Christopher W. Morgan is Professor of Theology at California Baptist University and Senior Pastor of First Baptist Church of Barstow California.

Copyright © B. Dale Ellenburg & Christopher W. Morgan

ISBN 978-1-84550-335-2

10 9 8 7 6 5 4 3 2 1

Published in 2008
in the
Focus on the Bible Commentary Series
by
Christian Focus Publications Ltd.,
Geanies House, Fearn, Ross-shire,
IV20 1TW, Great Britain

www.christianfocus.com

Cover design by Daniel Van Straaten

Printed and bound by
CPD Wales

Contents

Dedicated with gratitude to our wives,
Constance and Shelley,
for their love and support.

Acknowledgments

Special thanks to California Baptist University for generously granting me (Chris) a sabbatical to work on this project. CBU is a special school, and it is my pleasure to be a part of it. I also want to express my gratitude to Jeff Kennedy – my co-pastor, father-in-law, and friend – for modeling what it means to spend and be spent for Christ and His church. Thanks also to the pastors at The Grove Church in Riverside, California, who helped me wrestle with the meaning and significance of James.

Warmest appreciation to Kirby Woods Baptist Church in Memphis, Tennessee, where I (Dale) had the privilege of preaching the Word throughout the writing of this commentary. You modeled for me what the body should be and do, and I thank my God upon every remembrance of you.

We are grateful to Beth Ann Brown for first-rate editorial assistance, to librarians Terry Brown and Barry Parker for their assistance in research, and to Tony Chute, Chris Compton, Don Dunavant, Robert Peterson, Dan Wilson, Matt Leonard, and Jonathan McCormick for reading the manuscript and offering suggestions.

Thanks again to Malcolm Maclean, Willie MacKenzie, and the team at Christian Focus Publications for their Christian convictions, wise counsel, and accommodating flexibility.

We also want to express our appreciation for pastors around the world who are faithful to their call to preach the Word, love the church, and lead God's people. May the Lord continue to use them to honor His name, strengthen His churches, and reach the lost. May the epistle of James encourage and challenge them as it has us.

Introduction

Why Study James?

The interview process and trial sermon went well, the vote was taken, and now Michael[1] has accepted the call to pastor his first church. 'Pastor Michael, that has a nice ring to it,' he muses. As he dreams of what this church could be, he gladly hangs his freshly printed seminary degree on his new office wall and puts his commentaries on the shelves. He looks out his window at his name that now appears on the church sign. He has high hopes that this church will be like the church of the New Testament – vibrant, holy, unified, and centered on God and His truth.

One year later Pastor Michael realizes that the church leaders were not completely forthright with him about their problems. He finds that some in the church are more interested in religion than following Jesus. They enjoy studying the Bible but never seem to get around to doing what it says. Pastor Michael also observes that some church members display an obvious prejudice against a certain group or groups of people who attend – they are believed to have the wrong color of skin, the wrong socio-economic background, live on the wrong side of the tracks, or in some cases are simply not in the 'insider' clique. The young minister discerns that several suppose that they should be seen as spiritual leaders, but their character and spiritual maturity do not match their view of themselves. And recently, Pastor Michael has received attacks of gossip,

---

1. This story combines those of a few friends and former students. The name is changed.

slander, and criticism – sometimes seemingly innocent but other times unmistakably evil and malicious. Too many people in the church pray for the success of their particular goals and programs but apparently have no interest in the good of the overall church. 'Is this really prayer, or simple rivalry, ambition, and pride in disguise?' he wonders. But the majority of members are not that way, Pastor Michael concludes. They reflect a different sin. Instead, they wear their insincere smiles as they enter the sanctuary and when they are asked how they are doing they express some 'Christianese' platitude or assert that they are 'fine,' even when on the inside they are falling apart. They have exchanged real community for plastic hypocrisy.

Pastor Michael is not sure how to feel or what to do. He knows the New Testament well enough to know that churches are not supposed to be like this. Yet he has heard from his professors, his pastoral mentors, and is finding from his experiences that churches in real life are too often like this – they are not yet fully what God has called them to be. Thankfully, Pastor Michael is convinced of God's call on his life so he does not allow the discouragement to lead him to squelch his commitments by quitting the ministry. But he wants to see something better, something authentic, something effective. He longs to experience the church as it was intended to be. He wants to experience what he sees as the New Testament church: a healthy, vibrant, unified, God-centered, evangelistic covenant community.

So Pastor Michael studies afresh the New Testament to ascertain what this near-perfect New Testament church looks like, but as he does he discovers a frustrating truth – the New Testament does not depict a perfect church and not even a nearly perfect one! He had always assumed that the portrait of the church by Luke in Acts 2 was the norm. But after more careful study, he recalls that even the churches in Acts had tensions related to money, culture, power, tradition, personalities, leadership style, and missionary qualifications and strategies. He then remembers the mess that the church at Corinth had become. Other churches had problems, too, such as Jew-Gentile tensions in Rome, cultural divisions and heretical teaching at Corinth, disunity in Philippi, misunderstandings about Christ in Colosse, and so forth. How had he failed to notice that the apostle Paul addressed the concerns he did because the church needed to hear them? He knew that context mattered but never perceived how that applied to the doctrine of the church.

Like so many others, Michael discovered that the church is not yet what it should be. And this discovery was disheartening. That the church is not what it is supposed to be is not all that surprising for some of us who have served in it for a number of years. To us it is no longer surprising but it remains disturbing.

One book of the Bible that helped me (Chris) come to a better understanding of this hard reality is the epistle of James. Although I had read James many times and had preached from it a few times, I had not detected how James' letter addressed real-life churches with real-life problems. The church that James addressed had a tendency to substitute the performance of religion for a life devoted to Jesus and obedience to His commands. The church struggled with favoritism toward the rich and looked down on the poor, even though most of them were poor themselves and even though the rich exploited them! This believing community had in their ranks people who supposed they were spiritual leaders but were only deceiving themselves because they failed to display genuine spirituality and wisdom through a peaceable spirit, unity, and love. This church had people whose words were so vicious that James points to hell as their source, so vindictive that James equates their words with murder, and so slanderous that he reminds them of the future judgment that will take into account their actions and their speech. This church was composed of some people whose prayers God refused to answer because of their self-seeking, proud, and contentious hearts.

After my careful reading of James, my assessment about the church in the New Testament and today is more realistic. The church is in the now and the not yet, I am finding. It exists in the historical gap where the new age has dawned but has not been realized fully. I knew that of myself and my own Christian pilgrimage but somehow forgot to see the church in that light. This perspective helps me keep my realism from turning to pessimism because I remain convinced that Christ is building His church and is making His bride increasingly more holy. It also keeps me from deeming the status quo as acceptable. It helps me push on to lead the church that Christ, the Chief Shepherd, has entrusted to my care. It leads me to long to pastor God's flock with a wise and seasoned resolve. The church is not yet what it is supposed to be, but neither am I. This perspective pervades James.

In addition to helping us understand the realities and purposes of the Christian community, James addresses other struggles we face in life: trusting God in the midst of our suffering, refusing to give in to temptation, controlling our anger, making sure that we employ our words to edify and not to destroy, maintaining consistency in the Christian life, caring for and ministering to the oppressed, loving people who come from a different socio-economic background, choosing peace over self-centeredness, depending on God in all things, and growing in patience. James deals with all of these and more.

How to Use This Commentary

This commentary is designed to supplement (not be a substitute for) your personal reading and study of James. Our primary purpose is to explain the teachings of James in a way that is helpful to pastors, college students, beginning seminarians, lay teachers and church members. In doing so, the commentary has three parts: 'James in Context' (written by Chris), Commentary (structured by Chris, written primarily by Chris through 1:18, and written primarily by Dale from 1:19–5:20), and 'Theology of James' (written by Chris).

'James in Context' is important because it enables the reader to understand the context of James. Reading without knowing the context is like listening to one part of someone else's conversation – we may only understand a portion of it. So in the introduction, we address questions like: Who wrote this? Who is James? When was it written? To whom was it written? What type of writing is it? What is the style of its writing? How is it structured? What is its primary theme and themes? Seeing the context of James' authorship, date, audience, literary form, structure, and themes will enable the reader to grasp the message of James more carefully and clearly.

Upon this foundation, the reader is encouraged to read the commentary. The commentary contains chapters divided according to the major divisions ('pericopes') of James. For each division, there is a title that is designed to help the reader see the central topic of the particular biblical passage. Each chapter has headings and most have sub-headings. These divisions should help the reader observe the flow of the passage as well as assist teachers and preachers as they wrestle with how to outline or organize their teaching and preaching. Each verse of James will receive comment and explanation in the natural flow of the specific passages. A 'Wisdom to Live By' section is included at the end of each chapter that seeks to point out principles and raise application-oriented questions. If you are reading this individually, hopefully these principles and questions will help you see the central ideas of each chapter and assist you in the living out of the message of each chapter. If you are reading this as a group, then this section will provide discussion topics and study questions.

The third major section seeks to explain the themes and context of James' thought. 'Theology of James' is designed to help the reader see the larger themes and teachings of James. In particular, special attention is given to James' themes of (1) wisdom for the community, (2) consistency in the church and the Christian life, (3) suffering and testing, (4) the poor and rich, (5) words, (6) love and mercy, and (7) prayer. To understand the message of James, these themes need to be grasped. After the primary themes of James are recounted, the teachings of James will be compared to that of other biblical writings/writers. It is here that assessment will be given of how James' message relates to the Old Testament wisdom literature, the Old Testament prophets, the teachings of Jesus, and the writings of Paul (especially addressing the issue of justification by faith).

I

James in Context

Authorship

Who wrote James? At first glance, the answer might seem obvious. The author identifies himself in the letter's greeting as 'James, a servant of God and of the Lord Jesus Christ, to the twelve tribes in the Dispersion: Greetings' (1:1).

New Testament scholars, however, have offered a variety of opinions concerning the authorship of James. Detailed explanations of these authorship debates go beyond the purpose of this commentary. Those investigating such matters can find much helpful material in the best of the more academic commentaries by Peter Davids (New International Greek Testament Commentary), Douglas Moo (Pillar New Testament Commentary), and Ralph Martin (Word Biblical Commentary). For our purposes, we will highlight three major views.

1. James, the brother of Jesus

The epistle claims to be written by someone named James, but it does not elaborate on his identity. This omission suggests that the author was well-known among Christians in the first century.[1] The historic view is that James, the

---

1. Douglas J. Moo, *James*, Tyndale New Testament Commentaries (Grand Rapids: Eerdmans, 1985), 19-20. Herein called Moo (TNTC).

brother of Jesus, is the author.[2] He was the most prominent leader named James in the early church (Matt. 13:55f; Mark 6:3).

Since James is mentioned first on both lists of brothers ('James, Joseph, Simon, and Judas'), it is likely that he was the oldest of those four. This would make him the second oldest of the brothers, after Jesus of course. Though James and the other brothers occasionally accompanied Jesus at particular times in his ministry, both in Galilee (John 2:12) and in Jerusalem (John 7:1-10), they did not believe in Jesus during his earthly ministry (Mark 3:13-21; John 7:5).

But sometime after the resurrection Jesus' physical brothers believed and became his spiritual brothers. John Stott observed: 'It is remarkable, therefore, that during the ten days which elapsed between the Ascension and Pentecost, the brothers of the Lord are specifically mentioned by Luke as finding their place in the believing, praying company of expectant Christians (Acts 1:14).'[3]

What happened? In Paul's testimony of Jesus' resurrection appearances, we catch part of the story:

> For I delivered to you as of first importance what I also received: that Christ died for our sins in accordance with the Scriptures, that he was buried, and that he was raised on the third day in accordance with the Scriptures, and that he appeared to Cephas, then to the twelve. Then he appeared to more than five hundred brothers at one time, most of whom are still alive, though some have fallen asleep. Then he appeared to *James*, then to all the apostles. Last of all, as to one untimely born, he appeared also to me (italics mine; 1 Cor. 15:3-8).

So it is reasonable to conclude that James believed after encountering the risen Christ.

---

2. Because of the virgin birth, it could be argued that this James might be better described as the half-brother of Jesus. For the sake of style, I will refer to him simply as James, the brother of Jesus.

3. John R. W. Stott, rev. by Stephen Motyer, *Men with a Message: An Introduction to the New Testament and Its Writers* (Grand Rapids: Eerdmans, 1994), 120.

As early as AD 44, James was viewed an important leader in the early church, especially among Jewish Christians. For example, after the angel of the Lord rescued Peter from being imprisoned by Herod (who had just killed James, the brother of John), Peter said, 'Tell these things to James and to the brothers' (Acts 12:17). Paul referred to James as an 'apostle' (Gal. 1:18-19) and as a 'pillar' along with Peter and John (Gal. 2:9).

Acts 15 also describes the important role James played in the early church. A major theological and missiological dispute emerged. Some Jewish leaders were maintaining that circumcision was necessary for salvation. Paul and Barnabas opposed these leaders and their views and 'were appointed to go to Jerusalem to the apostles and elders' and address this question (15:2). At this so-called 'Jerusalem Council,' Paul and Barnabas spoke, declaring how God had been genuinely converting the Gentiles. Some Jewish Christians who belonged to the Pharisee's party opposed Paul and Barnabas and their conclusions. Then after much debate among the apostles and elders, Peter delivered a powerful case for God's acceptance of the Gentiles. Paul and Barnabas testified again, and then James spoke. He declared:

> Brothers, listen to me. Simeon has related how God first visited the Gentiles, to take from them a people for his name.... Therefore my judgment is that we should not trouble those of the Gentiles who turn to God, but should write to them to abstain from the things polluted by idols, and from sexual immorality, and from what has been strangled, and from blood. For from ancient generations Moses has had in every city those who proclaim him, for he is read every Sabbath in the synagogues (Acts 15:13-21).

At that point the apostles and elders commissioned a letter to Gentile believers saying essentially what James had just asserted. It is important to note how central a leadership role James played among early Jewish Christians. He had a major seat at the table (maybe the chair?) during the Jerusalem Council, his conclusions regarding the Jewish-

Gentile controversy won the day, and his speech served to solidify the council's decision.

Several of James' followers evidently took their leader's emphasis on Jewish Christianity too far. Some were snubbing table fellowship, and likely refusing to participate in communion, with the Gentiles. Paul confronted the misguided followers of James and insisted on the full acceptance of believing Gentiles (Gal. 2:1-16).

Acts 21:17-26 recounts another episode that involved both Paul and James. Paul and Luke arrived in Jerusalem and went to see James and the elders. Paul told stories of what God had done among the Gentiles. Upon hearing the stories, James and the elders glorified God (21:20). But they also informed Paul that many Jewish Christians had been hearing false reports of his teaching and ministry. The word on the street was that Paul had been undermining the law by telling Jewish Christians not to circumcise their children and not to follow traditional customs. So they encouraged Paul to go into the Temple and publicly perform the rites of purification, which would help silence the rumors and demonstrate his clear commitment to the law of God. At their request, Paul did so.[4]

Beyond these accounts, the information on James is sketchy and based on various reports by early historians. They mention that he was considered the first 'bishop' of Jerusalem and nicknamed 'James the Just' because of his devotion to prayer and faithfulness to the law.[5] Josephus,

---

4. This story is instructive at several turns. First, it shows how people misinterpreted Paul's teaching concerning the law. Paul preached that justification was by faith in Christ, not by the works of the law. But many Jewish Christians likely construed that Paul said the law was unimportant. Paul taught that circumcision was not necessary for salvation, but these rumors maintained that Paul was telling Jewish Christians not to circumcise their children. Second, it also shows how by ministering in Jerusalem, James had to address these concerns (Acts 21:20-21). Paul was preaching the gospel to Gentiles and declaring that Gentiles could be saved apart from the Jewish works of the law. James was preaching the gospel to Jews and needed to show how Christianity is consistent with, the extension of, and the climax of the law and its teachings. Third, it shows Paul's commitment to the spread of the gospel. He did not need to comply with James' request, but realized that doing so would be helpful to James and the others who were sharing the gospel in a largely Jewish context.

5. Moo (TNTC), 20.

the early Jewish historian, stated that James was martyred in Jerusalem in AD 62. Josephus recounted that James was highly regarded by the people of Jerusalem, but feared and hated by the priestly aristocracy that ruled the city. The High Priest, Ananus, had James brought before the Sanhedrin, tried, and stoned.[6]

So then, it must be asked, why is this James, the brother of Jesus, a strong candidate for the author of this letter? First, this James is the only viable James mentioned in the New Testament writings. Second, the testimony of the ancient church supports this as the historical view.[7] Third, the Greek of this epistle contains some striking similarities to that of the brief speech by James recorded in Acts 15:13-21, and to the letter sent under his authority (Acts 15:23-29). Moo maintains:

> The epistolary 'greeting' (*cairein*) occurs in James 1:1 and Acts 15:23, but only one other time in the New Testament; the use of name (*onoma*) as the subject of the passive verb 'call' (*kalew*) is peculiar, yet occurs both in James 2:7 and Acts 15:17; the appeal 'listen, my brothers' is found both in James 2:5 and Acts 15:13; and there are other slight similarities. These parallels are certainly not numerous enough to provide proof of common origin, yet they are suggestive when taken in conjunction with the first two points.[8]

Fourth, the Jewish flavor of the epistle seems consistent with what we know about James, the brother of Jesus. The Old Testament allusions, proverbial nature of the wisdom sections, the prophetic style of admonitions, the reference to the synagogue, and strong monotheistic emphasis all resonate with the biblical accounts of this James.

Fifth, the teachings of Jesus, especially in the Sermon on the Mount, reflected in this letter are striking. This too would be appropriate from the brother of Jesus who was with Him on certain parts of His earthly ministry.

---

6. Stott, 121-23.
7. Moo (TNTC), 22.
8. Moo (TNTC), 22. See also J. B. Mayor, *The Epistle of St. James*, 2d ed. (London: Macmillan, 1913), iii-iv.

Finally, James' leadership position in the early Jewish Christian church would have made it natural for him to address authoritatively the needs and concerns of the 'twelve tribes in the Dispersion' (1:1).

2. Another James or unknown Christian leader

Some scholars believe that certain characteristics of this epistle are inconsistent with the traditional view of James, the brother of Jesus, being the author. So they suggest another James or an unknown Christian leader in the early church as the author. Below are three of their major arguments against the traditional view.

First, some scholars maintain that it is hard to believe that the brother of Jesus would not have mentioned, or at least alluded to, that relationship in the letter. Such a relationship would have only bolstered his authority to speak and the audience's likelihood to follow his instructions.

Second, some scholars also point to the language and cultural background of the epistle as inconsistent with the author being James, the brother of Jesus. Ralph Martin contends:

> Aside from the issue of direct authorship, the most secure conclusion is that this document – whether in epistolary form or not – betrays a debt to the literary conventions and idioms of Hellenistic Judaism. It may have some connection with James in Jerusalem; but its final author, whether as redactor or amanuensis, was well versed in the bilingual vocabulary and writing techniques of the Roman provinces.[9]

Though not personally holding to the view, Moo recounts the argument clearly: 'James is written in idiomatic Hellenistic Greek, with some literary flourishes (cf. the incomplete hexameter in 1:17), and occasionally employs language derived from Greek philosophy and religion (e.g. 'the cycle of nature' in 3:6).'[10]

Third, some suggest that the theological use of law in the epistle varies from the heavy commitment to the law

---

9. Ralph P. Martin, *James*, Word Biblical Commentary (Waco: Word, 1988), lxx.
10. Moo (TNTC), 24-25.

found in James, the Lord's brother. The epistle depicts the law (i.e. Torah) as 'the law of liberty' (1:25; 2:12) and 'the royal law' (2:8) and focuses on the moral law, with no mention of the ceremonial law. This, it is argued, does not fit together well with Jesus' brother's emphasis on the law, including his particular stress on the ceremonial and ritual aspects of the law.[11]

So what are their alternative suggestions? A few argue that it was written pseudonymously (written under the false name of James by someone or a community in the tradition of James for the purpose of authority and the continuing of the legacy of his teaching). Peter Davids dismantles that hypothesis: 'Against the theory of pseudonymous authorship stands the simplicity of the greeting, the lack of exalted titles ('brother of the Lord,' 'elder in Jerusalem,' or 'apostle of Christ'); for a pseudonymous author would most likely identify his James better and would stress his authority.'[12] And in our opinion, the claim for a pseudonymous author seems rather inconsistent with James 1:1 and a verbal, plenary view of the inspiration of Scripture.[13]

Others maintain that the author could have been another James mentioned in the New Testament, or maybe even one who went unmentioned, since James (*jIakobos*) was a common name. The New Testament records at least three distinct men named James, besides Jesus' brother.

First, there was James, the son of Zebedee. This James became a follower of Christ near the outset of Christ's ministry (Mark 1:19). One of the twelve disciples, James was often mentioned with his more legendary brother John, and evidently was a member of Jesus' inner circle (with John and Peter). James, the son of Zebedee, was beheaded at the command of Herod Agrippa I in AD 44 (Acts 12:1-2).

---

11. Martin, lxx-lxxi. For an assessment of these arguments, see Moo (TNTC), 23-28.

12. Peter H. Davids, *The Epistle of James*, New International Greek New Testament Commentary (Grand Rapids: Eerdmans, 1982), 9.

13. For a case for the acceptability of pseudonymous or pseudepigraphal writing of New Testament documents, see James D. G. Dunn, 'Pseudepigraphy' in *Dictionary of Later New Testament and Its Developments*, eds. Ralph P. Martin and Peter H. Davids (Downers Grove, IL: InterVarsity, 1997), 977-84. Dictionary herein called *DLNT*.

A second James was the son of Alphaeus (Mark 3:18). He too was a member of the twelve. He is only mentioned in Mark 3:18, unless he is the same person as James the 'lesser' or 'younger' referenced in Mark 15:40 (simply 'James' in the parallel in Matt. 27:56).[14]

There was a third James who was the father of Judas. This Judas, distinguished from the infamous Judas Iscariot (John 14:22), is listed as one of the twelve disciples in Luke 6:16 (cf. Acts 1:13). Evidently, this Judas is also called Thaddaeus in Matthew 10:3 and Mark 3:18.

These alternatives, however, are problematic. James, the brother of John, is an unlikely author because he was beheaded at the command of Herod Agrippa I in AD 44. It is highly unlikely that this letter was written before then. Most scholars also reject the latter two James because they would have needed to explain their identities if the 'twelve tribes in the Dispersion' were expected to submit to their authority. Nevertheless, it remains a possibility that another James or unknown Christian leader penned this epistle.

3. Two-stage development: teaching from James, the brother of Jesus, and the later redaction of the teaching into an epistle

The third major view seeks to combine the best of both of the previous positions and is sort of a middle-ground position. It holds that James, the Lord's brother, is responsible for the teachings of the letter, but that the letter itself may have been composed by another person or by a Christian community. Various forms of this view exist. Two prominent scholars who defend a two-stage development view are Ralph Martin and Peter Davids.

Martin suggests that the letter originated with the teaching of James, the brother of Jesus, who was martyred in approximately AD 62. Then after the Jewish War of AD 66–70, the community of which James had been a part left Palestine and settled in Syria. There they continued to

14. Moo (TNTC), 19.

follow the teachings of James, refined them, and created a letter, the epistle we know as James, to address a pressing pastoral problem (which will be discussed later in this chapter).[15]

Davids maintains that some of the material in James points to an early date, between AD 40 and the Jerusalem Council in about AD 50. He supports this from the self-designation of the author, the strong Jewish influence, the use of a preliterary tradition of the words of Jesus, and the lack of a developed Christology. Yet Davids also finds evidence of a later date from the Greek idiom, the contextual factors that would occasion such strong teaching on poverty and wealth, and some similarities to the Apostolic Fathers. He theorizes that the teachings of James, the Lord's brother, stands behind the source material, but that he received assistance in the editing of this material, either during his lifetime or that his material was edited at a later date (perhaps after his death) as the church spread beyond Jerusalem and began to use Greek more exclusively.[16]

To conclude, though it seems possible that an unknown James wrote this letter, and though the two-stage hypotheses of Martin and Davids have merit, both are unnecessary. We are most convinced by the historic view, namely that James, the brother of Jesus, stands behind this entire epistle.

Date

If James, the brother of Jesus, is indeed the author of this letter, then it must have been written before AD 62, the date Josephus reported for James' martyrdom. The lack of any reference to the issues surrounding the Jerusalem Council (e.g. Law, Gentiles, kosher food, etc.) seems to point to a date prior to the Jerusalem Council, which occurred in approximately AD 50. The references to severe poverty would especially make sense if the letter of James were written after AD 46 and the time of the famine in Jerusalem (Acts 11:28). This would also coincide with the initial versions of the social, political, and religious upheavals that

15. Martin, lxvii-lxxvii.
16. Davids, 22.

culminated in the Jewish war of rebellion in AD 66–70.[17] This dating also seems consistent with the strong emphasis on the traditions of Jesus' teaching, with the church depicted as a 'synagogue,' and the letter's dependence on Jewish sources.[18] Thus, we tentatively propose a date between AD 46 and 49. If this is correct, James would be the earliest book written to be included in the New Testament.[19]

Audience

Though a detailed understanding of the historical situation and audience cannot be gleaned from James, a basic reconstruction of the recipients is possible and does lend some insight for interpreting the letter. The letter indicates information about the audience, sometimes explicitly, but most often implicitly.

One characteristic of the audience is clear: the recipients were primarily, if not exclusively, Jewish Christians. Throughout James are references to Jewish institutions and beliefs. These Christians met in a 'synagogue' (2:2) with 'elders' (5:14). They worship a God who is immutably holy (1:13-15) and are committed monotheists (2:19). They view God as the unique Judge and Lawgiver (4:12). James expects them to deem as authoritative his references to Abraham, Rahab, and Elijah. They also understand Old Testament imagery of the marriage relationship as a covenant between God and His people (4:4). It also seems that James 1:1 corroborates that the recipients were primarily Jewish Christians.

Where did these Jewish Christians live? James 1:1 states that the letter was addressed, 'To the twelve tribes in the Dispersion.'[20] Most scholars view this literally, as referring to Jewish Christians who were scattered among the nations. Other scholars are quick to point out that this phrase was

---

17. Douglas J. Moo, *The Letter of James*, Pillar New Testament Commentary (Grand Rapids: Eerdmans, 2000), 25-27. Herein called, Moo (PNTC).

18. Moo (PNTC), 26.

19. This of course also depends on how one dates the Gospel of Mark and Paul's epistle to the Galatians.

20. For an insightful article on the Diaspora, see P. R. Trebilco, 'Diaspora Judaism,' in *DLNT*, 287-300.

used in intertestamental Judaism as a reference for the true people of God in the last days. It was also used in this way by Peter (1 Pet. 1:1). So it is unclear whether these Jewish Christians were located in Palestine and given this label as an encouragement to stand firm through the trials because of the eschatological hope they possessed, or whether they were literally scattered among the nations and lived the realities of Diaspora Judaism.[21]

A careful reading of James provides other insights into the audience. We find that these Jewish Christians were a part of a local congregation ('synagogue' in 2:2) with teachers (3:1) and elders (5:14). Evidently James is addressing a particular church with specific problems. These believers were experiencing significant trials (1:2f) and serious oppression (2:6; 5:1-11). Some in their ranks were claiming they had faith but had little concern for personal holiness (1:22-25; 4:4) and failed to assist the poor or the marginalized (1:26-27; 2:1-13; 2:14-26). The congregation also included others who were quarrelsome, creating factions rather than peace (3:13-4:10).

It is difficult to reconstruct with precision the socio-economic level of the recipients. James 1:9-11 refers to 'the lowly brother' who will ultimately be exalted. This suggests recipients who were low on the socio-economic scale. Yet James 2:1-13 evaluates how these recipients have treated the rich who attend their assembly in comparison to those who come and are poor with 'shabby clothes.' Some of the members of the church gave preferential treatment to the rich and dishonored the poor, which was particularly problematic since most of them were poor (2:6). It also seems from the commands in James 2:14-26 that the recipients were generally able to meet the needs of those fellow church members who were poorly clothed and in need of daily food. From this it appears that there was a certain minority in the church who had major financial needs, but also a larger group that was not severely poor.

---

21. For a helpful article on the interpretive options and ramifications concerning James' meaning of the twelve tribes of the Diaspora, see Robert W. Wall, 'James, Letter of,' in *DLNT*, 548-51. Herein called Wall (*DLNT*).

The majority at least had decent clothes and daily food, and even enough resources to help their fellow believers. There also must have been some who were wealthy enough to receive James' exhortation in 4:13: 'Come now, you who say, "Today or tomorrow we will go into such and such a town and spend a year there and trade and make a profit."' Such an exhortation makes little sense unless there were at least some in the congregation who were merchants. James also addresses the rich in 1:9-11 and 5:1-6, and from this some have concluded that the congregation must have included wealthy landowners. That is highly improbable, though, since James depicts such people suffering future punishment in hell. Instead, it is more likely that James is using the rhetorical style reminiscent of some of the Old Testament prophets and condemning people outside the fellowship.

In conclusion, this reconstruction of the audience suggests four distinct groups referred to in this epistle:

- The poor (the majority in this believing community)
- The severely poor (those referenced as without decent clothes and often in need of daily food)
- The merchants (those who were tempted to be over-confident in their ability to buy, sell, and make a profit)
- The wealthy landowners (those who were exploiting and persecuting the poor in the believing community).[22]

The congregation itself was composed of the first three groups, with the majority being poor.

---

22. More than one hundred years before the writing of James, the Roman general Pompey had cut Judean territory and left many Jewish peasants without land. Later the extreme taxation by Herod the Great drove more small farmers out of business. The result was that in the first century many peasants worked as tenants on larger, feudal estates while others became day laborers in the marketplaces, hoping to find good work and often finding it only seasonally (around harvest). Resentment against aristocratic owners was significant and often well deserved. See Craig Keener, *The IVP Bible Background Commentary* (Downers Grove, IL: InterVarsity, 1993), 688.

Literary Form and Style

Language and Style

Most New Testament and Greek scholars agree that James is written in a fairly elevated form of literary Koine Greek. Peter Davids asserts:

> This can be concluded from a host of observations: the use of subordination (with conjunctions) and participial constructions rather than coordination, the careful control of word order (e.g. the placing of the stressed object before the verb, the separation of correlated sentence elements for emphasis as in 1:2; 3:3, 8; 5:10), the relative lack of barbarisms and anacolutha [i.e. an abrupt change in grammatical structure], the use of the gnomic aorist (1:11, 24), and choice of vocabulary.... All of these point to a developed literary ability.[23]

James is also characterized by an unusual vocabulary. J. B. Mayor pointed to 63 New Testament *hapax legomena* (a word only found in James, not in any other New Testament document) in the letter.[24] Davids maintains that 13 of these 63 appear in James for the first time in Greek, while 45 are found in the Septuagint, a pre-Christian Greek translation of the Old Testament.[25]

It also seems that the language of James includes Semitisms. Some examples of the Hebrew influence on the style include the use of the passive to avoid stating God's name (1:5, 5:15) and parallelism (1:9, 11, 13; 4:8-9; 5:4). Further evidence of Jewish background includes that the believers gather in the synagogue (2:2), acknowledge Abraham as their 'father' (2:21), and know God as 'Lord of hosts' (5:4, the only time this is used in the New Testament). At minimum the thought world of James incorporates Jewish concepts and ideas.[26]

In addition, James' use of analogy is especially prominent. He makes analogies of waves driven and tossed by the sea (1:6), withering plants (1:10-11), looking into a

---

23. Davids, 58.
24. Mayor, ccxlvi-ccxlviii. I owe this insight to Davids.
25. Davids, 58-59.
26. Ibid, 59.

mirror (1:23), a dead body (2:26), bridling of a horse (3:3), a rudder turning a ship (3:4), a forest fire (3:5-6), taming wild beasts (3:7), the absurd fountain of fresh and bitter water (3:11), the absurd vine of grapes and figs (3:12), the vanishing vapor (4:14), clothes eaten by moths (5:2), and farmers waiting for the harvest (5:7).[27]

One of the most striking literary features in James is his use of hook words or phrases that link together clauses and sentences.[28] For example, notice how patience (1:3-4), maturity (1:4-5), asking (1:5-6), testing/temptation (1:12-14), lust (1:14-15), and anger (1:19-20) are used in this way.

Form

As is evident from James 1:1, the genre of James is *epistle*. It opens with an address that clearly mentions its author, recipients, and general occasion.

Though James' primary form is as an epistle, other literary forms can and should be detected within its epistolary genre. For example, James is also *paraenesis* (exhortation). Paraenesis is 'a genre of ancient moral literature characterized by various collections of moral sayings and essays, loosely held together by common themes and linking catchwords but without literary rhyme, theological reason or specific spatial location.'[29] Its dominant mood is imperative, and the primary exhortation is virtuous living. It often points to moral truth that all should accept and heroic examples that all should imitate. This approach characterizes James.

Many scholars also suggest that James in some ways bears the imprints of oral composition. It is possible that the material was originally a collection of *sermons* by James later put into writing as a letter under his authority and oversight.[30]

---

27. Kurt A. Richardson, *James*, New American Commentary (Broadman & Holman, 1997), 24.

28. This is called duadiplosis, or paronomasia.

29. Wall (*DLNT*), 551.

30. C. L. Church, 'A Forschungsgeschichte on the Literary Character of the Epistle of James,' (Ph.D. diss., The Southern Baptist Theological Seminary, 1990), 255-61.

Davids maintains that a variety of elements in James not only demonstrate the author's literary skill, but also his accomplished rhetorical style and ability in oral composition. He bases this on James' overall flow and rhythm, along with the particular usage of paronomasia (1:1-2), parechesis (1:24), alliteration (1:2), rhyme (1:6), and similarity in word sounds (3:17).[31] There are also several indications of an oral style in James. Davids makes this observation because of the relatively short sentence structure, frequent use of the imperative (49 in 108 verses), the forms of direct address (17 occurrences of the vocative, primarily 'brothers'), vivid examples, personification (1:15, 23), simile (1:6, 10-11; 5:7), rhetorical questions (2:6-7, 14, 17; 4:1, 5), and negative terms (2:20; 4:4, 8).[32] Davids concludes, 'All of these examples together show that despite its careful literary crafting, the letter partakes of the characteristics of oral rather than written discourse.'[33]

Structure

Attempts to uncover a structure in James have resulted in several different conclusions. First, some find little or no literary strategy and structure. The German Reformer Martin Luther represented this approach when he complained that James threw things together chaotically.[34] In a more modern and careful way, Martin Dibelius approached James as having minimal structure, viewing it primarily as paraenesis and thus a loosely strung together collection of exhortations.[35] Others, however, have correctly noted structure and progression. Following the trajectory of Fred Francis,[36] Davids argues that James is a

---

31. Davids, 58.
32. Ibid, 58.
33. Ibid, 58.
34. Martin Luther, 'Preface to the New Testament' (1522), in Luther's *Works* 33:397. I owe this insight to Moo (PNTC), 43.
35. Martin Dibelius, *A Commentary on the Epistle of James*, rev. by Heinrich Greeven, Hermeneia Commentary (Philadelphia: Fortress, 1976), 1-11.
36. Fred O. Francis, 'The Form and Function of the Opening and Closing Paragraphs of James and 1 John,' *Zeitschrift für die neutestamentliche Wissenschaft* 61 (1970): 110-26.

'carefully constructed work.'[37] Finally, some scholars like Moo proffer that James does display key motifs that are replayed and interwoven throughout the letter, but that his structure is not as neat as some suggest.[38]

A few of the more insightful structures proposed by top scholars are listed below. Robert Wall puts forward the following structure:

1. Thematic Introduction (1:1-21)
2. The Wisdom of 'Quick to Hear' (1:22–2:26)
3. The Wisdom of 'Slow to Speak' (3:1-18)
4. The Wisdom of 'Slow to Anger' (4:1–5:6)
5. Concluding Exhortations (5:7-20)[39]

Peter Davids proposes:

1. Epistolary Introduction (1:1)
2. Opening Statement (1:2-27)
3. The Excellence of Poverty and Generosity (2:1-26; develops the theme of 1:9-11, 22-25)
4. The Demand for Pure Speech (3:1–4:12; develops the theme of 1:5-8, 19-21)
5. Testing through Wealth (4:13–5:6; develops the theme of 1:2-4, 12-18)
6. Closing Statement (5:7-20)[40]

Ralph Martin suggests the following plan for the letter:

1. Address and Greeting (1:1)
2. Enduring Trials (1:2-19a)
3. Applying the Word (1:19b–3:18)
4. Witnessing to Divine Providence (4:1–5:20)[41]

Douglas Moo sees James as developing themes surrounding spiritual wholeness:

---

37. Davids, 25.
38. Moo (PNTC), 45.
39. Wall (*DLNT*), 557-59.
40. Davids, 22-29.
41. Martin, ciii-civ.

1. Address and Greeting (1:1)
2. The Pursuit of Spiritual Wholeness: The Opportunity Afforded by Trials (1:2-18)
3. The Evidence of Spiritual Wholeness: Obedience to the Word (1:19–2:26)
4. The Community Dimension of Spiritual Wholeness: Pure Speech and Peace, Part 1 (3:1–4:3)
5. A Summons to Spiritual Wholeness (4:4-10)
6. The Community Dimension of Spiritual Wholeness: Pure Speech and Peace, Part 2 (4:11-12)
7. The Worldview of Spiritual Wholeness: Understanding Time and Eternity (4:13–5:11)
8. Concluding Exhortations (5:12-20)[42]

Perhaps the best recent proposal for James' structure has come from Mark Taylor and George Guthrie.[43]

1:1   The Opening of the Letter

1:2-27 Double Introduction: Living by Righteous Wisdom
    1:2-11   Handling Trials with Righteous Wisdom

        1:2-4   The Spiritual Benefit of Trials
        1:5-8   The Need for Righteous Wisdom
        1:9-11   Wise Attitudes for the Rich and Poor

    1:12   *Overlapping Transition: Blessings for Those Who Persevere under Trial*

    1:13-27   The Perils of Self-Deception

        1:13-15   Temptation's True Nature
        1:16-19a   Do Not Be Deceived: God Gives the Word
        1:19b-21   Righteous Living through the Word
        1:22-25   Do Not Be Deceived: Be Doers of the Word

---

42. Moo (PNTC), vi-vii, 43-46.

43. Mark E. Taylor and George H. Guthrie, 'The Structure of James,' *Catholic Biblical Quarterly* 68 (2006): 681-705. See also Mark E. Taylor, 'Recent Scholarship on the Structure of James,' *Currents in Biblical Research* 3 (2004): 86-115; idem, *A Text-linguistic Investigation into the Discourse Structure of James* (London: T & T Clark, 2006). See also Luke L. Cheung, *The Genre, Composition, and Hermeneutics of James* (Waynesboro, GA: Paternoster, 2003).

1:26-27   *Transition: Self-Deception Regarding Speaking and Acting*

2:1–5:6 Living the 'Law of Liberty'

A 2:1-11 Body Opening: Violating the Royal Law through Wrong Speaking and Acting Inappropriately toward the Poor

B 2:12-13 *So Speak and So Act as One Being Judged by the Law of Liberty*

C 2:14–3:12 Wrong Acting and Speaking in Community

C1 2:14-26   Wrong Actions toward the Poor

C2 3:1-12   Wrong Speaking

D   Righteous vs. worldly wisdom

CA 4:1-10   Prophetic Rebuke: A Call to Humility and Repentance

CA1 4:1-5   Rebuke of the Community: Wrong Speaking and Acting

CA2 4:6-10A   Call to Repentance

BA 4:11-12 *Do the Law, Do Not Judge It*

AA 4:13–5:6   Body Closing: Twin Calls to the Arrogant Rich (Presumption/Oppression)

AA1 4:13-17A   Rebuke of Arrogant Presumption

AA2 5:1-6   Judgment on the Arrogant Rich

5:7-20 Conclusion: Enduring in Righteous Living in Community

5:7-11   The Need for Patient Endurance
5:12   Transition: An Exhortation against Oath Taking
5:13-20   The Need for Righteous Words in Community

Themes

The epistle of James develops many themes: trials and temptations, the Word and Law, faith and works, words, peace, pride and humility, poverty and wealth, eschatology, patience, and prayer. These themes will be addressed in the commentary as the text of James itself raises them and more fully in the theology section that follows, so there is no need for redundancy here. Two important considerations, however, should be noted before moving to the textual commentary: James' approach to these topics and a central theme.

James' Approach to Thematic Topics

James moves from topic to topic quickly, in a way that leaves most readers who seek to uncover his primary structure scratching their heads. Notice how many topics are addressed in these five chapters: trials and temptations, the Word and Law, faith and works, words, peace, pride and humility, poverty and wealth, eschatology, patience, and prayer. Most topics are treated with at least one paragraph, yet many are interwoven from time to time in a brief, loosely connected way.

It is also helpful to note how Davids understands the structure of James and how he makes connections between topics that are disconnected in the text at times. Davids sees intentional repetition of three major themes touched upon in James 1. The opening statement, he says, introduces these themes and then the rest of James develops them: the first section on poverty and generosity (2:1-26) develops the theme of 1:9-11, 22-25; the section on pure speech (3:1–4:12) develops the theme of 1:5-8, 19-21; and the section on testing through wealth (4:13–5:6) develops the theme of 1:2-4, 12-18.[44]

Though these structural insights by Davids are quite valuable, the theme of poverty, generosity, and wealth may be a bit overemphasized. It could rather be argued that the poverty and wealth emphasis in James serves as both the contextual reality that shape the themes and topics of James and as a theme itself. Poverty and wealth is not the central theme, however, as James does not really develop a synthetic theology of wealth and poverty. Rather he assumes the Old Testament teaching and literary use

---

44. Davids, 22-29.

of the 'poor' as oppressed, cared for by God, and deserving of protection by God's people. The poverty context is crucial, however, since many of the challenges facing the church community evidently related to this: trials, favoritism, faith and works, conflicts, presumption, oppression, patience, etc.

A Central Theme: Wisdom for the Community

Biblical scholars have offered various centers of James – wholeness, faith, obedience, wisdom, caring for the poor, etc. While I am not proposing a center of James per se, I do believe that a central concern in James is wisdom. Wall suggested: 'In my view, wisdom is the orienting concern of this book by which all else is understood: after all, James refers to wisdom as the divine 'word of truth,' which is graciously provided to a faithful people to make sense of their trials and to guide them through those trials in order to insure their future destiny in the new creation.'[45] Taylor and Guthrie's structural analysis also displays how central wisdom is in James. It also depicts the centrality of the community in James. I believe that we should link the two and suggest that a central thematic concern in James is 'wisdom for the community.' In practical terms, what does this mean?

First, I mean that the letter of James has a background and focus that shows it to be an heir of Jewish wisdom literature.[46] Martin maintains that James is a teacher in the Israelite-Jewish tradition and consciously reflects the wisdom traditions. Occasionally James uses language that seems to reflect the Old Testament wisdom traditions when he describes how rich people 'drag' the poor into court (2:6; Job 20:15 LXX[47]), the 'withering' of riches (1:10-11; Job 15:30

---

45. Wall (*DLNT*), 522.

46. For more careful investigations concerning this relationship, see B. R. Halson, 'The Epistle of James: Christian Wisdom?' *Studia Evangelica* 4 (1968): 308-14; J. A. Kirk, 'The Meaning of Wisdom in James: Examination of a Hypothesis,' *New Testament Studies* 16 (1969): 24-38; R. B. Y. Scott, *The Way of Wisdom* (New York: Macmillan, 1971).

47. LXX refers to the Septuagint, a Greek translation of the Hebrew Old Testament, which evidently James used.

LXX), and the call to perseverance (James 1 and 5; Job 15:31 LXX). James also writes with pictures and metaphors that demonstrate his dependence on the Old Testament wisdom traditions. He discusses the brevity of life with the fading flower (1:11; Prov. 27:1; Eccles. 12:6; Job 13:28) as well as referencing the movement of the heavenly bodies (1:16-18; Job 38:33 LXX).[48] James also similarly links wisdom with themes such as the gift of God, peace, prayer, and faith. Thus, James is a Christian epistle with deep roots in the Old Testament wisdom tradition.[49]

Second, by 'wisdom for the community' I also mean that James has a primary concern to dispense wisdom and its practical results. David Hubbard put it well: 'Wisdom takes insights gleaned from the knowledge of God's ways and applies them in the daily walk.'[50] This approach to wisdom is at the heart of James. James applies the truths about God and His ways to such daily issues as trials, temptations, words, wealth, obedience, planning, brevity of life, etc. In doing so, James stresses that our response to these daily challenges must be consistent with God's person and ways. James' frequent opposition to being double-minded and his regular call for a unified wholeness and integrity are consistent with and highlight his practical wisdom approach. Living in a unified and consistent manner is wisdom rightly applied.

Third, I mean by 'wisdom for the community' that James is addressing Christian living from a community/church perspective. James is an ecclesiological document

---

48. Martin, lxxxvii-xc.

49. This is not meant to suggest that James is Jewish wisdom literature. James is thoroughly Christian, is not all that concerned with the intellectual search for wisdom, and does not fit many of the literary categories commonly associated with Jewish wisdom literature. James is a Christian epistle shaped by Old Testament wisdom literature and at most could be characterized as Christian epistolary wisdom literature. I am also not suggesting that its only background is Old Testament wisdom literature. James surely reflects the Old Testament prophetic tradition as is clear from its imperatives and passages like 5:1-6. James also quotes from the Pentateuch at least three times. For a careful approach to these matters, see also Dan G. McCartney, 'The Wisdom of James the Just,' *The Southern Baptist Journal of Theology* 4 (Fall 2000): 52-64.

50. David A. Hubbard, 'Wisdom,' in *The Illustrated Bible Dictionary*, ed. J. D. Douglas (Downers Grove, IL: InterVarsity, 1980), 1650.

that speaks to real-life community concerns. In a sense, most New Testament epistles could be characterized this way. Yet the majority of sermons and commentaries on James neglect this. I must confess that the first two times I preached through the epistle of James (in 1994 at Catron Baptist Church in Catron, Missouri; and in 2001 at First Baptist Church in Barstow, California), most of my sermons focused on the individual applications of the exhortations – facing trials at a personal level, dealing with temptation at a personal level, individual obedience with reference to words, money, etc.[51] Regrettably, I did not notice James' intensely community-centered perspective until the last sermon in the 2001 series. Since that time, however, it has become increasingly clear to me that James is writing with a community emphasis, dealing with church problems, and thinking from a church perspective.

Though some of James' exhortations can correctly be interpreted from an individual standpoint and can be applied individually, a careful reading of James reveals this community emphasis. These Jewish Christians were a part of a local congregation ('synagogue' in 2:2) with teachers (3:1), elders (5:14), and members in need of the church leadership's prayers (5:14-16). These believers were experiencing significant trials (1:2f) and evidently serious oppression (2:6; 5:1-11). Some in their ranks were claiming they had faith but had little concern for personal holiness (1:22-25; 4:4) and failed to assist the poor or the marginalized (1:26-27; 2:1-13). The congregation also included others who were quarrelsome, bringing friction rather than peace (3:13–4:10). Therefore, James is writing to address community problems. His solution? James responds by giving 'wisdom for the community.'

---

51. I am not saying that such sermons are necessarily incorrect. Preachers must give community and individual applications in their messages. I am saying that I failed to notice the intensely community-centered teaching of James and therefore did not adequately apply his teachings at the church level.

2

Address and Greeting
(James 1:1)

James, the brother of Jesus. As explained in 'James in Context' in the Introduction, we hold the traditional view that James, the brother of Jesus, is the author of the epistle (Matt. 13:55f; Mark 6:3).

James, a servant of God and of the Lord Jesus Christ
In a manner reminiscent of the apostle Paul, James' introduction does not stress his position as the leader of the Jerusalem church. He does not mention here that he encountered the risen Christ personally. James does not announce that he is Jesus' brother or Mary's son.[1] Instead, he simply refers to himself as 'a servant of God and of the Lord Jesus Christ' (1:1). In doing so, he demonstrates both humility and authority. The title 'servant' (*doulos*) clearly indicates that his esteem is not tied to his personal agenda but only to his Master. The recipients should listen to James because he represents God and the Lord Jesus Christ.

Yet the title 'servant' also carried with it a connotation of authority. John MacArthur said it clearly:

---

1. This curious lack of reference to his family relationship with Jesus, along with other reasons previously mentioned in 'James in Context,' has led many scholars to reject the traditional view of this letter's authorship.

To be a *doulos* (servant) of God was considered a great honor in Jewish culture. Such Old Testament luminaries as Abraham (Gen. 26:24), Isaac (Gen. 24:14), Jacob (Ezek. 28:25), Job (Job 1:8), Moses (Exod. 14:31), Joshua (Josh. 24:29), Caleb (Num. 14:24), David (2 Sam. 3:18), Isaiah (Isa. 20:3), and Daniel (Dan. 6:20) are described as God's servants. In the New Testament, Epaphras (Col. 4:12), Timothy (Phil. 1:1), Paul (Rom. 1:1), Peter (2 Pet. 1:1), Jude (Jude 1), John (Rev. 1:1), and our Lord Himself (Acts 3:13) all bore the title of *doulos*.[2]

James was 'a servant of God and of the Lord Jesus Christ' (1:1). This is the only place in the New Testament where this exact language is found.[3] If James indeed was written in the late 40s, then the use of the titles 'Lord' and 'Christ' demonstrates how the early Christians viewed Jesus.[4]

To the twelve tribes in the Dispersion
Who were the recipients of James' letter? James 1:1 states that the letter was addressed, 'To the twelve tribes in the Dispersion.'[5] Three main views have been posited by scholars concerning these scattered believers. Most scholars view this literally, as referring to Jewish Christians who are scattered among the nations (cf. Acts 11:19f). Other scholars are quick to point out that this phrase was used in intertestamental Judaism as a reference for the true people of God in the last days. Peter also used it in this way (1 Pet. 1:1). So it is unclear whether these Jewish Christians were located in Palestine and given this label as an encouragement to stand firm through the trials because of the eschatological hope they possessed, or whether they were literally scattered among the nations and lived the realities of Diaspora Judaism.[6]

---

2. John MacArthur, Jr., *James*, (Chicago: Moody, 1998), 12.

3. Martin, 4.

4. Moo (PNTC), 49. In his sermon on Pentecost, Peter also uses these titles of Jesus: 'God has made this Jesus, whom you crucified, both Lord and Christ' (Acts 2:36).

5. Though some of the material below was included in the authorship discussion in 'James in Context,' it may prove helpful to review it for the sake of interpreting James 1:1.

6. See Moo (PNTC), 49.

What other information does James give us to help us understand his audience? One characteristic of the audience is clear: the recipients were primarily, if not exclusively, Jewish Christians. Throughout James are references to Jewish institutions and beliefs. These Christians gather in a 'synagogue' (2:2) with 'elders' (5:14). They worship a God who is immutably holy (1:13-15) and are committed monotheists (2:19). They view God as the unique Judge and Lawgiver (4:12). They understand the Old Testament imagery of the marriage relationship as a covenant between God and His people (4:4).

A careful reading of James also provides other insights into the audience. We find that these Jewish Christians were a part of a local congregation ('synagogue' in 2:2) with teachers (3:1) and elders (5:14). So evidently James is addressing a particular church with specific problems. These believers were experiencing significant trials (1:2f) and evidently serious oppression (2:6; 5:1-11). There were some in their ranks who were claiming they had faith but had little concern for personal holiness (1:22-25; 4:4) and failed to assist the poor or the marginalized (1:26-27; 2:1-13). The congregation also included others who were quarrelsome, bringing friction rather than peace (3:13–4:10).

James 1:9-11 suggests recipients who were low on the socio-economic scale. Yet James 2:1-13 evaluates how these recipients have treated the rich who attend their assembly in comparison to those who come and are poor with 'shabby clothes.' Some of the members of the church gave preferential treatment to the rich and dishonored the poor, which made no sense since most of them were poor (2:6). It also seems from the commands in James 2:14-26 that the recipients were generally able to meet the needs of those fellow church members who were poorly clothed and in need of daily food. From this it appears that there was a certain minority in the church who had major financial needs, but also a larger group that was not poor in any severe sense. The majority at least had decent clothes and daily food, and even enough resources to help their fellow believers. There also appear to have been some who were wealthy enough to receive James' exhortation in 4:13: 'Come now, you who say, "Today or tomorrow we will go into such and such a town and spend a year there and trade and make a profit."' Such an exhortation makes little sense unless at least some in the congregation were merchants. In any event, it seems best to conclude that the audience of James' letter is largely lower class, with a few members who were severely poor and potentially a few members who were well-off financially.

3

Wisdom and Trials
(James 1:2-12)

Two tragedies are at the forefront of the minds of most Americans as I (Chris) stare at my computer. This coming weekend is the anniversary of 9/11 and it reawakens painful memories. Planes crashing. Towers falling. People running. Children crying. Dust covering. Fear intensifying. Firemen sacrificing.

This is also just a week after Hurricane Katrina pounded the Gulf Coast. The power of Katrina's winds and floods is mind-boggling. Electricity knocked out. Thousands of homes completely flooded. Transportation virtually impossible. Corpses floating. Families separated. Shelters overcrowded. Refugees displaced.

Unfortunately, experiences of human suffering are not new. The recipients of James' letter were all too accustomed to such trials. But they were suffering in part because of their Christian faith. Because we live in a sin-cursed, fallen world, we are subject to disasters. Christians, though, must face the reality that some persecution and tribulation will happen to us precisely because we are followers of Christ (cf. Jesus' words in John 16:2, 3, 33). Many believers in our world today understand all too well what James is saying – they too are experiencing persecution for their faith.

James refers to his suffering audience as 'the twelve tribes in the Dispersion.'[1] If we take this literally, which seems to be the most natural interpretation, these believers were exiles and likely experienced all of the trials associated with being forced into a new and strange situation.[2] What is clear is that most of these church members endured poverty, a few even to the point of having only 'shabby clothes' (2:2) and others evidently being destitute of clothes and food (2:14-17). Most of these church members also experienced religious persecution, oppression, and exploitation from the rich landowners. James 2:7 makes it clear that the wealthy were slandering Christ's name, exploiting many poor believers, and dragging them into court. James 5:1-6 also reveals that the rich were withholding daily wages from these believers and condemning them unjustly in the courts. Some may have even died from this exploitation (5:6).

So what encouragement does James offer this suffering community? At first glance, James' exhortation appears shocking, if not downright appalling! James encourages these troubled believers in five ways:

1. Consider it all joy.
2. Realize that perseverance is doing a divine work in you.
3. Ask God for wisdom.
4. View the rich and poor from an eternal perspective.
5. Remember the blessedness that comes from enduring life's trials.

1. Consider it all joy (1:2-3)
Consider it all joy (1:2)
Using a play on words (*charein*, translated 'greetings' in 1:1, is picked up by *charan*, translated 'joy' in 1:2), James urges his readers who faced such circumstances to 'consider it all joy' (the verb is an imperative). This is the heart of James' exhortation in 1:2-11.

---

1. See the comments on 1:1 for more about this designation.
2. Moo (PNTC), 54.

In the Greek text, joy, the object of the verb, is placed first for emphasis. 'Consider' (from *hēgeomai* – 'a deliberate, calculated decision') it 'all joy' (NASB), 'pure joy' (NIV), 'nothing but joy' (NRSV). Believers experiencing such trials are not told simply to 'hang in there' or even to be more detached, as a Stoic philosopher would say. Instead, James asserts that joy is the proper response and perspective for trials.[3] Those familiar with the New Testament find this as no surprise. Paul's teaching on the matter is similar:

> Therefore, since we have been justified by faith, we have peace with God through our Lord Jesus Christ. Through him we have also obtained access by faith into this grace in which we stand, and we rejoice in hope of the glory of God. More than that, we rejoice in our sufferings, knowing that suffering produces endurance, and endurance produces character, and character produces hope, and hope does not put us to shame, because God's love has been poured into our hearts through the Holy Spirit who has been given to us (Rom. 5:1-5).

Peter likewise stresses joy as the suitable response to trials:

> In this you rejoice, though now for a little while, if necessary, you have been grieved by various trials, so that the tested genuineness of your faith – more precious than gold that perishes though it is tested through fire – may be found to result in praise and glory and honor at the revelation of Jesus Christ (1 Pet. 1:6-7).

Yet sometimes we are so familiar with the biblical teachings related to suffering that we forget to be surprised by their claims: count it all joy when you face various trials. Joy? When suffering comes our way we tend to respond with personal tension, or frustration, or even fear – but joy? When trials come we feel a sense of helplessness, as if we are barely hanging on to a piece of driftwood in a sea with the waves taking us wherever they will, and all we feel we can do is hang on for the ride. In such times, how is joy a possible response?

---

3. Davids, 67.

To address this important question, it is crucial that we seek to understand what is and what is not intended from James' command here. James is not offering advice as some self-help or positive thinking guru. He is not saying: 'I know you are hurting, but be positive. Smile. Don't worry; be happy.' Further, James is not offering glib advice that too often comes from well-intentioned but unwise people at times such as funerals. Nor is James saying that suffering is good. The community suffering in view here in 1:2-4 seems to be that of being persecuted and exploited by wicked wealthy landowners. If that is indeed the case, then the suffering is a result of the sin and evil of those landowners. Such actions are castigated later by James in 5:1-6. No, suffering is not considered good here. In Romans 8:28 the apostle Paul corroborates this. It is not that all things that happen in life are good. Not at all. Instead, God works all things together for good to those who love God and are the called according to His purpose.

So what does James intend then? As he does so often in this epistle, James here echoes the teachings of Jesus on suffering and persecution in the Sermon on the Mount:

> Blessed are those who are persecuted for righteousness' sake, for theirs is the kingdom of heaven. Blessed are you when others revile you and persecute you and utter all kinds of evil against you falsely on my account. Rejoice and be glad, for your reward is great in heaven, for so they persecuted the prophets who were before you (Matt. 5:10-12; cf. parallel in Luke 6:22-23).

When you are persecuted on my behalf, Jesus says, rejoice, for you are blessed. The exhortation in James 1:2 to consider it all joy, as well as the emphasis in 1:12 on the blessedness of those who persevere through the tests (which will be treated later in this chapter), echo and reiterate Jesus' encouragement to this hurting believing community. So consider it all joy, James asserts, because, *first*, God blesses those who persevere under such pressure.

Second, not only does James stress the proper response of joy because of the future blessing for those who endure, but he also points to the good by-products of trials. Perseverance, completeness, and blamelessness are worthy effects that come as a result of people having faith in the midst of suffering (1:3-4).[4]

Third, it is important to note that James uses an eschatological contrast to encourage this believing community to consider it all joy even though they are faced with persecution and exploitation by the rich landowners. The rich exploiters will lose and God's people will win. The rich exploiters will be brought down and destroyed, but the humble believers will be exalted and blessed (1:9-11; cf. 5:1-8).[5]

In sum, while the suffering in view in 1:2-12 is a result of human evil, these believers can rest assured that God providentially guides all history and that they will be faced with no circumstance that He ultimately will not use for their good and His glory. Because of this, the believing community are obligated to consider it all joy when they encounter persecution.

Consider it all joy, my brothers (1:2)

Though James often comes across forcefully with his frequent admonitions and imperatives, his preferred address to these believers is warm: 'my brothers.'[6] He uses this throughout the letter (2:1, 14; 3:1, 10, 12; 4:11; 5:7, 9-10, 12, 19). Sometimes he even addresses the community as 'my beloved brothers' (1:16, 19; 2:5). This designation, though common in the New Testament, should not be overlooked. It indicates several important realities. First,

---

4. See also Romans 5:1-5, 2 Corinthians 1:3-7, and 1 Peter 1:5-8 for additional positive effects.

5. Note here what I (Chris) call 'the comfort of hell.' Biblical writers often point to hell as an encouragement to and comfort for the persecuted believers. Hell demonstrates that justice will prevail and reminds the persecuted believers that they will ultimately be vindicated. See also 2 Thessalonians 1:5-11; Revelation 14:9-11; 20:11-15; and 21:8.

6. Obviously, James' use of the masculine term 'brothers' was not intended to exclude the believing community's women, his 'sisters' in the Lord.

we clearly see that James is addressing Christian believers. Second, we should note that James is also stressing that he is united with them in the spiritual family of God. Third, the tone is undoubtedly affectionate, showing the oft-neglected warmth of James.

Consider it all joy ... when ... (1:2)

Notice that James does not say *if* you encounter trials, but *when*. Both the temporal construction (*hotan* with a subjunctive mood) and the verb 'fall' itself suggest the idea of unexpectedness, much like the man who 'fell among thieves' on the way to Jericho (Luke 10:30).

'Trials' comes from the Greek *peirasmos* and can carry either of two connotations: one, a testing or refining to prove one's character, and two, an enticement to evil. Clearly, the first connotation is in view here in 1:2-3 while the latter is the idea later in 1:13. 'Various,' rendered 'divers' in the KJV, is a 'colorful' term. It comes from *poikilos* and means variegated or multicolored. The LXX uses this word to refer to Joseph's coat of many colors in Genesis. Christians can expect challenges to their faith to come in many unexpected shapes, forms, and colors.

By referring to 'trials of various kinds,' James is likely referring to the community sufferings already mentioned (religious persecution, financial exploitation, and resultant poverty). But he also may be writing vaguely enough to ensure that his words apply to those experiencing trials of other forms – physical pain, sickness, death of loved ones, etc.[7] Even as I (Dale) write these words, my dear wife is undergoing chemotherapy following surgery for cancer. It was the last thing we expected and it has proved to be a crucible that has tested our faith in unexpected ways. But we know that God intends to work something good through it all (Rom. 8:28).

It is important to note that trials can and do come to faithful Christians and healthy churches. The proponents of the health and wealth theology need to read afresh passages such as James 1:2-12 and 5:1-8, as well as Romans 5:1-5,

---

7. Moo (PNTC), 54.

2 Corinthians 1:3-7, 1 Peter 1:5-8, and 2 Timothy 3:12. Christians should not be surprised when they face trials. Trials will come, and God aims to use those trials to mature His churches and His people.

Consider it all joy ... knowing ... (1:3)
One of the chief reasons these believers were commanded to consider it all joy when they faced trials was 'because you know that the testing of your faith develops perseverance' (NIV). In this rationale, do not miss the fact that James here associates trials with the testing of faith, which is interesting in light of the context. The trials in view here were brought on by evil, rich landowners. Yet in the midst of these oppressors' sin as the cause of these believers' suffering, James asserts that God is at work using the suffering as a testing of the faith of His people.

What precisely does James mean by the 'testing of your faith'? It is a different word altogether from 'trials' in verse 2. Douglas Moo comments:

> 'Testing' translates a rare Greek word (*dokimion*), which is found elsewhere in the New Testament only in 1 Pet. 1:7 and in the Septuagint only in Ps. 11:7 and Prov. 27:21. Peter apparently uses the word to denote the result of testing; the NIV translates 'genuine.' But the two Old Testament occurrences both denote the process of refining silver or gold, and this is the way James uses the word. The difficulties of life are intended by God to refine our faith: heating it in the crucible of suffering so that impurities might be refined away and so that it might become pure and valuable before the Lord. The 'testing of faith' here, then, is not intended to determine whether a person has faith or not; it is intended to purify faith that already exists.[8]

What does this testing do? It develops perseverance (*hupomonē*). *hupomonē* has been translated perseverance, endurance, steadfastness, fortitude, and patience. Patience is an acceptable translation as long as it is understood to be an active patience. The etymology of *hupomonē* paints a picture of successfully carrying a heavy load for an

---

8. Moo (PNTC), 54-55.

extended period of time. Like a muscle that becomes strong when it faces resistance from a weight, so Christians develop spiritual strength and stamina through facing trials.[9] It is hard to imagine how perseverance could be developed in any way other than by such resistance, since it seems that perseverance presupposes a pressure to endure.

2. Realize that perseverance is doing a divine work in you

When trials come, James says, consider it joy and recognize that God is developing in you perseverance and other good traits. It is also important to observe that the development of perseverance is a process. One event does not bring forth enduring character. It is the real life process of encountering trials and responding to them in faith that produces perseverance.[10]

Let perseverance have its complete work (1:4)

The language here is typical for James as he uses the third-person imperative to say 'let, allow'[11] perseverance to produce three indispensable godly qualities: **maturity, completeness, lacking nothing.** Perseverance is not only an end; it is also a means to further ends: **so that ....** Perseverance, that unswerving tenacity to endure under pressure, will fashion in us:

1. 'Perfection' or maturity. The term does not suggest that we will be faultless and flawless; rather, we will experience the reality that life's trials help us by grace to reach a level of maturity we would not otherwise attain.

2. 'Complete' indicates a fully developed character; 'entire' is a good sense for the word. Together the words describe a well-rounded believer who is mature beyond the norm in Christian growth.

When I (Dale) was working my way through college, I worked in a factory that made parts for the machines

---

9. Moo (PNTC), 55.
10. Davids, 69.
11. James uses this third singular imperative form ('let him, let her, let it') fourteen times in the epistle. Interestingly, seven of them are found in 1:4-19.

used in cotton mills. We took the raw steel and subjected it
to several processes before it was finally fashioned into the
specific parts. One process required that the raw metal be
heated to many thousand degrees and then plunged into
a vat of oil or brine. Through such a process the steel was
purged of its impurities and given a hardness that could
be produced in no other way. In much the same way, God
tempers us through tests and trials.

Let perseverance have its complete work, so that... (1:4)
God intends that the perseverance we learn from testing
and trials not only makes us 'perfect' or 'developed fully,'
but He also develops us into 'complete' believers. This
word comes from *holoklēros*, 'whole, fully furnished.' To
round out the contours of what God intends to accomplish
through such trials and tests, he says we can be 'lacking in
nothing.'

    3. 'Lacking in nothing.' What does God mean by
'lacking nothing?' In the midst of trials, we have received
full spiritual endowment to endure any trial which comes
our way. We lack nothing because we have received 'all
spiritual blessings.' Ephesians 1:3 states, 'Blessed *be* the
God and Father of our Lord Jesus Christ, who hath blessed
us with all spiritual blessings in heavenly *places* in Christ.'

Trials in believers' lives do not represent their spiritual
levels; rather, they provide the opportunity to reveal their
levels and then exercise spiritual attitudes in the situation.
Endurance is work that matures us. Accordingly, God uses
trials that build and repair us where we have breaches in
our spiritual life. Part of working out our salvation is the
enduring of trials that mature us when we approach them
with the proper attitude. The perfecting work of the trials
is the spiritual growth of believers as well as the believing
community.

3. Let anyone lacking wisdom ask God for it in faith (1:5-8)
If we have any hope of persevering under trials the way
James admonishes, we must have God's wisdom, the

ability to see life as God intends and to act accordingly.[12] James links verse 4 with verse 5 by a common theme: 'lacking nothing' in verse 4 with 'if you lack' in verse 5. James knew we would need God's perspective – His wisdom – on our trials if we hope to respond to them in a way that results in perfection and maturity (v. 4). Motyer described this need for wisdom well: 'You are in the thick of such a tangle of circumstances that there is no way it can seem to be anything other than a purposeless mess. There is no stretch of the imagination by which it even begins to look like a stepping-stone to maturity.'[13]

But if any of you lacks wisdom... (1:5)

James states that we need wisdom, *sophia*, not just knowledge, *gnōsis*. The literature on the ideas behind *sophia* in James' day is voluminous and we need not here rehearse it.[14] Real-life trials require real-life answers, and James has little interest in speculative, philosophical notions about wisdom. Here, without question, he speaks of wisdom as the practical use of the knowledge we have, the ability to respond to life's challenges from God's perspective. Or, as one sage put it, 'Knowledge tells us how to take things apart; wisdom shows us how to put them together.'

Let him ask God... (1:5)

Knowing that we need God's wisdom so that our trials will not be wasted, how then do we receive this needed virtue? Quite simply, 'Let him ask from God.' Here is another of James' imperatives; it is the present tense of *aiteō* and could be understood as 'let him keep on asking.' With encouraging and pointed simplicity, he says, 'ask for it and God will give it.'

---

12. For more on wisdom in James, see the 'James in Context' and 'Theology of James' sections of the commentary.
13. J. Alec Motyer, *The Message of James*, The Bible Speaks Today (Downers Grove: InterVarsity, 1985), 37.
14. See the valuable article by Arthur Patzia, 'Wisdom' in *DLNT*, 1200-3.

Let him ask God... and it will be given to him (1:5)
Those who ask will not be disappointed. James makes
three affirmations about this promise.

First, God will give this wisdom 'liberally.' This adverb
(*eaplōs*) occurs only here in the New Testament and its
precise connotation is unclear. Some commentators think
the idea is that God gives 'simply,' with no ulterior motives.
Others say, and we agree, that it refers to the abundant
and unconditionally generous way God gives.

Second, we can ask confidently because God will not
'upbraid' or 'rebuke' us for asking. The word is graphic:
'to cast in one's teeth.' We are assured that God will not
chide or scold us for asking, and for asking often!

Third, we have the simple and sublime promise that
God *will* grant what we ask when we seek His wisdom.

But let him ask in faith with no doubting (1:6)
Verse 5 is positive in tone in every way, but verse 6 issues a
challenge: this wisdom will not come automatically nor is
it gained by self-effort or perfunctory praying. If we want
to receive it, we must ask 'in faith.' 'Ask' is another third-
singular imperative, identical in its present tense to verse 5
and could be translated: 'let him *keep on asking*.' Here we
have an insistence to persevere in prayer.

The opposite of asking in faith is to 'doubt.' 'Doubt'
is from the verb *diakrinō*, meaning 'to judge between.'
To doubt is to have a divided mind that draws us in two
directions. In verse 8 we will see another related word
that describes this condition: 'double-minded.' This
person could be likened to a cork floating on a 'surge of
the sea, driven and tossed by the wind,' drifting first this
way and then that. 'Surge' is different from the normal
word for 'wave.' The only other occurrence of the word is
in Luke 8:24 when the disciples and Jesus are in a storm
at sea and the waves are 'surging' against the boat. That
story serves well to show us a vivid picture of this spiritual
condition of doubting.

Let not that man think he will receive anything... (1:7).
God answers prayer, but prayer that honors Him by our

complete trust. The kind of divided, seasick praying described above cannot expect a divine response. God delights in the person who, with confident faith, 'believes that He is and that He rewards those who seek Him' (Heb. 11:6). We all can sympathize with Jesus' disciples who were rebuked in Matthew 8:26 for their lack of faith. Often I find myself praying as the man who came to Jesus with the demon-possessed son in Mark 9:24, who confessed, 'Lord, I believe, but help my unbelief.' You can have complete confidence, James asserts, that God will give you wisdom if you genuinely desire it.

Being double-minded ... unstable in all his ways (1:8)
Three negative terms describe the person who prays half-heartedly and with uncertainty. 'Doubting' in verse 6 turns to 'double-minded' and 'unstable' here in verse 8. 'Double-minded' translates *dipsuchos*, a term perhaps coined by James and found in the New Testament only here and in 4:8. Literally, it means 'two-souled' or 'divided soul.' We can gain some sense of the idea with our derogatory adjective 'two-faced.' This is akin to John Bunyan's 'Mr. Facing Both Ways' in *Pilgrim's Progress*. Doubting, wavering praying arises from a person with a divided heart, wavering between confidence in a prayer-hearing God and whether it does any good to pray at all. This 'straddling the fence' person is also 'unstable,' an unsteady, fickle, staggering soul who is vacillating not only in prayer but also in his daily walk.

Remember that the immediate context is that of facing trials and difficulties. We need God's wisdom to respond to them correctly so that they will produce in us patience and maturity. We must be sure that God will give us that needed wisdom, because two-faced, double-minded asking means that we do not fully believe God's promises but depend on our own resources.

4. View the rich and poor from an eternal perspective
Continuing the theme of trials in life and our need for wisdom in facing them, James now reminds these poor

believers that being exploited is better than being the exploiters.[15] In this passage James introduces a common theme woven throughout Scripture and especially emphasized by Jesus. Richardson phrased it well, 'A cardinal teaching of the Gospels is the eschatological reversal of status experienced now in fellowship with Jesus (cf. Matt. 19:30; Luke 1:46-55). "Lift up the poor believers now; require the rich believers to humble themselves" would be a correct understanding of James' intent.'[16] In other words, our way of calculating true wealth is not the same as God's. Remember what Jesus said to the faithful church at Smyrna, 'I know your poverty, but you are rich' (Rev. 2:9).

Let the lowly brother boast in his high position (1:9)

Two words stand in contrast here. 'Lowly' is *tapeinos*; 'high position' is *hupsos*. The first means 'humble; of lowly status.' The latter means 'height, high or exalted station.' The 'lowly' brother is of low position, poor, undistinguished in position, power, and esteem. Most of the Christians in James' day faced difficult economic conditions. A vast number were slaves. They were 'lowly,' and thus, likely poor, oppressed, and seemingly unimportant individuals. Christ was literally their only hope.

But the humble brother is actually rich – rich in Christ. He is exalted spiritually. He has a heavenly dignity. He can glory in his high position with Christ. James says, 'So you do have something to **boast** in and that is your position in Christ. The humble person is exalted now. He enjoys his present spiritual status because of his relation to Christ. He has put his trust in Christ and can take His words to heart.' Jesus said, 'Seek first the kingdom of God and His righteousness; and all these things shall be added to you' (Matt. 6:33).

and the rich in his humiliation (1:10-11)

On the other hand, the rich should boast in his humiliation. The Greek is a bit disjointed here. The main verb is not

---

15. For more on the theme of the rich and the poor, see the 'Theology of James' section.
16. Richardson, 70.

repeated but the meaning is clear: God measures wealth and poverty in a very different way from us. Perhaps James is reflecting on a saying of Jesus recorded in Luke 14:11: 'For everyone who exalts himself will be humbled, and he who humbles himself will be exalted.' The rich (*plousios*) man is admonished to consider that he too is a sinner and is no better in the eyes of Christ than the poorest of people. And besides, the rich should remember the fleeting nature of human wealth. A. T. Robertson sums up the admonition wonderfully, 'The cross of Christ lifts up the poor and brings down the high. It is the great leveler of men.'[17]

Linguistically, it is not necessary to view the rich as a believer because the word 'brother' (used for the poor in verse 9) is not repeated. Theologically, it is wiser to interpret the rich as unbelievers because their fate is destruction and ruin. Plus, James' warning seems to echo Jesus' counsel to the rich fool in Luke 12:13-21 as well as the parables of reversal (e.g. Luke 16:19-31).

for as the flower of the grass he passes away (1:10)
The familiar imagery of a burning east wind from the Syrian desert as it dries and withers the grass of the field provides a picturesque description of the temporal nature of human riches. 'Flower of the grass' translates *anthos chortou* and may mean 'wild-flower.' Davids suggests it was like the common anemone or a type of primrose,[18] but at any rate the hot summer sun comes and scorches the fragile flowers. The humble believer has eternal riches but the rich fade away like cut grass on a scorching hot windy day.

scorching wind ... withers the grass ... flower falls off (1:11)
Verse 11 intensifies the gist of the parable by adding a few elements. The sun rises, and a 'scorching wind' withers the tender plants. 'Scorching' translates *kausōni* and refers to the dry, easterly sirocco. It withers the grass and the flowers fall off.

17. A. T. Robertson, *Studies in the Epistle of James* (Nashville: Broadman & Holman, n.d.), 44-47.
18. Davids, 77.

the beauty of its lovely appearance perishes (1:11)
James adds this final phrase to further strengthen the picture of the transitory nature of earthly wealth. 'Beauty' translates a word found only here in the New Testament: *eupeprēs*, meaning 'good or lovely appearance.' 'Appearance' is literally the word 'face.' A rose is a beautiful flower, but it is pitiful when it withers and its 'face' loses its life and color.

It is all too easy to lose sight of the transient worth of riches. They may seem to offer security, but James reminds us that to those whom they become a 'god,' they will perish like a flower in the scorching heat. Why does James include this? How does this relate to the believing community? As he does in 5:1-6, James' goal is to encourage the believers (who are largely poor) by reminding them that rich oppressors will not escape God's just judgment. The rich oppressors ultimately will be bankrupt and oppressed in hell. The poor (in context this refers to believers) will be rich in heaven.

5. Remember the blessedness that comes from enduring life's trials

Blessed is a man who perseveres under trial (1:12). As he does so often, James sounds much like Jesus with his beatitude *makarios*, 'blessed.' The sense is God's approval, quite in contrast to the man described in verses 9-11. We can translate *makarios* as 'blessed, spiritually prosperous, happy, joyful.' The blessedness is linked to persevering under trials. Some translations such as the NKJV render *peirosmos* (trials) with a negative connotation (tempt) here in verse 12, but it is more likely that it still carries the more neutral notion of 'testing or trial.' The negative sense will be James' focus beginning at verse 13 and he is using verse 12 as a transition.[19] The spiritually prosperous man perseveres under trial. It is the verb form of the noun used earlier in 1:3, 'patience.' This is the attitude that lives above

---

19. James often does this. For more, see 'James in Context' as well as the exegesis of 1:13-18.

the chances, changes, and circumstances in life. Such a person will 'consider it all joy when you encounter various trials.' It is only the one who endures that is blessed.

when he has been approved (1:12)

James calls us blessed, or happy beyond measure, because we have been 'approved.' This is the same word used for 'testing' in verse 3. It is *dokimos*, meaning 'approved by testing, tried and true, genuine.' We have passed the test and persevered through the pain to glorify Christ in our trials and suffering.

the crown of life (1:12)

God will honor our faithfulness with the crown (*stephanos*) of life when Jesus comes. James says, 'once he has been approved, he will receive the crown of life which *the Lord* has promised to those who love Him' (v. 12b). Jesus said in Revelation 2:10: 'Do not fear what you are about to suffer. Behold, the devil is about to cast some of you into prison, so that you will be tested, and you will have tribulation for ten days. Be faithful until death, and I will give you the crown of life.'

The crown spoken of here was a head wreath or garland that was given as a victor's prize in the Greek Olympic games. At times it was given to men whom the community wanted to honor, and it was worn in religious and secular feasts. Here it is a 'living crown' in contrast to a fading, perishable crown. It is the crown of life. The crown that consists of eternal life is contrasted with the fading away of earthly prosperity and fame.

Some commentators suggest that James is not only re-ferring to a future crown when we get to heaven, but also to the crown of a rich and full life to be enjoyed here and now. The fires of the furnace have burned away the dross and now our lives reflect the image of Christ. We experience it here and now because it is the life that proceeds from God and will be consummated when we see Jesus face to face. We received this gift of eternal life when we believed on Christ. It is real and lasting life. To endure trials is a proof of this kind of life. William Barclay wrote about this crown promised to those who love God:

> The Christian has a *joy* that no other man can ever have. The Christian has a *royalty* that other men have never realized, for, however humble his earthly circumstances, he is nothing less than the child of God. The Christian has a *victory* which others cannot win, for he meets life and all its demands in the conquering power of the presence and the company of Jesus Christ....[20]

Right now you may be facing head-on a hailstorm of trials that just will not go away. What kind of trials are you enduring? Perhaps it is a wound that can never be healed; physical or emotional scars are deep. They carry with them a weight that will never be lessened. Please remember, when you find yourself in the furnace of suffering, that God is sovereign, knows what He is doing, and wants us to believe the words of the cherished hymn:

> When through fiery trials thy pathway shall lie,
> My grace all sufficient shall be thy supply.
> The flames shall not hurt thee, I only design
> Thy dross to consume and thy gold to refine.

Wisdom to Live By

- We should prepare ourselves for future trials through building up our faith in the present. A fertile prayer life, memorizing Scripture, living in community with faithful believers, and reading the biographies of great Christians who have gone before us – all of these help us to be grounded when the storms of life come.

- We can memorize Scripture, like James 1:2-4, Romans 5:1-5, and Romans 8:18-28.

- We can ask God to use us to encourage someone who is presently facing a difficult trial. We can pray with that person, listen, encourage him or her in tangible ways like preparing a meal, helping with chores, offering financial assistance, etc.

---

20. William Barclay, *The Letters of James and Peter* (Edinburgh: St. Andrew Press, 1960), 57-58.

- Solomon had an open invitation from God to ask for anything he wanted. For what did he ask? Wisdom. God honored that request and was pleased that he asked. James teaches us to do the same – are we asking God for wisdom?

4

Wisdom and Temptation
(James 1:13-18)

Sam Storms quips: 'Death and taxes. If conventional wisdom is to be trusted, they're the only two things of which we may be certain. Well, so much for conventional wisdom. There's a third: temptation.'[1] He is right. None of us will ever completely avoid the lure of temptation.

But what is temptation? I (Chris) decided to see how our contemporary culture would answer that question. So in addition to the more traditional avenues of research, I typed 'temptation' in a Yahoo search on the Internet. It listed the following:

- The Temptations (music group)
- Temptation Island (TV show)
- Temptation (new wave rock magazine)
- Temptations Super Dance Club (bar catering to homosexuals)
- Sweet Temptations (bakery that makes cakes)
- Temptations Café (yogurt and food)
- Tall Temptations (women's clothes)

---

1. Sam Storms, *Pleasures Evermore: The Life-Changing Power of Enjoying God* (Colorado Springs, CO: NavPress, 2000), 247.

- Temptation Online Casino (gambling)
- Chic Temptations (jewelry)
- Wicked Temptations (sexy clothes)
- Various sites about overcoming temptation (Christian living)

Think about that list a minute. Notice what things are considered temptations: from chocolate cake to sex, from women's clothes to casinos, from jewelry to strawberry yogurt! Clearly, our culture uses 'temptation' loosely. Then it dawned on me. Our culture does not take temptation seriously because it does not take sin seriously. Further, it does not take sin seriously because it does not take God seriously.

So how do we contemporary Christians view temptation? Too often we gradually adopt our culture's light attitude about sin and temptation. We can determine if we too have undermined unintentionally the seriousness of sin by how we answer this question: which are we more afraid of – trials or temptation? Be honest. Most of us would have to admit that we are more afraid of a disruptive trial than a temptation. Yet C. H. Spurgeon reminds: 'Earnest Christian men are not so much afraid of trials as of temptations. The great horror of a Christian is sin.'[2]

Nevertheless, the most important question for us is not what our culture thinks of temptation, or even how many Christians view temptation, but what does the Bible teach concerning temptation? While verses that mention temptation abound, none is more thorough or more picturesque than James 1:13-18. Understanding James 1:13-18 is a prerequisite for appreciating the biblical view of temptation. Using the theme of testing as a bridge to the topic of temptation, James puts forth the following teaching:

1. The Nature of Temptation (1:12-13)
2. The Source of Temptation (1:13)

---

2. Tom Carter, ed., *Spurgeon at His Best* (Grand Rapids, MI: Baker, 1988), 203.

3. The Process of Temptation (1:13-15)
4. The Strength for Temptation (1:16-18)

Upon that foundation, James displays the nature of the new birth and offers hope to believers in overcoming temptation.

1. The Nature of Temptation (1:12-13)

Bible translators differ over the placement and interpretation of verse 12 as it relates to verse 13. The NIV translates 1:12: 'Blessed is the man who perseveres under trial, because when he has stood the test, he will receive the crown of life that God has promised to those who love him.' The NRSV reads: 'Blessed is anyone who endures temptation. Such a one has stood the test, and will receive the crown of life that the Lord has promised to those who love him.' As noted in the last chapter, some scholars suggest that 1:12 essentially summarizes 1:1-11 and should be considered with that section. But others maintain that it introduces the topic of temptation. In a sense, both could be right. James has a tendency to employ sentences as bridges from one thought to the next. For example, 1:12 repeats several words already used in 1:1-11: 'trial' (1:2), 'test' (1:3), and 'endure' (1:3-4). Peter Davids concludes: 'With verse 12 one begins the second section of the opening with each theme being repeated in order. Naturally, the author does not simply repeat, but indicates enough overlapping ideas to remind the reader of the previous section and then moves on to develop each concept further.'[3]

As explained in the previous chapter, *peirasmos* (the noun form of the verb translated 'tempted') has the basic meaning of trying, testing, or proving. The word itself is neutral. In 1:2-4, it doubtless carries the idea of being tested by a trial, problem, or difficulty. In 1:13, it clearly refers to temptation, the inducement to evil (see also Matt. 6:13, 26:41; 2 Pet. 2:9). However, biblical commentators differ over its precise connotation in 1:12. It could refer to

3. Davids, 78.

tests or temptations, but most scholars conclude that
it should be understood simply as tests. Regardless,
1:12-13 demonstrate the interconnectedness of tests and
temptation. After all, the primary difference is not in the test
itself but the person's response to it.[4] Warren Wiersbe puts
it well: 'What is the relationship between testings without
and temptations within? Simply this: if we are not careful,
the testings on the outside may become temptations on the
inside. When our circumstances are difficult, we may find
ourselves complaining against God, questioning His love,
and resisting His will.'[5] Since outward trials frequently
provide an occasion for the enticement of sinful attitudes
within,[6] it seems like a natural transition for James to blend
them into his thoughts concerning temptation.

2. The Source of Temptation (1:13)
Let no one say when tempted (1:13)
James uses a diatribe style of oratory by putting words in
the mouth of an imaginary detractor: 'I am tempted by God.'
James answers by saying God is not in the remotest manner
the source of temptation. Moreover, our text does not say
'if' we are tempted but 'when.' It is a present participle and
implies no sense of conditionality – we will face not only
trials but temptations as well, enticements to do wrong. The
next few verses show us why.

Knowing that it is our fallen human nature to place
blame on someone or something other than ourselves,
James first addresses the source of temptation negatively
in 1:13 before he does so positively in 1:14. *First, it is
important to realize that other people are not the source of our
temptations.* The tendency to 'pass the buck' is as old as the
Fall itself. Genesis 3:9-13 recounts the story:

> But the Lord God called to the man, 'Where are you?' He
> answered, 'I heard you in the garden, and I was afraid because

---

4. MacArthur, 45.

5. Warren Wiersbe, *Be Mature: An Expository Study of the Epistle of James*
(Wheaton, IL: Victor, 1982), 35.

6. Thomas D. Lea, *Hebrews and James*, Holman New Testament Commentary (Nashville: Broadman & Holman, 1999), 261.

I was naked; so I hid.' And he said, 'Who told you that you were naked? Have you eaten from the tree that I commanded you not to eat from?' The man said, 'The woman you put here with me – she gave me some fruit from the tree, and I ate it.' Then the LORD God said to the woman, 'What is this you have done?' The woman said, 'The serpent deceived me and I ate.'

When confronted with their sin, instead of confessing it, Adam and Eve tried to shift the blame elsewhere. Adam directly blamed Eve, 'the *woman* you put here with me.' Yet he also foolishly proposed that God Himself was partly at fault, 'the woman *you* put here with me.' Then Eve naturally followed suit, 'The *serpent* deceived me.' We have been playing this blame game ever since the Garden. But for James this will not do.

Second, we need to recognize that Satan is not the primary source of our temptations. That is right, you read that sentence correctly. Satan presents temptation but is not the primary source of it, as James makes clear in 1:14. The devil does not make us do it.

I am being tempted by God (1:13)
Third, and most importantly, God is not the source of our temptations (1:13, 16-18). The language here highlights the source of the temptation. 'One can never say,' James asserts, 'the source of this inducement to do evil is God.' The Bible does teach that God sometimes tests people. Biblical examples include Abraham in Genesis 22:1, Job, the nation of Israel in Judges 2:22, and King Hezekiah in 2 Chronicles 32:31. Yet while God may test or prove his people in order to strengthen their faith and dependence upon Him, He never seeks to induce sin.[7] This important distinction is commonly misunderstood. Those who stress the sovereignty of God in bringing trials into their lives could easily and falsely assume that God likewise brings temptations into their lives. (This would not be all that different from the contemporary theological blunder that

---

7. Moo (TNTC), 71-72.

if God is sovereign, then He is the author of sin). So James goes to great lengths to refute this error, tackling it in verse 13 and again in verses 16-18.

Why is it impossible for God to be the source of our temptations? James' answer centers on the biblical doctrine of God: God is not the source of temptation because He is completely good and holy. We see this in four ways.

for God cannot be tempted by evil and He Himself tempts no one (1:13)

First, God cannot be tempted to do evil. James uses a rare passive adjective (*apeirastos*) that means 'untemptable.' He is completely holy and without the possibility of sinning. He never solicits us to do evil. Some years ago I (Dale) was serving as a pastor of a church in Tennessee. A lady came to me and said, 'God is leading me to divorce my husband and begin dating a man with whom I work.' After my initial shock I tried to compose myself and asked, 'Why would you think that?' Her response was, 'This man I work with is not a Christian and I need to be a witness to him.' I assured her that God never leads us to do what is wrong so that we might do what we think is right.

Second, God does not tempt anyone. The Greek is forceful: '*He Himself* tempts no one.' Evil repulses Him! He does not tempt anyone. God tests us for our good, but never tempts us so that we might sin. There is a big difference between testing to prove you are genuine and tempting to do evil. God says He never entices anyone to evil. When God tests us He does so to cause us to stretch and grow in our Christ-like character.

Third, He is Light – pure and without shadows (v. 17). 'Father of lights' is a unique designation of God in the Bible. This sense of God as 'Father' (*patēr*) in the inanimate realm has parallels in Job 38:28 (Father of rain), 2 Corinthians 1:3 (Father of mercies), and Ephesians 1:17 (Father of glory). Numerous Old Testament passages present the concept of God as Creator/Father of the heavenly bodies (*lights* is plural).[8]

---

8. Cf. Genesis 1.

James' emphasis here is to show that God operates solely in the realm of light – both physically and morally. Sin and darkness are concepts that go together like a hand in glove. But God is diametrically opposite to this – He is the Creator of all light sources and He is absolute moral and spiritual light. He could never be the Father of sin and darkness.

Fourth, He is unchangingly good (v. 17). In Him there is no 'variation.' He does not alternate between good and evil or between light and darkness. He is not moody or capricious; He does not act differently today than He did yesterday. In theological studies this is called the *immutability* of God: He does not change because He is perfect and need not change (Mal. 3:6; 1 John 1:5). God cannot change for the worse because He is holy; He cannot change for the better because He is already perfect.

We cannot claim we are the victims of temptation. Our depravity (own desires) is the primary source of our temptation (1:14-16). Jeremiah 17:9 asserts, 'The heart is deceitful above all things and desperately wicked. Who can know it?' Mark 7:21 further clarifies: 'For from within, out of the heart of men, proceed evil thoughts, adulteries, fornications, murders, thefts, covetousness, wickedness, deceit, lewdness, an evil eye, blasphemy, pride, foolishness. All these evil things come from within and defile a man.' Sin infects every part of our lives – our minds, wills, emotions, desires, and choices. Our depravity is the source of our temptations. So how does this work, then? How does temptation come to us?

3. The Process of Temptation (1:14-15)

drawn away by his own desires (lusts) and enticed (1:14)
Temptation begins with our own 'lust' or 'desire.'[9] The compound Greek word is descriptive: *epithumia,* literally 'to burn with heat.' Unfortunately, lust almost always has

---

9. We all know the dangers of the drug LSD and have heard, perhaps seen, the horrors of what the drug does to a person. LSD is a useful acronym for remembering the process of temptation: lust leads to sin, and sin brings about death. Lust – **S**in – **D**eath: spiritual LSD.

sexual connotations in our modern culture, but the word here refers to any sinful craving. We all have natural desires (physical, sexual, emotional, etc.) but those desires are also affected by the Fall. For example, the marriage bed is honorable and undefiled. That is, sex is good as long as it is in the bonds of marriage. Attraction to the opposite sex is good and necessary; it makes marriages stronger and it produces babies to continue the human race. But outside marriage, God says that such desires must be held in check.

'Enticed' (*deleazomenos*) is an old Greek word that literally refers to luring and catching by the use of bait or a trap, like baiting a hook. The fish sees the worm covering the hook, swims around, bites it, gets reeled to the shore, is killed, cleaned and eaten! And all the while, the bait keeps us from seeing the hook! So it is with sin – it never shows us the end result of 'taking the bait.'

when desire has conceived it bears sin (1:15)
Good desires are easily misused and misunderstood. Eating is good; gluttony is sin. Sleep is good; laziness is sin. Work is good, but focusing on work rather than God and your family is sin. How often good things are distorted and corrupted! Lust is when desire starts taking over, and when we act on those wrong desires, sin is the result. A wise sage said: 'You cannot help birds flying over your heads in the air, but do not let them land and build their nests in your hair.'

Sam Storms asserts, 'The focus of Satan's efforts is always the same: to deceive us into believing that the passing pleasures of sin are more satisfying than obedience.'[10] Sin is the decision or the act of disobedience. It is giving in to the temptation. While we are free to choose our actions, we are not free to decide the consequences of our actions.

So the first step is our unrestrained lust. Then James uses the interesting parallel of human conception: when we choose to obey these lusts 'conception' takes place. In the same way that the seed of the father impregnates the egg of the mother and a baby is conceived, so it is when our will

10. Storms, 247-48.

is joined with lust. Lust conceives and has a baby: sin. R. V. G. Tasker notes, 'Just as a child is alive before the actual moment of its birth, so sin does not begin to be sinful only when it is manifest in a specific, visible action, though some such sinful action is bound sooner or later to emerge, once the lustful thought has been entertained and cherished.'[11]

The word 'sin' occurs more than 400 times in our English Bibles. But the general word 'sin' encompasses an ugly array of offenses toward God. Sin is ignorance (*agnoema*), failure to observe the laws of God (*anomia*), transgression (*para-basis*), and missing the mark (*hamartia* – the word used here in v. 15). We sin actively and passively – sins of commission and omission. The end result of sin is death.

sin, when it is full grown, brings forth death (1:15)

The old saying is true: sin takes you farther than you want to go, keeps you longer than you want to stay, and costs you more than you want to pay. God warned Adam and Eve in the Garden that if they chose to disobey Him in the matter of eating from the forbidden tree, they would 'surely die.' They rebelled against God's will and were immediately separated from Him spiritually. And ultimately they died physically. They experienced the awful reality of sin when it is 'full grown.' The Greek word is *apotelestheisa*, a compound word found only here and in Luke 13:32. It means 'fully developed, complete in all its parts.' Death inevitably follows when sin is fully formed, for sin from its beginning carried death within itself.

This spiritual and physical death sentence was passed to all of Adam's progeny. Thus, when we are born, we bear the spiritual nature of Adam – separated from God and dead in our sin (Eph. 2:1-3). Paul stressed this reality in another way in Romans 6:23: 'The wages of sin is death.' Because we have the nature of Adam we commit acts of sin. As a boy growing up in rural South Carolina, I (Dale) often heard the older folks quip, 'What's down in the well comes up in the bucket.' In other words, we sin because

---

11. R. V. G. Tasker, *The General Epistle of James*, Tyndale New Testament Commentary (Grand Rapids: Eerdmans, 1957), 47.

we are sinners by nature, and what is in our hearts ultimately reveals itself in our actions. Spiritually, we are dead in trespasses and sins if we are without Christ, and ultimately our bodies die due to the introduction of sin into the human race by our first parents, Adam and Eve. This death sentence is starkly contrasted with the crown of life promised to enduring believers in verse 12.

4. The Strength for Temptation (1:16-18)

In stark contrast James moves now to provide us with strength to overcome temptations. James says, 'Do not be deceived.' Do not be led down the wrong path. We have a choice which way we will go. Do what you know to be the right thing to do. Sin often makes us believe a lie rather than acting on the truth.

do not be deceived (v. 16)

'Deceived' translates *planasthe* and means 'to lead astray, to cause one to wander.' James presents three motivations to help us not be led astray and to resist temptation. *First*, he warns us about the *judgment of God*. Sin leads to death, as shown in verse 15. There is no such thing as sowing a crop of wild oats and reaping a crop of righteous wheat. Death and hell claim their own – always – so do not be deceived.

Two examples come to mind. Both involve great men of the Old Testament who serve as living commentaries on this verse: David and Joseph. David's example is negative, and tragic consequences followed the sin. But Joseph serves as a positive role model we should emulate.

King David was enjoying a time of prosperity and peace in his reign. The story is simply told in 2 Samuel 11:1-27. 'Then it happened' introduces one of the saddest chapters in the Bible. It is the tragedy of a sinful look by a good man who put himself in the wrong place. The king should have been with his army defending the nation from invaders. Instead 'David stayed at Jerusalem' (v. 1) and at evening time he got up from his rest and walked around on the roof of his house, taking in the fresh air and relaxing. 'And from the roof he saw a woman bathing, and the woman was very beautiful in appearance' (v. 2). We do not know if that was David's habit and knew about the woman or if this was the first occasion when he saw the woman.

David could have dropped the matter right there, but instead of focusing on the affairs of state he 'sent and inquired about the woman' (v. 3). He now moved from the lust to the sin. He began to play with his passions and plot the fulfillment of his desires. 'So David sent and inquired about the woman' (v. 3). There was still time to stop the pursuit of his lust. When he investigated he found out she was already married. David's servant courageously informed David that she was 'the wife of Uriah.'

Rather than reeling in his lusts, 'David sent messengers and took her, and when she came to him, he lay with her.... And the woman conceived ... and said, "I am pregnant"' (v. 14). And this act of adultery progressed to intrigue, lying, cover-up and murder (vv. 6-21). 'But the thing David had done was evil in the sight of the LORD' (v. 27). This was the turning point in the life and reign of David. From this time onward his life went downhill.[12]

But thankfully we have another example – this one positive. Joseph was a teenager from a devout family who was sold by his brothers into slavery in Egypt. The captain of Pharaoh's bodyguards purchased Joseph to be a slave in his household. We are told 'The LORD was with Joseph, so he became a successful man' (Gen. 39:2). The Egyptian official saw that Joseph was blessed by God. Joseph became the 'personal servant' and 'overseer over his house, and all that he owned he put in Joseph's charge' (v. 4). As with David, Joseph was experiencing the blessings of God and success. The LORD even 'blessed the Egyptian's house on account of Joseph' (v. 5). Potiphar profited from Joseph's walk with the LORD God. Potiphar had such confidence in Joseph that 'he left everything he owned in Joseph's charge and did not concern himself with anything except for the food which he ate.' Confidence, trust, integrity, and power were all in Joseph's hands.

---

12. Thankfully, David later found forgiveness, as Psalms 32 and 51 indicate.

'Now Joseph was handsome in form and appearance' (v. 6) and Potiphar's wife noticed. The bait and the opportunity were now present: '... his master's wife looked with desire at Joseph, and she said, "Lie with me" (v. 7). He was like any other red-blooded man. He had natural physical desires he had to hold in check. Like David, he could have acted on his lusts or he could resist the temptation.

'He refused' (v. 8). It was not as if this was the only opportunity with temptation. She kept it up day after day (v. 10). Listen to Joseph's reasoning: he refused and said to his master's wife, 'Behold, with me *here*, my master does not concern himself with anything in the house, and he has put all that he owns in my charge. There is no one greater in this house than I, and he has withheld nothing from me except you, because you are his wife. How then could I do this great evil and sin against God?'

As she spoke to Joseph day after day, he did not listen to her to lie beside her *or* be with her. Now it happened one day that he went into the house to do his work, and none of the men of the household was there inside. She caught him by his garment, saying, 'Lie with me!' And he left his garment in her hand and fled, and went outside (Gen. 39:8-12). She set him up, pursued him, and when her plot failed she cried rape.

Joseph did not pursue the passion. Even though he was enticed daily, he would not be alone with her; he fled and went outside (vv. 9, 10, 12). Joseph was persuaded by higher goals (vv. 21, 23). 'How could I do this great evil, and sin against God' (v. 9). 'But the LORD was with Joseph' (v. 21). 'The LORD was with him; and whatever he did, the LORD made to prosper' (v. 23). Unlike David, Joseph realized the horror of sin and refused to succumb to temptation.

every good gift and every perfect gift comes down ... from the Father of the Lights (1:17)

Second, the *goodness of God* motivates us to resist temptation. Contrary to being the source of temptation, God is good and He desires what is best for His children. He is the author of all good gifts. James uses two different words for gift: the first is *dosis*, which usually denotes the act of giving. The second is *dōrēma*, which generally refers to the thing given. James probably does not intend a significant distinction but rather uses the synonyms for rhetorical purposes. All that God gives is good and perfect. The wages we receive from sin is death, but the gift of God is eternal life (Rom. 6:23). Not only does God give us salvation, He also graciously provides for us everything we need for life and godliness (2 Pet. 1:3).

Furthermore, His gifts are *consistently* good. He is the Father of 'lights.' Two ideas are expressed about God here. First, the construction James used is interesting: 'lights' is plural and it has the definite article (lit., 'Father of *the* lights'). This indicates that James is referring to the heavenly luminaries that give light to the universe. These good gifts do not come to us by chance or from some impersonal stroke of fate. The Creator God is the supplier of these good gifts.[13]

The second idea expressed about God in verse 17 is found in the phrase 'in whom there is no variation or shadow cast by turning.' This distinguishes God from the luminaries He created. 'Variation' is from *parallassō*, found only here in the New Testament and meaning 'to alternate or cause to vary.' Even though the heavenly bodies are amazingly stable in their created places, they still are subject to change. Not so with God. He changes not (Mal. 3:6). Quite contrary to being the source of evil in verses 13-16, God, by nature, can only be the author of good gifts.

of His own will He brought us to birth by the Word of truth (1:18)

The *third* motivation that gives us strength over temptation is salvation, that is, a new birth. It is the greatest of all gifts.

---

13. But a moral implication could be included here as well. God is not only the creator of the lights; He Himself is by nature pure light and no darkness encircles Him. Christ embodied that light as He came to shine and penetrate spiritual darkness (John 1:9; 8:12; 9:5; 1 John 2:8; Eph. 5:8). The light of God's truth and righteousness remains constant. There is never any shadow of the turning sun on His character. There is no shadow of darkness with Him. He remains constant with no variations.

Notice that James used birth as a picture of desire leading to sin (1:15). Now he uses the same verb (*apokeuō*) to explain how God is the Father of our new birth. Normally we think of conception and giving birth in terms of the biological role of the mother. But here it is God the Father, and He alone, who is the source of our new birth. James asserts three truths about this new birth.

First, God is the *source* of this new birth. The divine Creator of the heavenly lights is the One who makes us new creations in Christ (2 Cor. 5:17). This may be the most theologically weighty verse so far in the epistle. 'Of His own will' translates an aorist participle (*boulētheis*) placed first in the sentence for emphasis. The God who acted freely and without external constraints is the God who graciously took the initiative to give us new birth. Sin brought death (1:15), but God resolutely willed not to let us perish in sin. Having willed it, God acted freely to save us, a fact wholly inconsistent with the notion that God tempts us to sin. No human merit or effort could supply what is needed for spiritual conception to take place (John 1:13).

Second, 'the Word of truth' is the *agent* of new birth. This phrase has been variously identified by interpreters as the Old Testament, the gospel, or even Christ Himself. Certainly in the Old Testament God's Word and truth are frequently joined (Deut. 22:20; 2 Sam. 7:28; Ps. 15:2; 118:43; Jer. 23:28; Prov. 22:21). And Jesus asserted that He is the source of truth (John 14:6). But it seems best to agree with Tasker, 'Men are made His sons when they hear and respond to the gospel of salvation, here called the Word of truth as in Eph. 1:13; Col. 1:15.'[14]

that we should be a kind of firstfruits of his creatures (1:18)
Third, the *purpose* of the new birth is that we should be firstfruits of his creatures. What James has in mind here is debatable, as the meaning of 'firstfruits' is dependent on the identity of 'we.' James may have been referring to his fellow first-generation believers who represented many more to follow. Others think that James has in mind

14. Tasker, 49.

Christians of all ages who are the choicest and finest of God's creation.

Wisdom to Live By

- Do we refuse to blame others for our own sin?
- Do we recognize the depravity of our own hearts and not underestimate our own evil desires? Are we careful not to allow our desires to get out of control?
- Do we remember the horror of sin and are we careful to avoid places where we are tempted?
- Do we access God's power in Christ to overcome temptation?
- Do we make good decisions now to keep ourselves away from temptations later? It is reported that Phillip Brooks said: 'Some day, in the years to come, you will be wrestling with the great temptation, or trembling under the great sorrow of your life. But the real struggle is here, now.... Now it is being decided whether, in the great day of your supreme sorrow or temptation, you shall miserably fail or gloriously conquer. Character cannot be made except by a steady, long, continued process.'

5

Wisdom and the Word
(James 1:19-27)

'Now hear this!' These are typical words that introduce important announcements. With just such a command James introduces this third section of his epistle. Numerous seams weave this section into the previous one:

(1) having introduced the Word of God as the agent of our new birth like a baby in the womb, he now speaks of it as seed in the soil;

(2) having held before us the glorious promise of a *future* crown of life in verse 12, he now invites us to experience fully a *present* salvation in verse 21;

(3) having made us aware that this life is one of bondage to trials and temptations, he now encourages us by asserting that God's law is one of liberty in verse 25.[1]

In all of this he now admonishes his readers as 'beloved' fellow believers. Born of the same Father, they share a fraternal relationship. He calls them to lay aside sin and receive the Word with meekness, obeying it in the daily pursuits of life.

Today Christians in the West have access to the Word through countless sources: radio, TV, churches, CDs, conferences, seminars, etc. But sadly many Christians never

---

1. Motyer, 42.

get beyond hearing the Word to actually *doing* the Word. How sad it is that so many of us take the Word for granted while many fellow believers live with little access to the Scriptures, and many are persecuted and ostracized when they make their faith known. To whom much is given, much will be required. James' argument in this section is: 'Now that you have been born again your new life should have the characteristics of that new kind of life. This new life must be in obedience to God and in order to do that we must be ready to hear and apply God's Word.' The section can be summarized in four instructions:

1. Be eager to hear the Word (1:19-20).
2. Lay aside sin through repentance (1:20-21).
3. Receive the Word with meekness (1:21).
4. Obey the Word consistently (1:22-27).

1. Be Eager to Hear the Word (1:19-20)

this you know (1:19)

This terse phrase translates the Greek word *iste*. It may be an indicative ('you know this') or an imperative ('know this'). The sense is probably indicative and refers to the previous section. His readers knew the power of the Word to give birth and they knew that all who are born again are firstfruits of God's abundant grace. In this way, the phrase links the former section with what follows: 'You know the truth of what I have stated. But now we must go beyond this elementary knowledge and be eager to hear and obey this life-giving Word.'

Let everyone be quick to listen, slow to speak, slow to get angry (1:19). Three grammatically parallel exhortations serve to prepare our hearts to 'receive the Word' (v. 21) properly. *First*, we must be *quick to hear*. 'Quick' translates the Greek *tachus*. The idea is that of swiftness, eager to hear so that we may heed. We need to sit silently and listen to God's Word opened to us. We need to meditate on and ponder over words and sentences. We need to weigh the nuances, examine it word by word, and listen carefully so we can comprehend its meaning. A. T. Robertson captures the sense well: 'Poor listening will make poor preaching of a really good sermon. Good listening will come near to making a good sermon out of a poor one. The writer of Hebrews complains that his readers have become dull of hearing. "Dull" means "no push." They had no push in their ears, no energy in listening, were already half asleep.'[2]

Second, we should be *slow to speak*. We have often heard the saying, 'God gave us two ears and one mouth to remind us to listen more than we speak.' We learn while listening, not while speaking. We must learn to spend time in silence preparing our hearts for true worship. We need to keep our mouths closed so our minds will be ready to hear. Proverbs 17:27 reinforces this bit of wise advice: 'He who has knowledge spares his words.'

The *third* admonition in preparation for receiving the Word is to be *slow to get angry*. The Greek word is *orgē* and generally refers to an infuriated disposition while another Greek word, *thumos*, implies more of a sudden and violent rage. Two insights are in order here about anger. Generally, there is a clear connection between talking and anger, and words spoken in anger are more often than not injurious and harmful. A person who keeps up his talking is a poor listener, and a poor listener is subject to failure in keeping anger in check. I am reminded of Peter in the Garden of Gethsemane with Jesus. When the mob came to arrest Jesus, Peter was slow to hear, quick to speak, and quick to anger – he was even ready to kill a man (John 18:10)!

But specifically, James seems here to speak of anger as it relates directly to the life-giving Word. He warns us not to be angry at God's Word because it reveals our sin and challenges our behavior and values. Like a man who stones the prophet for delivering God's message, this man becomes angry at the Word because it reveals God's truth to him.

James is not implying that there is no place for justifiable anger. Jesus exercised righteous indignation (Mark 3:5)

---

2. Robertson, 61.

but it was a holy and compassionate anger. Anyone who cannot get angry at injustice and wrongdoing has little energy to fight against it. But even then, godly anger can be controlled and it does not express itself inappropriately. Paul exhorted us not to let the sun go down on our anger (Eph. 4:26).

for the wrath of man does not work out (bring about) the righteousness of God (1:20)

Once again we can hear James echoing the words of his blessed Master in Matthew 5:21-22. Righteousness does not spring out of our wrath. Interestingly, James changed the word for man from *anthrōpos* (mankind) to the more specific *anēr*. It moves us from a general, overarching statement to a personal level: 'An individual's acts done out of fury and rage do not bring about God's righteous standards.' At least three thoughts lie behind this verse: (1) an angry Christian certainly does not reflect God's righteousness; (2) wrath does not promote the course of righteousness; (3) wrathful man does not practice the kind of conduct approved by God.[3] 'Work out' translates *ergazesthai*, and means 'to effect, bring about, produce' as in 1:3 where testing *brings about* patience.

We should note that James' words might have application to a specific occasion in the church community. Perhaps it was the free conversation style of the early Christian worship services that James had in mind and some of the members were taking advantage of this freedom of expression. There was serious wrangling going on in the service. Robertson notes, 'Such violent talkers break up the spiritual life of a church. The less they know, the more they talk. They have opinions on every subject of politics or religion. They know how their neighbors should act in the smallest details and criticize everybody and everything. They are happiest when all is agog with talk of some sort; and the more gossipy it is, the better they like it.'[4]

---

3. Tasker, 50.
4. Robertson, 63.

2. Lay Aside Sin through Repentance (1:20-21)

Some months ago my (Dale) wife had to undergo surgery several times. I stayed with her right up until the time she was taken to the actual surgical table. The environment in the surgical area was immaculately clean and sterile. Indeed I would have been most concerned to see dirt and filth and unclean, rusted surgical implements! Such things are simply out of place in an operating room. In the same way, sin is out of place in the heart of one who desires to hear and do the Word of God.

therefore ridding [yourself] of all filthiness and all that remains of evil (1:21)

Our English translations make this phrase an imperative, but the only imperative verb in the verse is 'receive.' 'Ridding' is a participle that carries more of an adverbial sense: *'after* ridding yourself ... receive the Word' or *'by* ridding yourself ... receive the Word.' 'Filthiness' is a rare word in the New Testament; in fact, it is used only here and in 2:2 where James talks about the man with dirty, filthy clothes. It was also a medical term used at the time for earwax, which, if allowed to build up, could cause dull hearing.[5] This idea fits quite well here.

'Evil' (or wickedness, malice) is sin with a vicious nature that is bent on doing harm to others. It is the depravity of a mind that is opposed to humanity and just dealings. This 'wickedness' refers to hidden sins, motives, and attitudes that corrupt the behavior of people. The expression 'all that remains of evil' is a tautology (deliberate overstatement) that sums up this call for a complete moral reformation necessary to receive the Word aright.

Before we can receive the Word we must confess our sins. We must put aside all filthiness and wickedness that remains in our lives that we are aware of. Removal of 'all that remains of wickedness' refers to the sin that shaped our motives and attitudes and that lies beneath the surface of our lives. Every believer brings into the new life inconsistent behaviors and attitudes to this new life

5. Martin, 48.

in Christ. This is the battle of the old and the new nature. Wiersbe described this verse by comparing our hearts to a garden: 'If left to itself, the soil would produce only weeds. James urged us to pull out the weeds and prepare the soil for the implanted Word of God.'[6]

3. Receive the Word with Meekness (1:21)

receive with meekness the implanted word which is able to save your souls (1:21)

'Receive' carries with it a sense of urgency and it denotes more than just the act of acceptance; the idea is that of a warm welcome (cf. Rom. 14–15). Three aspects are spelled out about warmly receiving the Word.

First, the *manner* in which the Word should be received is 'with meekness' or humility. It is the opposite of being 'quick to speak and quick to be angry' (v. 19). We do well to ask ourselves: 'Do I come with a gentle, open, and teachable spirit. Do I welcome God's truths into my heart? Do I entertain it in my mind and will?' Simply agreeing with the truth is not the same as obeying it. We must act on what we hear, and be obedient to it.

Second, the *nature* of the Word is that it is 'implanted' or 'engrafted.' The adjective is found only here in the New Testament and comes from *emphuton*, a compound term meaning 'to grow or plant in.' God graciously brought us to birth through His Word and now He desires to implant more of it in our hearts so that our Christian experience matches the new birth we received. Peter uses language quite similar to this: 'Therefore, laying aside all malice and deceit ... as newborn babes desire the pure milk of the Word that you may grow by it' (1 Pet. 2:1-2).

Third, the *motive* for receiving the Word is that it is able to 'save your souls.' Three aspects of salvation are in view here. The *past* aspect is that of salvation – God used His Word, the truth of the gospel, to bring us to birth. The *present* aspect is that the Word aids in our sanctification – it is a constant resource that builds up the believer and gives

---

6. Wiersbe, 53.

him freedom from sin's dominion. The Psalmist averred, 'Thy Word have I hid in my heart that I might not sin against Thee' (Ps. 119:11). Finally, the Word has power to keep us for a *future* salvation – our glorification when we are in Christ's presence and forever free from the presence of sin!

4. Obey the Word Consistently (1:22-27)

In authentic Christianity we as believers ought to strive daily for increased obedience to the Word that has been implanted into our hearts. There is a spiritual danger in just hearing without acting on what we know to be true. We can even deceive ourselves at the point of our own salvation. Doers of the Word have the right attitude toward God's Word that leads to action. The remaining verses in James 1 present the right attitude toward the Word. In verses 22-27 we have: (1) a command to be *doers* of the Word; (2) an illustration of one who is a hearer but not a doer; and (3) a practical application of what it means to be doers of the Word.

become doers of the Word and not hearers only (1:22)

As a little boy growing up in church Sunday school, we learned a song that used James' phrase 'be ye doers of the Word' that I (Dale) can still remember after all these years. But the command here is not simply 'be,' but 'become' (from the verb *ginomai*). And it is present tense: 'become people who do the Word and continue in it.'

James has shown the wisdom of good listening; now he balances the injunction with the negative: 'not hearers only.' There is life in the Word of God; it pulsates with life-giving energy. It is living and active and sharp (Heb. 4:12), and wise are the ones who order their lives according to it. 'Hearer' (*akroatai*) was used in ancient times to refer to those who were 'professional' listeners, following lecturers and orators around to listen to them, but never being moved by their words. Hearing without doing is useless. It is self-deceptive. James may even be referring to sympathetic hearers in the synagogues who never became real disciples. Be quick to receive and continue humbly in the implanted Word. Those who 'hear the word of God, and keep it' are the ones who receive God's blessing (Luke 11:28).

who delude themselves (1:22)

The word James uses for 'delude' (*paralogizomai*) means 'to reason beside the point, to misjudge, to miscalculate and therefore to deceive oneself by fallacious reasoning.' He deludes himself by cheating himself in his reasoning processes. Robertson poignantly describes these people:

> Some people have a sort of religious dissipation in attending [church] services and imagine that they have accomplished a great deal if they simply go. People easily acquire itching ears that love to be tickled with some sensation. The Word takes no root in the heart of such [people]. They run from church to church to get some new word, a sort of soda-water habit. They deceive themselves and no one else.[7]

James paints a verbal picture to amplify and illustrate what he has said about hearing and doing the Word. He pictures a man looking into a mirror – he sees himself but what he sees makes no impact upon him.

for anyone who is a hearer of the Word and not a doer is like a man looking at his natural face in a mirror (1:23)

'Mirror' is from *esoptrōi*, a compound form from *eis*, 'into' and *optō* 'to look.' Ancient mirrors were made of polished metal (usually silver, copper, or tin). The Word of God is like a mirror as it reflects what is taking place in our hearts. It shows us areas in our inner lives that need to be corrected. 'Natural face' is literally 'face of his birth, the face he was born with.' James then goes on to state the problem: he does nothing about what he sees.

He glances at himself, goes away, and immediately forgets what sort (of person) he was (1:24)

James used tense changes in this verse to describe vividly what this person is like. 'Looking' in verse

---

7. Robertson, 68.

23 is present tense, but now he switches to the aorist (action stated simply with no continuation): he merely 'glances' at himself, has now gone away (perfect tense – happened and remains that way) and straightway 'forgets' what he saw. 'Just a glance and off he goes.' All that he saw in the Word of God is now out of sight and out of mind. If we do not act quickly on what we see or hear in God's Word we may forget it and not be obedient. Our tendency is to forget what we do not like in ourselves when we come under the steady, pure light of God's truth.

To contrast this, James drops the imagery of looking into a mirror and states the matter plainly:

but he who looks intently [gazes] into the perfect law of liberty and remains in it (1:25)
Different verbs are used here for emphasis. 'Gazes' is *parakupsas*, 'to stoop and gaze intently into.' It is the same verb used when Peter and Mary peered into the empty tomb (John 20:5, 11). This person gazes (not glances) into the 'perfect law of liberty.' This designation resembles the teachings of Jesus and shows that the law and liberty can and do coincide. Three thoughts about the Word are expressed by this phrase. First, it is 'perfect.' Second, the Word of God is the law in the sense that it is the sole body of truth that reveals the will of God for His people. It is the rule or standard by which the Christian life is to be regulated. Third, 'liberty' (*eleutherias*) expresses the liberating power of the Word.

The laws that God has woven into His universe give liberty. Music does not result from a random banging on a keyboard. Art does not come from childlike splashing of paint on a canvas. Airplanes fly only when certain and determined laws are observed. In each instance, failure to follow particular laws results in chaos. So it is with God's perfect law of liberty. God's law in the Old Testament prevented Israel from living in anarchy. In a much greater way, Christ's new law sets us free inwardly and outwardly to live as we ought. In what sounds like an oxymoron to a sinful world, it is only through God's law that we can really live free.

Human words fail to adequately describe God's Word. James has called it 'seed' which implants life, a 'mirror' that shows what we truly are, and the 'perfect law' which, when followed, will result in a person being **blessed in all he does** (see also 1:12). One can hear James echoing the words of His Master again – 'blessed' is the word *makarios*, the word Jesus used in the Beatitudes in Matthew 5.

The good listener takes time and the trouble to 'look intently' or 'gaze' into God's Word and consider the implications for his life. He takes his time and peers into the Word to grasp its meaning and make application to his personal life. Robertson writes:

> The man remains by the side of the roll of the law spread out before him and unrolls page after page with the keenest interest and zest until he rightly grasps the meaning of God. Thus he puts the Word into practice. He has it stamped on his mind and heart. He is a Christian pragmatist. He ... practices the presence of God. He translates the word of truth into his own life and becomes a living epistle.[8]

James moves now from the general to the particular. The transition from verse 25 to verse 26 seems abrupt. Granted, there is no connective to tie them together. But the transition is not as disjointed as it may seem. Verse 22 stated how easy it is to be self-deceived about true spirituality. So, to strengthen his case, he applies the injunction to be 'doers of the Word' to three specific concerns: (1) controlling the tongue, (2) showing compassion to the needy, and (3) manifesting moral purity and integrity. No doubt James isolated these three because of problematic situations in the community of faith to which he wrote.

If anyone thinks himself to be religious (1:26). 'Religious' is from the Greek *thrēskos*, which refers to external religious rituals, ceremonies, liturgies, and the like. The term is found elsewhere only twice in the New Testament (Acts 26:5; Col. 2:18), each with negative connotations.

8. Robertson, 70.

By contrast, the word normally used for genuine, God-honoring worship is *eusebeia*. But James uses the word positively by setting it in the context of practical, genuine Christianity. True religion expresses itself in at least three ways.

but does not bridle his own tongue (1:26)

First, true religion that 'does' the Word involves *controlling the tongue*. The application weaves together what has already been said (v. 19) and what he will say in a more expanded form in chapter 3. 'Bridle' is a vivid compound word (*chalinagōgōn*), meaning 'to lead with a bridle' like one would do with a horse. James regards the tongue as an unruly horse that needs bit and bridle held fast by the master to take control of it. The unyielding tongue is allowed to run loose and say whatever pops into the mind of a spiteful heart. MacArthur notes, 'It has been estimated that the average person will speak some 18,000 words in a day, enough for a fifty-four-page book. In a year that amounts to sixty-six 800-page volumes! Up to one-fifth of the average person's life is spent talking.'[9]

deceives his own heart and his religion is empty (1:26)

Religious activity minus a disciplined tongue reveals a heart that is deceived. James says take control of the tongue using the image of a man putting a bridle in his own mouth to restrain himself, not an animal or someone else. There is nothing so empty as pouring forth a great flood of religious words with little reality of personal experience in them. Such religion is *mataios*, 'empty, vain, comes to nothing.' James' word is the same as the one used in the Septuagint (the Greek translation of the Old Testament) for the worship of idols. In other words, religion without controlled, godly speech is empty and pointless, as unprofitable as bowing before an idol.

Second, being a doer of the Word means *showing compassion to the needy*.

---

9. MacArthur, 88.

Religion that is pure and undefiled before our God and Father is this: to visit orphans and widows in their distress (1:27)

Attending church services, doing volunteer work, tithing, observing rituals and ceremonies, saying prayers ... all of these outward expressions of religion are well and good. But *true* religion, that which pleases God, means we are willing to be selfless and have genuine concern for the welfare of others, especially those in need. 'Pure' is from *katharos*; its synonym is *amiantos*, 'undefiled.' Cleanliness and the absence of contamination are what James has in mind. And this purity of religion must pass the litmus test of **our God and Father**. For religious performance to impress other people is one thing; to be judged by God as pure and undefiled is quite another.

'To visit' is from *episkeptomai* and means 'to look in on, to inspect.' It is present tense – this should be the habit of one's religious life. *Orphanos* means bereft of father or mother or both. It is used only here and in John 14:18. Together with widows, orphans represented all those who were without defense, protection, or provision. We must remember that no social security or welfare or government aid existed in those days. The loss of a husband or parents often meant total disaster. The text calls for more than a single instance of helping those in need; the idea is that of the church assuming responsibility for the support of those truly bereft.

Third, the practice of true religion means *manifesting moral purity and integrity*:

and to keep oneself free from the contamination of the world (1:27)

'To keep' translates a present tense Greek infinitive. The idea is 'to keep on keeping oneself' uncontaminated by the world. 'Free from contamination' is a bit tedious, but it serves to relate accurately what James has in mind with his use of *aspilos*. The idea is that of being 'unstained or unspotted' by a world full of moral filth and slime. Paul challenged us to be 'blameless and harmless children of God in the midst of a crooked and perverse generation' (Phil. 2:15). The word 'world' (*kosmos*) carries a wide range of meaning in the New Testament (i.e. the created order, the 'world' of mankind, etc.), but James uses it in the sense of the spirit of the age – every age – which reflects a godless and immoral agenda against Christ.

We live in a world filled with hedonism, relativism, and humanism. Our world today resembles the one Paul described in Romans 1 that God has given over to depravity, degradation, and disgrace. Surely, if there is to be any light in this dark world, it must be the light radiated by the people of God. James has no use for a religion that does not emphasize moral and spiritual purity.

Two caveats come to mind. *First*, James is not suggesting here a theology of 'sinless perfection.' As long as we live in this fallen world we will be susceptible to sin. Thank God for 1 John 1:9. But a person who has experienced true saving grace will forever have a different attitude toward sin – he will eschew it and desire to be more like his sinless Lord.

Second, this admonition is not a call for the followers of Jesus to withdraw and sequester themselves away from the lost world in which we live. Jesus prayed in John 17 that the Father would not take us *out* of the world but that He would keep us *from* the evil one (John 17:15). Rather, he calls for Jesus' followers to live radically different lives so that we may point people to Christ. Edgar Guest stated this exhortation in poetic form:

> I'd rather *see* a sermon than hear one any day;
> I'd rather one walk with me than merely tell the way.
> The eye's a better pupil and more willing than the ear.
> Fine counsel can be confusing, but an example's always clear;
> And the best of all the preachers are the men who live
>   their creeds,
> For to see good put into action is what everybody needs.[10]

---

10. Edgar A. Guest, 'Sermons We See,' in *Collected Verse* (Chicago: Reilly and Lee, 1934).

Wisdom to Live By

- Are we controlling our words? Or do we have an unruly horse wandering around in our mouths? James regards the tongue as an unruly horse that needs bit and bridle held fast by the master to take control of it.

- Do we have control of our anger? What actions can we take to resolve sinful anger?

- Are our lives holy, 'undefiled' and 'uncontaminated' from the world?

6

Wisdom and Prejudice
(James 2:1-13)

Earthly possessions and how we use them reveal our spirituality as much as anything in life. Many of Jesus' parables dealt with wealth and possessions. He reminded us, 'where your treasure is, there your heart is also' (Matt. 6:21). Paul warned Timothy that the 'love of money is a root of all sorts of evil and that those whose ultimate goal in life is to get rich fall into temptation and a snare' (1 Tim. 6:9-10). Perhaps no other barometer more accurately measures our spiritual priorities than the way we use earthly riches.

In Chapter 2 James continues his emphasis on being 'doers' of the Word. His specific injunctions in 1:26, 27 are supplemented now by a command to avoid showing favoritism and partiality when it comes to wealth and possessions. Even in the earliest Christian communities social, financial, and racial distinctions already caused tension. James 2 presents for us two tests of genuine faith: (1) true faith is not prejudiced (2:1-13), and (2) true faith always makes itself evident by practical works (2:14-26).

The Jewish Christians to whom James wrote had received the gospel, been converted, and now needed much help in how to exercise their newfound faith. Their religious thought and temper were still largely controlled by the traditions of their Jewish heritage. Their assemblies for religious worship and teaching were still called synagogues, and probably the customs and structure of the Jewish synagogue were largely preserved at the time James wrote. The great majority of these new Christians were poor, and most of the wealthy Jews were bitterly hostile to the Christian faith. Throughout the epistle the rich as a class are described as enemies of the Christian church.

Apparently James had heard that in the Christian synagogue(s) the poor were being treated with contempt and the wealthy with ostentatious demonstrations of respect. So he wrote to correct the problem, citing four principles:

1. Prejudice is inconsistent with the example of Jesus.
2. Prejudice is inconsistent with the grace of God.
3. Prejudice is inconsistent with the command to love.
4. Prejudice is inconsistent with the nature of the judgment.

My brothers (2:1)

James softens his rebuke with this warm and familiar address, which he used twelve times in the epistle (1:2; 2:1, 14; 3:1, 10, 12; 4:11; 5:7, 9, 10, 12, 19). Combine this with the more endearing 'my beloved brothers' which he used three times (1:16, 19; 2:5) and one can sense James' pastoral heart.

1. Prejudice Is Inconsistent with the Example of Jesus

do not hold your faith in our glorious Lord Jesus Christ with [an attitude of] prejudiced favoritism (2:1)

A Command

James closed the last chapter by talking about true religion. Though he now changes terminology, he stays with the same thought. Faith in our Lord of glory *is* true religion and it consists of more than conformity to a set of outward standards – it is first and foremost a heart relationship that expresses itself in outward behavior. 'Our glorious Lord Jesus Christ' is a much-debated phrase. The literal word order in this string of genitive-case words is 'the Lord our Jesus Christ of glory.' Martin suggests four possible interpretations: (1) 'faith in the glory of our Lord Jesus Christ'; (2) 'faith in our Lord of glory, Jesus Christ'; (3) 'of glory' is a genitive of apposition: 'faith in our Lord Jesus Christ, the Glory'; (4) 'of glory' [*tēs doxēs*] is an adjective: 'faith in our glorious Lord Jesus Christ.' The latter option is the simplest and it makes the most sense. What is clear is that James attributes to the Lord Jesus the splendor that is peculiar to God Himself.[1]

'Prejudiced favoritism' is one of the most technicolor words in the New Testament. *Prosōpolēmpsiais* is a compound word that literally means 'to receive or lift up the face.' It is found in Romans 2:11, Ephesians 6:9, and Colossians 3:25; in each case denying any partiality or favoritism with God. The verb form is found in the New Testament only in James 2:9. Such an attitude makes a quick judgment about a newcomer to the congregation. An instant evaluation takes place about the person socially, educationally, and economically.

In the 1980s I (Dale) was pastor of a church in a little town in South Carolina. One day a rather unkempt-looking poor man whom I had befriended entered the sanctuary and an usher, a bit unnerved, made sure he took a seat in a back corner of the sanctuary. That same day, the mayor of the small town visited as well, and oh, the fanfare he received as he and his wife were escorted to the front of the church to sit in a seat of honor. I thought about these words in James and I realized something of the sinful mindset he sought to correct.

Jesus practiced just the opposite of this 'prejudiced favoritism.' 'How,' James asks, 'can you say you are a follower of Jesus and yet show prejudice and favoritism toward people?' Jesus had little use for the religious elite of His day and intentionally made Himself a friend of sinners. Peter had to learn this truth in Acts 10 when he was commanded to go to the home of the Gentile Cornelius. Peter learned his lesson well: 'Truly I now perceive that God shows no partiality' (Acts 10:34).

---

1. For a concise yet cogent discussion, see Moo (PNTC), 101.

for if a man comes into your synagogue wearing a gold ring and dressed in splendid clothes (2:2)

James pictures two men coming to church; perhaps they were visitors or maybe new converts. They enter the 'synagogue,' a common word for early Jewish Christians who gathered for the purpose of worship (see Luke 12:11). But there is evidence that in some places the physical building in which they met was a local synagogue (Luke 4:15, 20, 28). It may seem odd that a Christian church be termed a synagogue, but remember the early date and the Jewish milieu in which these new believers found themselves. Jewish Christians who were new to the faith would naturally carry over into their new worship the terms and symbols with which they were familiar.[2]

One man appeared looking as though he had stepped out of a fashion magazine, with gold rings and an expensive suit. Literally, the text reads *having gold rings on his fingers* (*chrusodaktulios*) *and in a bright toga* (*en esthēti lamprai*). In ancient times, gold rings were a quintessential symbol of affluence – some people even rented them to give the outward impression of being a person of means. The word used for 'splendid or fine' clothing is used of the apparel of heavenly beings (Acts 10:30; Rev. 15:6). He was an impressive figure indeed!

In sharp contrast **a poor man also enters** the same worship assembly **in filthy clothes**. The 'poor' man (*ptōchos*) was one who barely lived at the subsistence level, one who needed help just to get enough food and clothing to survive. The text does not indicate that the two entered simultaneously, though that would have made the incident more dramatic. This poor person wore dirty, shabby clothes (*ruparai*).

And you pay special regard to the man in splendid clothes and say 'Sit here in a good place' (2:3)

Those greeting the well-dressed individual show 'special regard' to him. The word is *epiblepō*, 'to gaze upon,' and

---

2. 'It is quite possible that the Jewish Christians still attended worship and heard Moses read in the synagogue (Acts 15:21), as Christians belonged to the synagogue of the Libertines (Acts 6:9) and the early Christians worshiped still in the Temple.' Robertson, 78.

is found elsewhere only in Luke 1:48 and 9:38. The man is invited to occupy what would have been well recognized as a seat of honor in the synagogue setting (as in Matt. 23:6).

The poor person, on the other hand, is treated with disdain and even contempt: **You, stand there or sit under my feet (2:4)**.
'You' is emphatic in the Greek, conveying an attitude of pointing out the poor man and telling him to stand 'over there' (*ekei*), away from the speaker's location, or to sit at his feet. The latter relegated the undesirable visitor to the rank of servants, people of submission and social disgrace.

Are you not divided in your own minds, and have you not become judges with evil reasoning? (2:4)
In posing the question in verse 4 James gives us the principle he seeks to drive home. If we are guilty of the behavior described in verses 2 and 3, then the only way we can answer verse 4 is in the affirmative. James is saying, in effect, 'You believe in the Lord Jesus, the Lord of glory, don't you? Well then, follow His example, and obey the teaching He gave about wealth and concern for the poor. If you really believe in Him, then you will want to have His mind in you.'

The Lord Jesus never looked at people's outward appearance and assessed their worth by it. Rather, Jesus looked at everyone with love and saw them as those whom He longed to serve. To show favoritism and to be snobbish are contrary to Jesus' love because they mean that we classify people in our minds, and we make false assumptions concerning them on the basis of their appearance. In fact, we set ourselves up as judges to assess others, forgetful of the Savior's warning: 'Do not judge, or you too will be judged. For in the same way you judge others, you will be judged, and with the measure you use, it will be measured to you' (Matt. 7:1-2). Obedience to the Word of God produces a determination to have the same attitude toward people as that of our Lord Jesus Christ, and that attitude rules out all favoritism and snobbishness.

2. Prejudice Is Inconsistent with the Grace of God

James captures his readers' attention by beginning verse 5 with **Hear this, my beloved brothers (2:5)**.

The command is from *akouō* – 'hear this and listen well!' The use of beloved (*agapētoi*) underscores again James' affection for this congregation.

Did not God choose the poor in this world [to be] rich in faith (2:5). Jesus taught that the kingdom was especially designed for the 'poor' (Luke 6:20). However, these to whom James wrote were denigrating the poor and arbitrarily exalting the rich. It must be understood that God's grace is the only basis for anyone's salvation (Eph. 2:8-9). 'Choose' is from *eklegesthai* and is in the middle voice, denoting that God's choice is of special significance to Himself. The poor are not chosen simply because of their financial condition, no more than the rich rejected because of their wealth. All have the same invitation and are called in precisely the same way – the gospel is God's means of calling (2 Thess. 2:14). But the poor often experience a special sense of needing God, while the rich are often complacent and independent.

James said that these chosen ones who respond to God's gracious offer of salvation are privileged in three ways. *First*, they are *chosen* by God. Though rejected by the world in so many ways, they are of supreme worth in God's sight. *Second*, despite being virtually bankrupt in this materialistic age, they are *rich in faith*. We should not judge individuals based on what they have, but on who they are. True riches are not deposited in vaults; they are deposited in human hearts who are rich in Christ and who are already seated with Him in heavenly places (Eph. 1:7; 2:6).

Third, God's 'poor' are **heirs of the kingdom promised to those who love Him (2:5)**

When the spies from Israel returned from the Promised Land bearing the grapes and pomegranates and figs (Num. 13), the people were able to taste the good things God had in store for them upon entering the land of

Canaan. Likewise, the Christian, though poor by this world's standards, realizes he is indeed spiritually rich. God's 'down payment' of the indwelling Holy Spirit is the promise of greater things to come (Eph. 4:30). The poor of this world can become rich in faith by God's grace. When we become children of God, we also become heirs (*klēronomous*) of His kingdom.

In verses 6-7 James makes a pointed rebuke and then asks two questions to show how his readers' behavior is inconsistent with God's grace. In so doing he gives two reasons why we should not discriminate against the poor.

You have disgraced the poor (2:6)
First, to discriminate against people based merely on social wealth or status *disgraces* those to whom God has granted grace. In effect, we place our standard of estimation higher than God's! 'You' (*humeis*) is emphatic and is the 'dear brother or sister' of verse 5. The word translated 'disgraced' or 'despised' (*ētimasate*) means more than to ignore. The idea is that of degradation and shame. The Bible teaches against such treatment of the poor and directs us instead to show mercy (see Prov. 14:21).

His *second* reason for avoiding partiality, found in 6b-7, comes in the form of three parallel questions, each expecting a positive answer. James fumes at his readers for their contradictory behavior. He is not suggesting a favor for a favor (like a *quid pro quo* argument). He stresses that showing the rich flattery and favoritism to 'get ahead' is wrong. These three questions leveled a three-fold charge against the non-believing rich.

a. Do not the rich oppress you? (2:6)
Godless, affluent people exploited the Christians who courted their favor. 'Oppress' is from a rare compound word (*katadunasteuō*). It is used in Acts 10:38 when the devil oppressed Jesus. The Old Testament contains many references to wealthy people who exploited the poor, and in every case God condemned it (see, for example, Amos 4:1; 8:4-6). Just as Amos did, James rebuked the Christian who favored the wealthy.

b. and drag you into the courts? (2:6)

Those to whom James' readers gave the best seats at the synagogue returned the favor by dragging Christians into court, likely having already 'bought off' the judgment. 'Drag' is a vigorous word for violent treatment. This brutal treatment is the kind found in Luke 12:58 and Acts 8:3, where the same word is used. On the pretext of some trumped-up civil or criminal charges, the secular rich exploited the poor this way. James probably had in mind cases involving debt, rent, property disputes and the like.

c. Do they not blaspheme the beautiful name by which you were called? (2:7)

James saved the worst accusation until last. We derive our word blaspheme as a transliteration of the Greek. It means 'to speak evil of, slander, to be intentionally irreverent.' One can imagine rich Jewish unbelievers slandering the followers of Jesus as disciples of a cursed criminal. 'How,' James mused, 'could you show undue preference to those who insult the poor or the followers of Christ or both?' James did not mention Jesus' name but he spoke of the honorable or beautiful (*kalos*) name of Jesus. 'By which you were called' is from a compound verb, 'to put a name upon.' Martin notes that the use of the word refers to the occasion when the name of one person is spoken over another's to designate the latter as property of the former.[3]

The name Christian is a powerful and precious designation of one who belongs to Christ. It is a name we should take care to honor and protect. Managers of the once infamous Louisiana Lottery approached Robert E. Lee after the close of the American Civil War. They posed a proposition to him as he sat on his porch in his rocking chair, crutches by his side. They indicated that they wanted to use his name as part of a shady deal that would make all involved very rich. He could not believe his ears and asked them to repeat, wanting to make sure he understood what

3. Martin, 66.

they were suggesting. Lee straightened up in his chair, buttoned his old gray tunic around him and bellowed, 'Gentlemen, I lost my home in the war. I lost my fortune in the war. I lost everything in the war except my good name, and it is not for sale.'[4] More than our own name, we should seek to honor and protect the name of Jesus. The wealthy to whom James wrote were not doing this, nor did they appear to be concerned that they failed to do so.

3. Prejudice Is Inconsistent with the Command to Love

So far James has shown the Christian community how their actions were inconsistent with the example of Jesus and with the grace of God. In these verses James turns to the royal law – the law of love – to persuade them to avoid partiality and prejudice.

Indeed, if you fulfill the royal law according to the Scriptures (2:8)

'Indeed' (*mentoi*) ties James' argument to what has gone before. The example of Jesus and the grace of God call for love on the part of the followers of Christ. James reached back to the Old Testament and pulled out a universal maxim that should govern all our behavior. The law of love mandates compassion and concern for everyone, not just for those considered important or worthy. In this verse James imagines a detractor who argues with him about his directive against partiality (called a 'diatribe' style). James takes up one of the Old Testament summaries of the second table of the Ten Commandments, 'Love your neighbor as yourself (Lev. 19:18).' The law is 'royal' (*basilikon*, kin to the word for 'king' and 'kingdom') for two reasons. *First*, the King, God the Father, gave it. He pronounced it in the Decalogue and Jesus reiterated it to His disciples in John 13:34. *Second*, it denotes a law fit for kingdom citizens who would do well to follow it. Jesus said that on the law of love hang all the Law and the Prophets (Matt. 22:40).

---

4. J. Wallace Hamilton, *Ride the Wild Horses* (Westwood, NJ: Fleming H. Revell, 1952), 122.

You shall love your neighbor as yourself (2:8)
James reminds his Christian readers of the priority and
binding nature of this commandment. Righteousness and
love go hand in hand in God's kingdom. To do the right thing
and to love are two sides of the same coin. As believers, we
make it our goal to please the Lord (2 Cor. 5:9), and in order
to please Him we must pursue love, aiming always at doing
the right thing in regard to others. To show favoritism is in
total opposition to the summary of the second table of the law
– 'Love your neighbor as yourself.'

You do well (2:8)
The word translated 'right, well' is not the usual word
dikaios but *kalōs*. The word used here points to what is
pleasing to God, what He likes or gives Him joy.

But if you show prejudiced favoritism, you commit sin (2:9)
The use of 'but' (*de*) anticipates a reversal of thought from
verse 8. 'Prejudiced favoritism' is the verb form from
the noun in verse 1. The word is found nowhere else in
the New Testament. The opposite of the 'royal law' is
'prejudiced favoritism,' and James speaks quite plainly that
the contrast is between 'doing well' (v. 8) and 'committing
sin.' For other straightforward indications of moral evil in
the community see James 4:17; 5:16-17, 20. For James, the
action of showing partiality, though inconsequential to
some, is a serious affront to God.

being convicted by the law as transgressors (2:9)
According to Paul in Galatians, to fail in keeping the law in
one point brings one under the condemnation of the whole
law (Gal. 3:10). 'Being convicted' is from *elegchō*, a strong verb
meaning 'to expose so that one has to acknowledge guilt.' To
break the law of love through an act of favoritism is to make one
a 'transgressor' (*parabatēs*, 'to step over the line' in rebellion).

**For whoever might keep the whole law and yet stumble
in one [point] has become guilty in all [points] (2:10)**
James' readers failed to understand that even if they
meticulously kept the law in all other points, yet failed in

the royal law of love, they 'stumble' (*ptaiein*, found also in
3:2 and only two other times in the New Testament) in all
its points. Stumbling and 'stepping over the line' (v. 9) are
interrelated. They undercut the basic essence of God's will
in our dealings with others. We cannot pick and choose
what we wish to obey and what we will set aside. To
violate any part of the divine law shows lack of reverence
and transgresses both the whole law and the Lawgiver.

4. Prejudice Is Inconsistent with the Nature of Judgment

In light of God's stern requirements, every believer should
live daily with an eye toward the Final Judgment. An old
preacher said it this way, 'That which a man spits toward
heaven will fall back on his own face.' Jesus said it more
precisely in Matthew 7:2, 'With what judgment you judge
you shall be judged.'

Verse 10 states James' case in a general way; verse 11
makes it individual and personal:

The One who said 'Do not commit adultery' also said 'Do not murder' (2:11)

Two extreme examples of breaking God's law are now
cited: adultery and murder. 'He who said' reminds the
readers that this is *God's* law and it has inherent power
because of the One who uttered it. Critical to the argument
is that we have not just a text, but also *Someone* speaking.

James reversed the two prohibitions from the way
they are found in the Old Testament (Exod. 20:13-14;
Deut. 5:17-18). Some think that James emphasized murder
because it was particularly apropos to his readers' situation,
assuming literal murder taking place in the particularly
destructive Jewish strife that preceded the rebellion against
Rome.[5] But that view may be a bit pressed. It seems better,
in agreement with Moo, to understand this prohibition
against murder in the light of the 'deeper' sense which
Jesus gave to it (Matt. 5:21-26).[6] The 'murderous' attitude
of the heart is the issue. The one who avoids adultery but

---

5. For a full discussion of this possibility, see Martin, 70.
6. Moo (PNTC), 115.

commits murder, whether literally or as a wrong spiritual attitude, is nevertheless a lawbreaker.

you become a transgressor of the law (2:11)
A rock thrown through a window strikes the glass at only one point, but it can cause the whole window to shatter. So it is with the law. The lesson for these people in the first century remains the same for us today: Christians must not judge and treat others simply based on shallow considerations. James drives home the point introduced in verse 10: the law is broken in its entirety when only one point is 'transgressed' (the same word as in v. 10). We must remember 'that which is highly esteemed among men is an abomination in the sight of God' (Luke 16: 15). The sin of James 2:1-13 was respect of persons and consequent sinful treatment simply based on manifest economic differences between the two visitors.

So speak and so act as those who are about to be judged by the law that sets free (2:12)
After a detour to show that those who show prejudiced favoritism are lawbreakers (vv. 10-11), James now returns to his exhortation toward practical behavior. Three facts arise about the 'law that sets free.' *First*, it is the *royal law* (v. 8), the law of the King and we should wish to obey it. *Second*, it is the *law of God*, and we must obey it. *Third*, it is the law that 'sets free' – corresponding to the law of liberty in 1:25 – and we *can* obey it.[7] God gave the Law to His people to safeguard the liberty He secured for them when He delivered them from Egypt (Exod. 20:2). I believe James' thought here is similar to Paul's in Romans 8:2: 'The law of the Spirit of life in Christ Jesus freed us from the law of sin and death.' As Christians, we have been set free from bondage to sin just as surely as the Old Testament people of God were freed from bondage to Egypt. In this freedom we are not antinomians – living as if no moral/spiritual law presides over us. No, we have been set free to do as we ought; we have a new power within to obey Christ that we did not possess before.

---

7. We summarize here the helpful discussion by Motyer, 71, 101.

'About to be judged' is a reminder that the certainty of the Judgment Seat of Christ (2 Cor. 5:10) calls us to a careful and diligent walk in light of God's Word. Jesus is the only source of true liberty, and we as followers of Christ must walk in and reflect that liberty that comes from participation in God's blessings of redemption.

For judgment is merciless to the one who has shown no mercy (2:13)

'For' connects this verse to the preceding one, but the pronouns change from second person in verse 12 to third person here. James points the finger of criticism toward those in the church who have not shown mercy to the poor and outcast. In the Day of Judgment they will have the tables turned on them. The person who practices unprejudiced, impartial love toward all fulfills the royal law.

In contrast to the warning of 13a, James expresses great hope in 13b: **yet mercy triumphs over judgment**. God's mercy is stronger than the condemnation passed by the law.[8] Jesus expressed this same principle in Matthew 5:7: 'Blessed are the merciful, for they will receive mercy.' 'Triumphs over' could also be translated 'to exult or glory over.' It is used again in 3:14 where James warns not to boast against the truth. God forgives enormous sins, but He will not excuse a lack of mercy (see Jesus' parable in Matt. 18:21-35).

The manner in which we deal with others – including our displays of favoritism, partiality and snobbishness (whether secret or displayed) – will all influence the judgment we shall receive as the servants of our Lord Jesus when we stand before Him. When we live in obedience to God's Word, we strive to deal with others as God deals with us.

Wisdom to Live By

- Are we willing to identify any areas of partiality and prejudice and genuinely repent of it?

8. Martin, 72.

- What actions do we need to take to address the sins of partiality and prejudice in our churches?

- How can we intentionally involve ourselves with the poor and outcast and be 'friends of sinners' like Jesus was?

- Are our churches places where *everyone* is genuinely welcome?

- Imagine a non-Christian resisting the truth that he is a sinner, saying, 'There are only little things wrong in my life.' How could we use verse 10 to help him understand the truth about himself and about God?

- We are to 'speak and act as those who are going to be judged by the law that sets free' (2:12). Words and actions: to which do we give the greater attention or care? In which do we sin more easily?

7

Wisdom and True Faith
(James 2:14-26)

Anyone familiar with James' epistle knows the importance of the section before us. Chapter 2:14-26 is the
most theologically disputed passage in the entire letter. In
chapter 1 James challenged his readers to be 'doers' of the
Word. In 2:1-13 he applied that general exhortation to the
specific sin of prejudiced favoritism. Now, in masterful language and logic, he shows what true faith and wisdom are
– they go beyond empty recitation of religious platitudes
and express themselves in tangible acts of obedience.

Also, most readers are familiar with the supposed dis-
crepancy between James' argument here and Paul's grand
description of justification by faith alone (Rom. 3:24;
5:1; Gal. 2:16-18; 3:11). Failure to understand James' reasoning in this section can lead to many an error. Even the
great reformer Martin Luther termed James an 'epistle of
straw' because he thought that James contradicted Paul's
great doctrine.

But James did nothing of the kind. Quite the contrary,
he shows the interaction of true saving faith and resultant
works.[1] Ten times in this paragraph faith and works are
mentioned together. Faith and works are not enemies of

---

1. For a more detailed analysis of how the teaching of James relates to Paul's
doctrine of justification, see the 'Theology of James' section of this commentary.

one another; rather, righteous works authenticate true saving faith. This truly is an important discussion, for to be wrong here affects our doctrine of salvation. What kind of faith truly saves? Is it necessary to do good works in order to be saved? How do we know when we are exercising genuine faith? We will analyze James' answer to these crucial questions under three divisions:

1. A description of useless faith (2:14-20)
2. The manifestation of saving faith (2:21-25)
3. The union of faith and works (2:26)[2]

1. A Description of Useless Faith (2:14-20)

This section begins with a rhetorical question of tremendous significance. Anticipating a negative answer, he asked whether faith without works can really be saving faith.

Verse 14 asks two rhetorical questions. **My brothers, of what use is it if someone says he has faith but does not have works?**
'Of what use' abruptly begins the argument. James seems to be combating a problem that had surfaced within the congregation. The issue at hand is the nature of true, saving faith, and given that he addresses the 'teachers' beginning in chapter 3, perhaps some type of erroneous and destructive heresy threatened the church. James' imagined 'interrupter' claimed to have genuine faith. The word 'faith' sometimes in Scripture emphasizes a warm, personal trust in Christ. At other times, faith signifies the body of beliefs a Christian holds. James' imagined opponent, which he constructs here for the purpose of describing genuine faith, claimed to have habitual,

---

2. Our goal in this commentary is to provide an exegetically correct, devotionally warm presentation of the epistle. Without taking much time to be overly technical, allow me (Dale) to state four conclusions that will underlie our discussion of the 'James vs. Paul dispute': (1) Paul and James both believed in salvation by God's grace alone through faith; (2) Paul insisted in many places that true faith produces righteous deeds; (3) Paul and James used the key words faith and works with significant differences in emphasis; and (4) Paul and James fought different opponents, not one another.

personal faith in God. So this leads us to the first insight in
this section on the description of useless faith.

This man had a wordy but worthless faith. Words
without deeds characterized his life, and James questioned
its worth – 'what use is that, what does that profit?' It
is devoid of any operative energy to produce anything
beneficial. As we shall see, James looks upon works as
proof of faith, not as a means of salvation.

That faith cannot save him, can it? (2:14)
Obviously, a negative answer is expected. The kind of faith
just described, faith without works, is not able to save.
Robertson expresses this well:

> How can a man know that he has any faith? The mere
> assertion is all one has at first. In the beginning the claim
> to faith is accepted, but the life must confirm the claim if
> people are to believe it. God can read the heart, but even God
> demands that the outward life reflect the inward heart.[3]

The illustration in verses 15 and 16 fleshes out the principle
of this verse: **If a brother or sister is inadequately clothed
and lacking in daily food (2:15)**
James uses his creative ability to describe a scene and
asks us to envisage a situation where fellow believers in
need of basic necessities such as food and clothes come
into contact with the church. 'Inadequately clothed' does
not mean 'totally naked' but insufficiently clothed. These
people are also without adequate food supplies. 'Lacking'
is from *leipein,* meaning 'to leave off, be deprived.' These
are people who literally live day-to-day wondering where
their basic necessities will come from.

Instead of receiving the help commensurate with
the love of a Christian community, all they receive is a
mouthful of pious platitudes:

**and someone from among you says, 'Go in peace; be
warmed and be filled' (2:16)**
'Go in peace' was a common Jewish farewell – *shalom*
(Judg. 18:6; 1 Sam. 1:17; 20:42; 2 Sam. 15:9). In other words,

---

3. Robertson, 94.

the Christians wanted them 'out of sight and out of mind.' 'Be warmed' and 'filled' could be either middle or passive voice. So, the meaning could be 'warm yourselves' and 'feed (*chortazō*) yourselves.' Instead of warm clothes and satisfying food, all they get is religious banality. Their words speak of grace, but even as they speak they fail to minister grace. How can they go in peace when in reality they will go hungry and cold?

Even so faith, if it has no works, is dead, being by itself (2:17)
The bottom line is this, James argues: faith apart from works is dead. It is pious talk without reality. It is 'by itself,' like an engine without fuel. Some essential components are present, but it is useless and inoperative without the fuel that enables it to fire and run. Jesus did not merely preach about faith, He served and healed and helped and died to show us what Christian faith is all about. As long as we go on in our religious business but 'pass by on the other side' to avoid 'getting our hands dirty' to minister to the less fortunate, we are in no way better than the priest and the Levite in Jesus' Good Samaritan parable. We are saved by faith and not by works, but be sure that true saving faith will exhibit itself *through* our works.

A second insight into this description of useless faith lies in verses 18-20. Here James shows that a faith may be very orthodox and yet be useless. Orthodoxy alone is not a guarantee of living faith. I (Dale) like to warn people, 'You can be theologically as straight as a gun barrel, but spiritually be twice as empty.' In dramatic form James puts words in the mouth of an imaginary person:

But someone will say, 'You have faith and I have works' (2:18)
James' flow of thought here has generated quite a bit of discussion. The problem centers on the identity of the 'someone' (*tis*) who speaks. Basically, three possibilities exist: (1) some interpret the imaginary speaker to be an ally who takes up James' argument and carries it forward, and the 'but' would then be translated as 'indeed'; (2) others understand the speaker as opposing James and the 'but'

(*alla*) is a strong adversative; (3) still other interpreters take the 'you' and 'I' to refer to representative positions in the church – some have faith and some works. The other part of the problem is how much is to be included in what the interlocutor says? Is it only 18a or all of the verse?

It seems best[4] to take the view that this is an imaginary objector (the second view mentioned above) whose objection covers only the first part of the verse. Then 18b-19 gives us James' reply to the objector. Taken this way, the objector challenges the faith of James since he has put such an accent on works. The objector thus claims to have both faith and works but implies that James has only works and no faith. Martin notes well two matters that support this view that James is the 'I' of the argument and the objector is the 'you.' *First,* the heart of the issue is what James regards as true faith, that is, true faith is inseparable from deeds commensurate with it. *Second,* full force can then be given to the indictment against the opponent in verse 20.[5] The rest of the verse, then, as well as the next, are the author's answer to the challenge.

Show to me your faith without [apart from] works and I myself will show to you my faith by my works (2:18)
James' response in 18b-19 says that the supposed faith can be: (1) dead (2:18b), but also (2) no better than that of the demons (2:19). Here he argues that living faith cannot be separated from deeds. The people of God cannot be divided into two camps – those who are more passive in their faith and those who are more active 'doers.' So, James challenges the objector to show his faith in a tangible way. 'Show' forms a forcible part of the rhetorical argument. It can be translated with the stronger sense of 'prove,' since it has that force in the contexts of Matthew 7:16-17, John 10:32, and Hebrews 8:5.[6] And this is the sense of the word where it is found the only other time in James 3:13.

'I cannot see your faith apart from works,' James argues, 'but I am willing to *prove* my faith by what I do.' The only

---

4. Robertson, 96-97, is very helpful.
5. Martin, 88.
6. Richardson, 134.

certain proof of faith is the life lived after such profession of faith. Is this not what Jesus said in Matthew 7:16-17 and 7:21: 'Not everyone who says to Me "Lord, Lord" will enter the kingdom of heaven, but he who *does* the will of My Father'?

James goes on to highlight the possibility and the danger of faith being not only dead, but of being no better than the demons!

Do you believe that God is one? You believe well! (2:19)

Any devout Jew would recognize these words as rooted in the *Shema,* a confession embraced by Jews and Christians alike based on God's solemn revelation of Himself in Deuteronomy 6:4. But James' audience is struggling with the verse that follows: 'You shall love the LORD your God with all your heart and with all your soul and with all your might' (Deut. 6:5). James used a hint of sarcasm, saying 'Excellent, you do well,' but faith in Deuteronomy 6:4 without obedience to Deuteronomy 6:5 exposes that your faith is dead and worthless. In fact, even the demons know and believe that much!

the demons also believe and they shudder (2:19)

As far as doctrine is concerned, demons are monotheistic – they all know and believe there is but one God. Furthermore, they are very much aware that Scripture is God's Word; Satan himself admitted as much in the wilderness temptations of Jesus (Matt. 4). They know and believe that Jesus is God's Son and that He has authority over them. Each time they confronted Him in the Gospels they knew exactly who He was and they acknowledged His authority over them. They know and believe that salvation is by God's grace through faith, that Jesus died, was buried, was raised to atone for the sins of mankind, and that He ascended to the right hand of the Father in heaven. They know quite well that He will return to earth and they believe in a literal hell!

Because of this, they 'shudder,' a word that means to bristle and tremble in the face of great fear. MacArthur aptly reminds, 'Orthodox doctrine is immeasurably better than heresy, for it is true and points to God.... But mere assent to it as true cannot bring a person to God and to salvation.'[7]

Are you not willing to know, O empty-headed man, that faith apart from works is barren? (2:20)
The diatribe form of argument continues here. James appeals to the objector to acknowledge that the conclusion just reached in verse 19 is valid, but the verse has a transitional character. James is preparing to marshal forth two specific examples to demonstrate his point. 'Empty-headed' carries the idea of vain or deficient, much as Paul used 'fool' in 1 Corinthians 15:36. The problem is that there is no such thing as inoperative faith. We must understand this even in light of Paul's declaration in Romans 3:28: 'We maintain that a man is justified by faith apart from observing the law.' There is a clear contextual difference between the two apostles. For Paul, the issue was justification before God; for James the goal was a useful, practical faith. In the Romans context faith will not be allowed to boast in its own works of righteousness. The context here argues that saving faith must not be allowed to boast in self-sufficiency apart from accompanying acts of righteousness.[8]

2. The Manifestation of Saving Faith (2:21-25)

Having denounced dead and demon-like faith as useless and destitute of saving power, James now begins to confirm from Scripture the positive truth that saving faith reveals itself through tangible acts of righteousness. In doing so he effectively brings forward two people who could not be more disparate. These examples of true faith that works are Abraham and Rahab – a patriarch and a prostitute, a Jew and a Gentile, a godly man and a godless woman.

James shows *first*, that Abraham's faith was accompanied by works (v. 21), *second*, the fruit of that faith (vv. 22-23), and *third*, a conclusion from Abraham's example.

---

7. MacArthur, 132.
8. See Richardson here for a good discussion, 136-37.

Was not Abraham our father justified by works in that he offered up Isaac his son on the altar? (2:21)
First, Abraham could not be a more forceful example of faith-plus-works righteousness to his Jewish readers. We often need a concrete incarnation of faith to depict the theological information about faith. No one ever questioned Abraham's faith; to both Jews and Gentiles alike he was the embodiment of faith. He is the 'Father of all who believe' for the Gentile no less than the Jew (Rom. 4:11). 'Was not' is from the common negative *ouk*, and James expected an affirmative response. The passive verb 'justified' directs the reader to God as the active agent expressing the verdict of justification. It is a concept of utmost importance in the New Testament. It involves not just the forgiveness of sin but the declaration by God that we are in right standing with Him based on the merits of Christ on our behalf. The verb is aorist, or historical. It records the divine verdict upon Abraham's faith-prompted action.

Thus with Abraham, faith was shown to be alive, not dead, and fruitful, not barren. It should be noted that 'offered up' is from *anenegkas*, and referred to only the binding of Isaac. He did not carry through with the sacrificial 'offering up,' but he was willing. So the Scripture from Romans 4 was fulfilled in the case of Abraham. Robertson observes: 'Paul in Romans 4 lays emphasis on the word 'believed,' and James stresses the obedience which proves the reality of the faith.'[9]

Second, James shows the *fruit* of that faith: **Do you see that faith worked through his deeds and that faith was perfected by his deeds (2:22)**.
'Do you see' may not be a question at all, but it makes little difference. It has the connotation of 'understand for yourself,' and it is singular in number. Every person has to come to the realization that true faith manifests itself in action. Spiros Zodhiates tells the story about a boy walking home with a bucket of honey. The bucket had a small hole in it and the boy repeatedly wiped the drops

9. Robertson, 100.

from the hole with his finger and ate it. A man asked him, 'Son, what is it you have there?' 'A bucket of honey,' the boy replied. 'Is it good honey?' the man queried. 'Oh yes, very good.' After a while the man asked the boy how he knew it was so good. 'Here,' said the boy, pointing to a drop just about to fall from the hole, 'taste for yourself.'[10] That is the message of James, and indeed, the message of the New Testament: taste and see that faith is living and vibrant and active.

The fruit of Abraham's faith is expressed in a three-fold way. *First*, his faith was 'perfected' by his deeds. A careful use of tenses helps to form James' emphasis here. 'Faith was working' (*sunērgei*) is an imperfect verb that suggests continuous, ongoing action. 'Perfected' is from the Greek *eteleiōthē*, an aorist tense verb that carries the idea of completed action. So, his ongoing works resulted in his faith being perfected and proven to be legitimate.

Second, the Scripture was fulfilled concerning Abraham's justification: **and the Scripture was fulfilled which says, Abraham believed God and it was accounted to him for righteousness (2:23)**
James wanted to show that Abraham's faith was not an idle, passive matter. The Scripture to which he alludes is Genesis 15:6, but in Genesis 22 Abraham demonstrated the active, tangible nature of his faith. We stated earlier that James and Paul were in agreement regarding the basis of justification before God. Paul quotes Genesis 15:6 in his arguments for justification by faith in Romans 4:3 and Galatians 3:6. 'Accounted' could also be translated 'imputed' or 'reckoned.' Adamson explains, 'Whereas Paul employs the example of Abraham to demolish the notion of justification by works, James uses him to illustrate the futility of dead faith.'[11]

10. Spiros Zodhiates, *The Behavior of Belief* (Grand Rapids: Eerdmans, 1959), 43.
11: James B. Adamson, *The Epistle of James*, New International Commentary on the New Testament (Grand Rapids: Eerdmans, 1976), 131.

A *third* fruit of his faith is that Abraham **was called a friend of God (2:23)**
This last phrase is not referring to any specific Scripture in the Old Testament. 'Friend' is from *philos*, a designation used only after Abraham demonstrated his willingness to obey God in verse 22. His faith led him to be willing to sacrifice Isaac, and James says that there was a covenantal relationship in which he could be called God's friend. What greater expression of justification could one receive than to be called God's friend?

Third, James draws a conclusion from Abraham's example: **You see that a person is declared righteous by works and not by faith alone (2:24)**
The conclusion he draws is that faith and works are inseparable. Any profession of being justified by faith must be proved by the works of the one making such a profession. James rejects a 'faith' that remains alone and produces no works. He insists upon a working faith. Jonathan Edwards asserts:

> The drift of the apostle does not require that he should be understood in any other sense; for all that he aims at, as appears by a view of the context, is to prove that good works are necessary. The error of those that he opposed was this: that good works were not necessary to salvation, that if they did but believe that there was but one God, and that Christ was the Son of God and the like, and were baptized, they were safe, let them live how they would, which doctrine greatly tended to licentiousness. The evincing the contrary of this is evidently the apostle's scope.[12]

John Calvin summarizes, 'Faith alone justifies, but faith that justifies is never alone.'[13]

In the same manner also (2:25)
To give another example of faith expressing itself through works, James uses a person least likely by a Jew to be called

12. Jonathan Edwards, *Works*, rev. Edward Hickman, 2 vol. (Edinburgh: Banner of Truth Trust, 1974), 1:650-52.
13. Quoted by Adamson, 133.

upon: Rahab. It is as if James feels that he needs to complete his argument by marshaling forth a quite common person to serve as an example of saving faith.

Rahab the prostitute (2:25)
Despite her less-than-upright vocation, she became a heroine of faith in Jewish tradition.[14] **was she not justified by works when she received the messengers and sent them out another way? (2:25).**
James deliberately designed the greatest conceivable contrast to the godly patriarch Abraham. Abraham was a Jew; she was a Gentile. He was a man; she was a woman. But Hebrews 11:31 honors her as a woman of faith. She confessed her faith clearly in Joshua 2:11. And she acted on that faith by harboring the Jewish spies who came to her city and sent them out by a safe way. As simple as her story of faith was, it was a faith that demonstrated itself in a tangible manner. By using such contrasting examples, James showed the necessity of proving one's faith by deeds. In fact, Rahab found herself a place in the genealogy of Jesus (Matt. 1:5)!

3. The Union of Faith and Works (2:26)
For just as the body without breath is dead, so also faith without works is dead (2:26)
'For' (gar) connects this statement to the testimony about Rahab – her justifying faith expressed itself in action. 'Just as' (hōsper) brings us again to James' 'circling fashion'[15] as he closes his argument with a concluding verdict. Creed and conduct cannot be separated any more than the body can be separated from its very life-breath and still be called alive. 'Breath' is from pneumatos, and many commentaries render it 'spirit.' We need not take the space to argue which is better – in the end, the result is the same: a corpse and not a living body! With this verdict James touches the

14. See Martin for Rabbinic traditions regarding her, 96. See also A. T. Robertson, *Word Pictures*, vol. 6, *General Epistles and Revelation* (Grand Rapids: Baker, 1933), 38. Cited as Robertson, *Word Pictures*. Robertson, *Studies in the Epistle of James* still cited as Robertson.
15. Adamson, 134.

root of the whole matter. The relationship between faith and works is like that between the body and its breath. Without breath, the body is a corpse. Without works, faith is dead. Religious words without accompanying works are worthless.

Wisdom to Live By

- This section of James has really taken us back to a key verse of the entire epistle – 1:22. Are we constantly narrowing the gap between what we know about the Word and how we apply it daily?

- How sensitive are we to the needy and deprived around us? What action needs to be taken to do like Jesus and get our hands dirty with real ministry to people in need?

- Does the way we live at home match what we confess at church? Bunyan's character in *Pilgrim's Progress*, Mr. Talkative, was a saint at church but a devil at home. He would be most uncomfortable with James' verdict in 2:17, 20, and 26!

- Further, we need to remember that this spiritual 'autopsy' needs to be applied not just on an individual level but to our faith community, the church, as well. Revelation 3:2 reminds us that churches collectively can have dead faith just as an individual can. We do well to ask ourselves afresh the little jingle, 'What kind of church would my church be, if every member were just like me?'

8

Wisdom and Words
(James 3:1-12)

James' Old Testament wisdom counterpart, the Proverbs, gives us this counsel about our words and speech: 'When words are many, sin is not absent, but he who holds his tongue is wise' (Prov. 10:19). This section is James' 'amen' to that verse. More than twenty-five years ago, a pastor/ friend/mentor talked to my wife-to-be and me (Dale) about the marriage relationship. He advised us, 'Keep your words warm and sweet. You may have to eat them some day!' Words have enormous power for good or for bad, and once spoken, they can never really be taken back.

We opened an earlier chapter ('Wisdom and Prejudice') by noting that nothing measures our spiritual priorities like possessions and how we use them. So, it was only natural for James to show that being 'doers of the Word' (1:22) involves measuring our use of wealth by godly standards. If the use of material wealth measures our priorities, then nothing measures our true heart condition like our words do. It is inevitable that a letter so devoted to practical wisdom would deal with words, speech, the tongue, and how they impact the community of faith.

I heard a story some years ago about a woman who came forward during the invitation in a revival service at her church. The Spirit of God was moving during the services in an unusual way. Her pastor, and indeed the entire church, knew what a gossiping, critical, divisive influence she was in the church body. She told her pastor, 'I have been convicted by God of the sinful way I have used my tongue, and I want to lay it on the altar.' The pastor could not resist saying to her, 'Sister, our altar is only twenty-four-feet long, but lay as much of it as you can there!' Words have the power to heal or to hurt, to help or to hinder, to build up or to tear down, to bless or to curse. But in this context, what drives James to address the community specifically regarding the tongue?

He has already cautioned them to be 'slow to speak' (1:19) and to bridle their tongues (1:26). Apparently this early church, still immersed in a synagogue milieu, was having significant problems with their words and how to control them. And this will not be his last directive regarding the tongue – he warns against slander in 4:11, empty boasting in 4:13, and grumbling in 5:9. Christian teachers were needed and apparently were arising in this incipient church. Higher standards were expected of these leaders and the risks were more acute. What James says to the teachers of this early church applies to all Christians in their use of words. Four general principles arise out of this section regarding the tongue:

1. Our words demonstrate our self-control.
2. Our words are powerful.
3. Our words can be destructive.
4. Our words reveal our heart.

1. Our Words Demonstrate Our Self-Control
Having just written about wrong actions, James follows it with wrong talking. Robertson summarized, 'Here he speaks against those who substitute words for works, a rather large class.'[1]

Let not many become teachers, my brothers (3:1)
The negative 'not' (*mē*) stands first in the sentence for emphasis. 'Teachers' (*didaskaloi*) need not be under-

---

1. Robertson, 104.

stood in the technical sense like the office of pastor-teacher (Eph. 4:11). In the Jewish synagogues the role of the teacher was an important and prominent one. Furthermore, wide latitude was granted to Jewish men who claimed to have a teaching ministry. Jesus took advantage of this practice often during His earthly ministry (Matt. 12:9; Mark 1:39; Luke 6:6). The ministry of teaching must never be discouraged or overlooked, but it can be easily abused.

knowing that we will receive a greater judgment (3:1)

There has never been a greater need in our churches for solid, biblically sound teachers. I (Dale) have served as a pastor to churches for almost twenty-five years, and it saddens me to say that the average Christian has never been more biblically illiterate. But those who teach must realize the greater responsibility and accountability we carry. Robertson explained: '[Teachers] are doctors of the heart and mind. They cannot escape their responsibility as spiritual surgeons, dealing with issues of life and death.'[2] Teachers, because they are prone to speak more words, are therefore more subject to erring in those words. Greater knowledge means greater responsibility (Matt. 18:6; Luke 12:48; James 4:17). 'Greater' could be translated 'stricter.' Though James does not say categorically that Christian teachers are measured against a higher standard than that required of other Christians, it appears that such a solemn emphasis is intended here.[3]

Knowledge is required of Christian teachers but so too is character. Anyone aspiring to be a teacher of the Word of God should approach the role with some trepidation because fulfilling such a responsibility means enduring a more rigorous judgment from God. It is no wonder that James, with his emphasis throughout on wisdom for the community, introduces this section on the tongue and speech by referring to teachers.

2. Ibid., 107.
3. See Martin, 108; Adamson, 141.

For all of us stumble in many ways (3:2)

We all stumble in many ways, but in nothing as frequently or more seriously as in matters of the tongue. 'Stumble' or 'trip' (*ptaiomen*) is the same word as in 2:10. The explanatory 'for' joins this verse to the preceding one as James justifies the serious warning he has just given.

If anyone does not stumble in his words, this one is a perfect man, able to bridle the whole body as well (3:2). The tongue is the most difficult member of the body to control; therefore, it is mentioned either directly or indirectly in every chapter in James (1:19, 26; 2:12; 3:1-12; 4:11; 5:12). James does not imply that the tongue holds the *only* potential for sin, for 'we all stumble in many ways.' All people trip up spiritually from time to time and James includes himself ('we') in this diagnosis. We can all sympathize with the songwriter who confessed, 'Prone to wander, Lord, I feel it; prone to leave the God I love.' Yet, we are nowhere more apt to stumble than in our speech.

James uses six verbal images to impress upon us the importance of controlling the tongue: a bit (v. 3), a rudder (v. 4), a fire (vv. 5-6), a poisonous animal (vv. 7-8), a fountain (v. 11), and a fig tree (v. 12). Repeating the principle from 1:26 James uses the same rare verb applied to the tongue: 'bridle' (*chalinagōgēsai*). Here the same metaphor is used. Just as the bit in a horse's mouth can control its whole body, so also a man who can control his tongue is able to control all the body's passions. The idea of a 'perfect man' reiterates the thought of 1:4. This is a Christian who is complete and mature, not sinless. James did not elaborate on this metaphor in 1:26, but here he does.

If we put bridles in the horses' mouths to make them obey us (3:3)

James uses illustrations about the potential power of the tongue that were curiously well-known in antiquity.[4] Everyone in that context understands the importance of keeping the horse under control; otherwise its power can

---

4. See the discussion by Martin, 110.

be destructive. One of the largest horses ever recorded in
history was a Belgian stallion that weighed 3200 pounds
and stood 19.2 hands tall! But that huge animal was useless
to its owner until a two-pound bit was placed in its mouth.
The noun 'bridle' in this verse is a cognate to the verb in
verses 1:26 and 3:2. If a person can control his tongue, he
can probably control his whole body.

we also turn their entire body (3:3)
When the rider or the charioteer turns the mouth of the horse
with bit and bridle, its whole body turns in that direction. In
the same way James directs us to 'bridle' our mouths with
the express purpose of controlling the words that come out.
Positively viewed, think of the wonderful service horses have
provided for mankind when they are controlled properly.
Our words can help, encourage, edify, and bless if we will
yield our mouths to the control of the Holy Spirit.

2. Our Words Are Powerful

'With great wealth of imagination James goes further to show
us the power of the tongue over the rest of the body.'[5]

In verse 4 the imagery is masterful: **Behold the ships,
being so large and driven along by powerful winds**.
The reality of a small object controlling a larger body is
reinforced with this second illustration. James invites us
to envision large ships being driven by rough, powerful
winds. He had no knowledge of the mammoth ships at sea
today, but his illustration was effective enough. The ship
on which Paul sailed to Malta held 276 people (Acts 27:37),
so the readers were familiar with large vessels.

**are yet turned by a very small rudder wherever the
impulse of the pilot chooses (3:4)**
The Greek text here is difficult to translate smoothly, but
the meaning is nevertheless clear. The pilot (from a Greek
verb that literally means 'to guide straight') of a vessel
knows the direction in which he wants the ship to go and

5. Robertson, 111.

he determines his course by a very small rudder. The only other New Testament use of 'rudder' (*pēdalion*) is in the Acts 27:37 passage mentioned above. The ship may be large, but the rudder still remains small in comparison. 'Small' is from *elachistos*, the superlative form of *mikros*. Even when the winds are strong and contrary to the ship's direction, the rudder continues to hold the ship on its determined course. The human tongue is like both the bit and the rudder in its smallness, and it far surpasses them in its power to influence, direct, and sway the course of people's lives.

Likewise also the tongue is a small member (of the body) and yet it boasts great things (3:5)

The tongue's boasts can be great indeed. History, as well as contemporary life, records tremendous achievements that have been inspired by words. Likewise, the pages of history are strewn with examples of the tongue's tragic power for evil. It was with five simple words, a lie notwithstanding, that Satan tempted Adam and Eve to sin and thus plunge the human race into disaster. In Genesis 3:4 the Serpent deceived Eve, 'You shall surely *not* die.' Adolf Hitler recorded his Nazi philosophy in the book *Mein Kampf*. For every word written in that dreadful treatise, more than 100 lives were lost in World War II. Yet Ronald Reagan's legacy as one of America's favorite presidents rests largely on his ability to talk straight to the American people, calming fears and inspiring hope. Words truly are powerful. Words affect the course of history.

'Member' is from *melos*, an old and common word used for parts of the body. Paul used it frequently when speaking of the body of Christ in 1 Corinthians 12. This is the only New Testament use of *aucheō*, 'to boast or brag.' Building further on his argument about the power of the tongue, James now employs a third simile.

Behold how a small fire sets a forest ablaze (3:5)

I (Dale) once served as a pastor of a small rural church in South Carolina. The parsonage had a wood stove and every so often the ashes had to be cleaned out. I used a little shovel to put them in a bucket and dumped them in a field next to the house. I did not give another thought to the menial chore until, about thirty minutes later, a man pounded on my door and shouted, 'Preacher, I hate to bother you but we have a fire out here.' I did not realize that the coals on the very bottom of that stove were still lit, and the winter day was dry and windy. In the span of half an hour, one little ember out of that stove had started a fire that consumed several acres before we could extinguish it. Our words can be like that.

We derive our prefix *puro* from the Greek word for 'fire.' 'Set ablaze' is from *anaptein*. Its only other New Testament occurrence is in Luke 12:49 where Jesus wishes that the fire He came to set on the earth were already kindled. James compares the tongue's destructive power to a wild fire out of control, a fire that can char people's lives and reputations.

The tongue is a fire, a world of unrighteousness (3:6)

Verse 6 is a striking one containing startling language. Commentators disagree on how the verse should be punctuated and thus translated.[6] Punctuation was not provided in the original documents of the New Testament. One thing is for sure: James now abandons simile and states the truth metaphorically, 'The tongue is not *like* a fire; it *is* a fire.' To make matters more difficult, James mixes his images. He moves from a fire to a 'world.' The translation problem is that James uses a series of five nouns, all in the nominative case, with only one indicative verb. Every combination has difficulties and deciding on the best translation is not easy. But we need not delve neck-deep in the minutia of the language, for James' intent is maintained despite the problems with the grammar.

'World' carries a wide range of meanings in the New Testament. It may mean the 'world' of humankind as in John 3:16, or the created order as in 1 John 2:15, or 'adornment' as in 1 Peter 3:3. The best view is to see 'world'

---

6. See Moo (PNTC), 156-58.

here as the sinful, fallen world-system that is in rebellion against God, as this is the use of the word everywhere else in James (1:27; 4:4). The tongue is a world of evil among the parts of the body (3:6). James seems to mean that every sort of unrighteousness found in the world finds an ally in an uncontrolled tongue.

As we ponder this statement we discover how profound a truth it is. Evil suppresses truth (Rom. 1:18), and men use their tongues in threats and other pressures to prevent truth from being known. Evil rejoices in evil and can make jokes about it (1 Cor. 13:6), and men use their tongues to express their pleasure in wrong things. Evil deceives and thinks nothing of giving a false impression (2 Thess. 2:10) and men use their tongues to deceive. In fact, the tongue corrupts the whole person (3:6). If we speak evil, we soon do evil. If we are bold enough to talk of sin, we shall soon be sufficiently bold to commit it. To declare that what we say is only talk amounts to self-deception. In fact, James goes on to say that the tongue can set the whole course of our life on fire.

Whereas the first two illustrations, the bit and the rudder are passive, waiting to be used, this imagery of fire moves into the blatantly active – a fire forces its own way in the most destructive manner.

being placed among the members of our body, it is a corrupter of the whole body and sets on fire the course of human existence (3:6)

Here we come to the problem mentioned earlier about the grammar. Should the comma in the translation be placed after 'fire' above and the rest read, 'a very world of iniquity being placed among the members...' or should the pause be after 'unrighteousness' and this section read 'being placed [or placing itself] among the members...'? As interesting as it is to ponder for some of us who are 'Greekers,' either way will not substantially affect where we wind up. The author posits four aspects of the 'fiery potency' of the tongue.[7]

_____

7. Motyer, 121-23.

First, he speaks of the *character* the tongue possesses. 'Being placed' is from *kauthistatai* and can be either passive voice or middle. Does James intend that the tongue 'is placed' by another or that it 'places itself' because that is its nature – aggressive and uncontrollable? This may very well be what the author had in mind. 'Members' is the same word as in verse 5, *melos*. It is the member that is the most inflammatory, doing its utmost to make the rest of the organs a 'world' that is hostile to God.[8]

Second, the author speaks of the tongue's *influence*: 'corrupter of the whole body.' 'Corrupter' is a participle from the verb *spiloō*, found elsewhere only in Jude 23.[9] The pervasive power of the tongue is that it can defile, corrupt, and besmirch the whole body so that every member is affected. Jesus taught this: 'that which proceeds out of the mouth, this defiles the person' (Matt. 15:11). Robertson captures the sense well: 'The tongue not only commits evil by lying, by defending sin, and by leading to sin, but it leaves a deadly stain in the very body and soul of the one who misuses it.'[10]

Remember that James is writing first and foremost to the community of faith, and he has stated that the tongue can corrupt or stain not only the individual but also the body of Christ. In fact, this thought is in line with 3:2 and 3:4. Martin is helpful here: 'The implication is that by irresponsible speech the whole body of Christ is stained.'[11] As pastors we can attest to James' burden. The local body of Christ can be hurt and hindered by careless and uncontrolled tongues in ways that are virtually unparalleled by any other sin.

Third, James notes the *evil force* of the tongue. It 'sets on fire the course of human existence.' F. J. A. Hort opined that this is one of the hardest phrases of the Bible.[12] James' concern is to show the magnitude of the tongue's destructive potential, but his language is nevertheless

---

8. Ibid.
9. The noun from, 'spot, blot,' is found in Ephesians 5:27 and 2 Peter 2:13.
10. Robertson, 116.
11. Martin, 115.
12. Quoted by Robertson, *Word Studies*, 6:43.

unusual. The verb is from *phlogizō,* 'to ignite, to set ablaze,' and 'course' is from *trochon,* a cycle or wheel. A paraphrase might cut through the fog here to show us James' meaning: 'The tongue sets on fire the entire complex of human existence in all its varied activities and relationships.' The verb tense indicates that the tongue perpetually, habitually causes human firestorms. The reference here may be to the familiar problem of a wheel that loses its lubrication. Of course, the friction that builds up from such a scenario would cause the wooden wheels of a chariot to burst into flames and to spread the flame wherever the chariot goes.

Fourth, we see the tongue's *affiliation:* **and is set on fire by hell (3:6)**
Motyer observes, 'The first feature of the tongue was that it was anti-God (the world); the last feature is that it is pro-Satan.'[13] Hell is *gehenna,* the term that originally denoted the valley of the sons of Hinnon, a ravine south of Jerusalem. There, according to later Jewish popular belief, the last judgment is to take place. In the Gospels it is the place of punishment in the next life (Matt. 23:33), the fiery destination to which the ungodly will be eternally condemned at the last judgment (Matt. 5:22; 18:9). The fact that this is the only place outside the Gospels where *gehenna* is used underscores the terrible source of the inflammatory power of the tongue.

But thank God that the tongue can be used for good just as well as for evil. All the news does not have to be bad for with the tongue we can bless and encourage and edify one another. In Acts 2 the tongues of the early church members were set on fire by heaven, not hell, and they preached the glorious gospel of our Lord Jesus!

James has so far used three verbal images to describe the power of the tongue: a bit (v. 3), a rudder (v. 4), and a fire (vv. 5-6). Now he draws on a fourth image: a poisonous animal.

---

13. Motyer, 123.

For all species of beasts and birds, of reptiles and sea creatures are being tamed and have been tamed by mankind (3:7)

'For' ties this verse to what precedes and elaborates on the wild and untamed nature of the tongue. 'Species' is from *phusis* and refers to kinds; the 'all' means 'all kinds; all you can think of.' James' fourfold list may be based on Genesis 1:26 and 9:2. 'Beasts' (*thērion*) referred to undomesticated animals[14] or to quadrupeds in general.[15] 'Birds' is from *peteinōn* and signifies all kinds of flying animals. 'Reptiles' (*herpetōn*) is from the verb 'crawl,' thus 'crawling, creeping things.' This is the only occurrence in the New Testament of 'sea creatures' (*enalion*), literally, 'things in the sea.'

James uses the present tense here: 'is being tamed.' The only other occurrence of this verb is in Mark 5:4 where the demoniac was beyond anyone's ability to tame. The ancient world took pride in the fact that humans were superior to animals. In fact, the Greeks believed that human reason overcame the strength and speed of animals.[16] It has always been God's design that man should rule over the created order. The nature of the animal has been domesticated by the nature of humanity. For example, humanity has expressed its ability to tame in dancing bears, trained seals, talking dolphins, acrobatic birds, and snake charming.

But no one is able to tame the tongue (3:8)

Not so with the tongue – it is a one-of-a-kind 'animal' that no one can tame. The change in subjects, 'no one,' makes the application here very personal. Even though mankind can tame the wild beasts, an individual faces quite a different proposition when it comes to taming his own tongue.

[It is] a restless evil, full of deadly poison (3:8)

The last part of verse 8 is especially strong. Most translations insert predicate nominatives: '*it is* a restless evil; *it is* full

---

14. Martin, 116.
15. Robertson, *Word Pictures*, 43.
16. Martin, 116.

of deadly poison.' But the Greek text suggests that these phrases be taken as exclamations: 'Restless evil! Full of deadly poison!' The adjective 'restless' (*akatastaton*) characterizes the tongue as being fickle and inconsistent; it cannot be trusted to stay in its place. The picture is of a caged animal, pacing back and forth. It is 'full' (*mestos*) of death-dealing poison.

As pastors we certainly would never consider turning wild lions or poisonous snakes loose on the dear people in Sunday morning worship. But we do not realize that our tongues are that way – poisonous tongues do great damage to people, families, and entire churches. When we tame a mighty horse we have a useful tool to work with, but a stallion untamed is useless, even destructive, to us. Only when the Spirit of God tames our tongue can He use it to bless others and glorify Christ.

3. Our Words Can Be Destructive
In his vivid manner James goes on to reveal the unstable, duplicitous nature of the tongue.

With it we bless the Lord and Father (3:9)
'That little bit of flesh between the jaws,' as the reformer Martin Luther called it, 'is a concealed and dangerous weapon.' According to the ancient Plutarch, an Egyptian king told one of his servants to cut out the best and worst meat of a sacrificial animal. In both cases, he cut out the tongue.[17] Such is the deceitfulness of the tongue: it can taste the Lord's Supper on Sunday and curse on Monday!

'We are blessing' (*eulogoumen*, from which we derive 'eulogy') is present tense, apparently indicating the pattern or continual practice of these hypocrites who express pious platitudes about God yet curse others. The Lord chided His people often in the Old Testament about how they honored Him with their words, yet their hearts were far from Him. The combination of 'Lord and Father'

---

17. Sophie Laws, *A Commentary on the Epistle of James* (New York: Harper & Row, 1980), 155.

is unique to the New Testament, the closest parallel being in 1 Corinthians 8:6.

and with it we curse others who are begotten in the image of God (3:9)
One of the most negative, critical, spiteful men I (Dale) have ever known was a pastor of a small church in North Carolina. He was a fine preacher, but outside the pulpit his tongue took on a completely different personality. I thought of this verse often as I listened to him disparage and criticize anyone and everyone in his path. 'Curse' is parallel to 'bless,' both in the present tense. Even unredeemed mankind retains an 'image of God.' The literal reading is 'being begotten in the likeness [similitude] of God.' It is this image which sets us apart as being superior to animals. When we assassinate the character of others with our tongues we trample God's image within them! James says the duplicity of the tongue is wrong because *first*, it *desecrates the image of God*.

Second, double talk *disobeys God's will*. **My brethren, these things should not be! (3:10)**
After repeating the almost unthinkable scenario ('**out of the same mouth come *both* blessing and curses**'), James condemns the dual deceit of the tongue. But here he changes the culprit to the 'mouth' (*stoma*). Most commentators think that the switch is due to the fact that the mouth is simply the place where the tongue is located, and in this way James can parallel the words of His Master, 'what comes out of the mouth defiles a person' (Matt. 15:11, 20). 'Should not be' translates *ou chrē*, 'it is not right, needful.' The verb is from *chran*, 'to give what is needed,' and is found only here in the New Testament. There can be no excuse for it; no reason can be concocted to justify it. One moment it is possible for us to use our tongues to praise God, our Lord and Father (3:9) and the next to curse people who are made in His image. John Bunyan, in his famous *Pilgrim's Progress*, described Mr. Talkative in these terms: 'He was a saint abroad and a devil at home.' When this

state of affairs exists in any measure in the home *or* the church, all is not well.

James turns to nature once again to draw a fifth verbal image of the tongue. In so doing he illustrates three contradictory phenomena: (1) a fountain that yields both fresh and bitter water, (2) a fig tree with olive berries, and (3) a vine with figs (3:11, 12). James argues his point with two rhetorical questions because he wants to carry his readers along with him in his argument. And in all of these illustrations we find the central truth, that *root* determines *fruit; source* is revealed by the *nature* of what it produces.

4. Our Words Reveal Our Heart

Does a spring from the same source pour forth both fresh and salt water? (3:11). Fresh water and bitter water do not flow from the same spring or fountain. James' readers knew the importance of a 'spring' to a dry Palestinian village or town. In fact, communities developed around such fresh water supplies. 'Source' is from *opē*, a crevice or open place in the ground. The word is found only here and in Hebrews 11:38 in the New Testament. The point is that the spring pours forth water in keeping with its nature. It is unthinkable that the same spring would give fresh water one day and bitter, brackish water the next. The *source* determines the *nature* of the water. Fresh water does not purify the bitter, but the opposite is true – a little bitter water can spoil the whole. One rotten apple spoils an entire basket of good ones. What cannot come from the same opening in the ground (no spring pours forth both salt water and fresh, v. 12b) can come from the mouth – bitter and sweet words can flow almost simultaneously. The tongue reveals what is in the heart like nothing else can.

The *second* contradiction James cites is a fig tree that produces olives. **My brothers, a fig tree cannot produce olives,** *can it***? (3:12)**
James' pastoral heart shines through in the address 'my brothers.' The key here is the word 'can,' which requires

a 'no' response. The root of the tree determines its fruit – fig trees produce figs and olive trees produce olives. The writer once again borrows from His Master in recalling His teaching that a good heart produces good fruit and an evil heart bears evil fruit (Matt. 7:16-20; 12:33-35; Luke 6:43-45).

My grandmother was a wise, godly woman who loved Jesus and shaped the lives of her grandchildren in significant ways. Among her many witticisms was, 'Pretty is as pretty does; ugly is as ugly does.' Her meaning was that like produces like. Angry hearts spew angry words. Hearts softened by the love of Jesus utter words in keeping with that love.

Third, James asks rhetorically, **or can a vine [produce] figs? (3:12)**
The fruit of the vine conforms to the nature of the vine, and vines do not produce figs – trees do! Vines produce grapes. The fruit of the lips reveals the root condition of the heart. It is just as inconsistent for a Christian to bless God with one breath and to criticize others with the next.

We would do well to yield our tongue to the Holy Spirit and ask Him to help us apply a threefold test to our words. *First*, is what I am about to say *true*? Many people possess a 'keen sense of rumor' and much of what they say is not really true or accurate. Much gossip would die in its tracks if we asked whether it is true. *Second*, is it *necessary*? Many times we fail to 'cover a multitude of sins' by repeating things about others that are not necessary to tell. Granted, a matter may be true, but is there any use in repeating it just to make idle chatter? *Third*, is it *kind*? How do the words I am about to speak fit with the second greatest commandment, 'You shall love your neighbor as yourself?' I do not know the source of the following rhyme I have used for years:

> There is so much good in the worst of us,
> And so much bad in the best of us,
> That it hardly becomes any one of us
> To talk about the rest of us.

Wisdom to Live By

- Are we taming our tongues? For the rest of the day, let's concentrate on measuring every word before it is spoken. Let's ask ourselves, what problems did we discover?

- Paul admonishes us to think on good things in Philippians 4:8. How do our words stack up to the barometer found there: true, noble, just, pure, lovely, of good report, praiseworthy?

- What ways can we recall that the tongue has hurt and hindered the body of Christ?

- How should the church body deal with a poisonous gossip? Are there actions we need to take to protect our churches from such gossips?

9

True and False Wisdom
(James 3:13-18)

Shortly after Solomon was inaugurated king over Israel the Lord appeared to him in a dream at night and said, 'Ask! What shall I give you?' What a blank check opportunity! What would you ask for? What would be the priority of your heart? Scripture tells us that Solomon made an honorable and noble request: 'Give to Your servant an understanding heart' (1 Kings 3:1-9, NKJV). Solomon asked for wisdom. And later, in Proverbs 2, he extolled the value of wisdom for making life beneficial and worthwhile.

So, it comes as no surprise that wisdom plays an important role in James' worldview. Remember, he presents it as the key to understanding life's varied experiences (1:5). It is likely that James here in 3:13-18 continues to address especially the teachers from verse 1. They carried a grave responsibility, as the section prior to this one demonstrated, and they needed wisdom to know what to say and how to say it. Genuine wisdom is contrasted with spurious wisdom in this passage. The author highlights three truths about false wisdom and three truths about true wisdom. They can be distinguished by their characteristics, source, and results.[1]

---

1. Note that the order in discussing false wisdom is: characteristics, results. But when James describes true wisdom the order is: source, characteristics, results. This emphasizes that true wisdom comes down from above, from God Himself.

1. False Wisdom: Its Characteristics
2. False Wisdom: Its Source
3. False Wisdom: Its Results
4. True Wisdom: Its Source
5. True Wisdom: Its Characteristics
6. True Wisdom: Its Results

1. False Wisdom: Its Characteristics

Who among you is wise and understanding? (3:13)
'Who' is the relative pronoun *tis*, used rhetorically here as in Luke 11:11. James brings two synonyms into play. 'Wise' is from the familiar *sophia,* a term that speaks of a general understanding of life's principles; here it refers to the practical teacher. 'Understanding' is a more technical word used only here in the New Testament. It speaks of an expert, a skilled and scientific person. The two adjectives are found together nowhere else in the New Testament. Moreover, true, godly wisdom will be very apparent in its demonstration of good works and meekness.

Let him demonstrate by good conduct his deeds [done] in the meekness of wisdom (3:13). James' language here is awkward as we try to translate it into English. But James' point is nevertheless clear: true, godly wisdom fleshes itself out in consistent Christian behavior. 'Conduct' translates the Greek *anastrophēs;* it denotes the behavior, the walk, the actions of a person. Paul used the word to summarize his entire life in Judaism (Gal. 1:13). True wisdom, far from being aloof or abrasive or belligerent, will exhibit itself by a meek and gentle demeanor.

'Meekness' is the same word as in 1:21 – just as the one receiving the word should do so with humble gentleness, so should the teacher carry out his ministry. One of the wisest men I ever knew was a layman in a church where I served as pastor. He had a gentle, homespun way about him; he never wanted to be the center of attention. But his gentle, godly wisdom and his insight into decisions that needed to be made were invaluable to me as a young pastor. How different this is from the 'worldly wisdom' that often infiltrates the church.

But if you have zealous bitterness and selfish ambition in your heart (3:14)
Zeal (*zelon*) is a good thing but the danger is that it can be terribly misdirected. Apparently the teachers in James' day were in particular danger of committing this error. Adamson observes, 'Both in politics and religion zeal can degenerate into mere partisanship.... The notorious zeal of the Jews (Acts 21:20) sometimes produced particularly harmful results.'[2] 'Bitterness' is *pikron*, and ties verse 14 to verse 11. The sins of the tongue reveal the animosity of the heart, and they can be most harmful. Wise, godly teachers will not fall into this trap.

Paul connected bitterness with 'selfish ambition' (*eritheian*) in his letters to the troubled Corinthian church. In fact, many interpreters argue that Paul's reference to both terms is a legitimate source for understanding the context of James' use of the words (1 Cor. 3:3; 2 Cor. 12:20; Gal. 5:20). The idea is that of a factious rivalry or party spirit. This kind of attitude relishes in the malicious, petty triumph of one group over another. A godly and meek spirit will never divide the body of Christ into factions.

do not boast about it and thus lie against the truth (3:14)
It seems that some people in this community of faith not only harbored bitterness and selfish ambition in their hearts, but, to make matters worse, they actually boasted about it. 'Boast' is from the same word as in 2:13; it carries the idea of one exulting over a person who is not as prominent or important. James informs them that when they do this they deny and lie against the truth that they ostensibly teach. 'Lie' or 'deny' is from *pseudomai*, from which we derive the prefix *pseudo-*. James drives home an important and needed lesson: by your conduct do not belie the truth that you teach.[3]

---

2. Adamson, 150.
3. Robertson, *Word Pictures*, 46.

2. False Wisdom: Its Source

James warns that such 'wisdom' derives not from heaven (God) but from below (earthly sources).

This wisdom does not come down from above but [it is] earthly, sensual, demonic (3:15)

This counterfeit wisdom has three characteristics. *First,* its viewpoint is of this world. 'Earth' is from *epi* and *gē,* literally 'upon the earth.' It does not have a heavenly point of view. *Second,* it is 'sensual,' or soulish (*psuchikos*) as opposed to spiritual. In fact, Martin notes that the five instances of the adjective, here and in 1 Corinthians 2:14; 15:44, 46; Jude 19, suggest a condition that is devoid of the Spirit of God. It looks more like unregenerate human nature than regenerate. *Third,* and even worse, this kind of bogus wisdom is 'demonic' (*daimoniōdēs*). This is an adjective found only here in the New Testament, and the indictment is quite serious. Demons are real personalities just as the devil or Satan himself.

Does James mean that those teachers who abuse with their tongues are 'demon-like' or that they are instigated by actual demons? We know that in the New Testament demons were responsible for evil thoughts and even outright hostility against God and man.[4] James seems to suggest that, in some cases at least, the fruit of these teachers' tongues resembled demons more than God.[5] James will tell the community in 4:7 to 'resist the devil,' and nowhere else are he and his minions more active than in using the tongue to tear down and mislead. Worldly 'wisdom' will destroy a church, a family, or a society in its attempt to exert its own will. And the source of such wisdom is hell itself.

3. False Wisdom: Its Results

Verse 16 calls attention to the results of this spurious wisdom.

For where bitterness and selfish ambition [are] (3:16)

'For' ties this verse to the preceding one and justifies the severe condemnation of this 'wisdom.' It is accompanied

---

4. Mark 5:1-13; 2 Thessalonians 2:9; 1 Timothy 4:1.
5. Adamson, 152.

by disastrous social results. Both 'bitterness' and 'selfish ambition' are used in verse 14 of those who claim to have wisdom.

When such a deleterious mindset is present, the outcome will be: **confusion and all kinds of evil deeds (3:16)**
James has used the word 'confusion' (*akatastasia*) twice already: in 1:8 and 3:8 to describe an unstable man and a restless tongue. Here the noun points to the restlessness, disorder and chaos produced in the assembly by worldly wisdom. God cannot be the author of such 'wisdom' that destroys the fellowship of the body.

'Evil' or 'vile' translates *phaulon,* an adjective marking the moral character of a person or activity. It is used in John 3:20 and Titus 2:8 of worthless, empty activity. James is concerned for the unity of the body, and where unruly tongues and worldly wisdom reign the result will be selfishness, confusion, and the like. Remember that this is James the peacemaker from Acts 15 and 21:18-25. He labored to keep the opposing parties together in Christ. It is that same spirit that breathes through this passage.[6]

The strong adversative 'but' (*de*) marks James' transition to discuss the source, characteristics, and result of true wisdom.

4. True Wisdom: Its Source
But the wisdom from above (3:17)
Unlike the spurious wisdom just depicted, true wisdom comes from 'above' (*anōthen*), or from God. Actually, James does not use a verb here but writes about 'the from above wisdom (*sophia*).' Martin comments, 'Strictly speaking James describes what true wisdom results in rather than what it *is*.'[7] James enumerates seven characteristics (or eight, depending on how we count them) of this true wisdom from God that is so needed in the community of faith.

---

6. Motyer, 135.
7. Martin, 133.

5. True Wisdom: Its Characteristics

is first pure, then peace-making, gentle, easily entreated, full of mercy and good fruit, impartial, and without hypocrisy (3:17)

The wisdom that God gives is 'first pure,' first in the sense of priority and rank. A key attribute of God that He desires us to remember is that He is holy, and that is the root word here (*hagios*). It means that God and His wisdom are free from fault, without deficiency, and devoid of anything sinful. God's wisdom loves peace and spreads it everywhere it operates. The Greek adjective is *eirēnikē*, from the familiar noun for peace, *eirēnē*. Here and in Hebrews 12:11 are the only instances of this adjective in the New Testament. 'Gentle' is from *epieikēs*, an old adjective meaning fair, reasonable, equitable. Robertson points out that no English word satisfactorily renders it.[8] It appears three other times in the New Testament (1 Tim. 3:3; Titus 3:2; 1 Pet. 2:18). English versions employ a variety of terms: 'considerate' (NIV, NEB); 'forbearing' (Moffatt); 'courteous' (Weymouth). However it is translated, it is a descriptive word describing greatness of character.

'Easily entreated' could be translated 'reasonable.' It occurs only here in the New Testament and speaks of a conciliatory nature – one that is open to reason. This quality, unlike the world's point of view, is not self-seeking and is ready to yield to others (Phil. 2:3). Not surprisingly, it is also 'full of mercy and good fruit.' The concept of being 'full of mercy' suggests one who is more than willing to help and minister to others. The same benevolence that God bestowed on us should be transferred to others. As God did for us, this kind of character is willing to 'get its hands dirty' in ministering to those in need. 'Good fruit' speaks of the good works that a righteous person will exhibit (Matt. 7:17-20). The fruit discloses the root; the tree will bear fruit in keeping with its nature.

The last two descriptions of wisdom from God are 'impartial' (*adiakritos*) and 'without hypocrisy'

---

8. Robertson, *Word Pictures*, 47.

(*anupokritos*). 'Impartial' occurs only here in the New Testament and refers to one who shows no favoritism. In this context it seems to mean that godly wisdom is consistent; it does not waver between convictions depending on the circumstance. It is the opposite of the duplicitous nature of the tongue in verses 9-12. A person of true wisdom is not shifty, turning to catch the prevailing winds that blow at the time. This attribute describes God – He does not change or waver. 'Without hypocrisy' or 'sincere' closes this telling description of true wisdom. It refers to being straightforward and is used to qualify love in Romans 12:9 and 1 Corinthians 6:6.

Wiersbe offers a helpful discussion on how we receive this wisdom. *First,* our wisdom comes from the Lord Jesus who saved us and indwells us through His Holy Spirit. In Him are hidden all the treasures of wisdom and knowledge (Col. 2:3). *Second,* the Word of God is a source of wisdom: 'Keep [the words of Scripture] and do them for this is your wisdom and understanding' (Deut. 4:5, 6). *Third,* we find wisdom through believing prayer, for God has promised to give it (1:5).[9] Our only source of true wisdom and understanding is God; to seek it from any other source – whether humanism, relativism, existentialism, or subjectivism – is to build our lives on an unstable foundation.

6. True Wisdom: Its Results

Verse 16 describes the evil results of worldly, spurious wisdom; now in verse 18 we see the results of true, godly wisdom. **Now the fruit of righteousness is sown in peace by those who make peace (3:18)**
The structure of this sentence leaves room for a wide variety of possibilities and the English translations reflect that fact. One concern is how to render the genitive 'of righteousness.' Is it appositional: 'the fruit which *is* righteousness'? Or is it subjective: 'the fruit which righteous living produces'? Either way James sums up the substance of all

---

9. Wiersbe, 107.

that he has been saying. He has spoken of good works and peace, of a living faith and not a dead creed. However we take the genitive phrase, righteousness is directly related to peace. This comes as no surprise as James writes to a congregation divided over rank, status, and wealth. 'Sown in peace' contains the present passive indicative of *speirō*, 'to sow.' The point of the grammar here is significant: one's life should consist of habitually sowing the seed of peace. Those who love peace innately sow peace everywhere they go. And nowhere is this peacemaking wisdom needed more than in the body of Christ!

The context of this passage demands that we appreciate that there may be two sorts of teachers. We must not forget that teachers were James' subject in the earlier part of the chapter. Teachers use their tongues more than most, and it is by our tongues, more than anything else, that we show the kind of wisdom that predominates in our life.

Teachers reveal by their tongues what kind of wisdom they possess. Self-appointed teachers, not called by God, will probably not be bothered very much if what they teach is not exhibited in their own lives. Their selfish motives may lead them to cause factions and disorder. Genuine Christian teachers, however, called by God and filled with His Spirit, though not perfect, will be most concerned about truth and their example (good life and deeds, v. 13). They will sow in peace and produce a harvest of practical righteousness in men's and women's lives by means of their consistent teaching and example.

Wisdom to Live By

- 'No one ever spoke the way this man does' (John 7:46). In what ways did the Lord Jesus exemplify the wisdom described in James 3:17?

- We do not and cannot deny the value of much human wisdom, and James does not do so. Rather, he criticizes human wisdom when it ignores God and is dominated by envy and selfish ambition. Taking human wisdom at its best, what are basic differences in viewpoint between the two wisdoms?

- Do we remember to associate wisdom with unity and peacemaking?
- In verse 18 James uses the words 'sow' and 'harvest.' What are the practical implications of the use of these words? What do they teach us about the nature of Christian growth and maturity?

10

Wisdom and Conflict
(James 4:1-12)

The message of the last verse in chapter 3 and the first verse in chapter 4 are in striking contrast to each other. James speaks much of peace at the end of Chapter 3; but the subject, as Chapter 4 begins, is war and conflict. Peace has its source in divine wisdom, but strife and conflict have their source in evil desire. James is not discussing war in the sense of conflict between nations or war as a social disorder. He is dealing specifically with strife and feuding and quarreling among members of the body of Christ.

James is deeply concerned about feuding and strife among the members of the church, as any pastor would be. So, James raises the question: why? His answer is that these people are being driven by their fleshly lusts and are not yielded totally to God. James lays out three principles that help us to understand conflict and how true wisdom combats it. He shows us its cause, course, and cure.

1. Conflict: Its Cause (4:1-3)
2. Conflict: Its Course (4:4-6)
3. Conflict: Its Cure (4:7-12)

1. Conflict: Its Cause (4:1-3)

King David was a godly, wise, capable leader over the nation of Israel. The books of 1 Samuel and 1 Chronicles record David's rise to the throne and his subsequent reign. He was a good man who followed after the Lord. But, tragically, his unrestrained lust led him to commit the heinous sin of adultery with Bathsheba and the murder of her husband Uriah (2 Sam. 11). The King sowed to the wind and reaped a whirlwind. He never imagined the conflict, tragedy, and pain that would result in his unchecked desires. And this is precisely what James warns us about here in Chapter 4.

Where do wars and conflicts among you come from? (4:1)
James' language here is intentionally repetitive. Literally, he asks, 'From where [comes] war and from where [come] conflicts among you?' He closed chapter 3 on a positive note – peace will come to those who make peace. But now he returns to the situation at hand: the body is torn apart by internal strife and fighting. As a master teacher, he uses a rhetorical question to address the problem, and then proceeds to elaborate on the perils of unrestrained lusts among the body of Christ. 'Wars' is from *polemoi* and 'conflicts' is from *maxai*, which could also be translated 'fightings.' The words show a duplication of thought – a real concern on the heart of the writer. Martin explains, 'Acrimonious speech, slanderous accusations, unrestrained anger – all depict a jealous and divided community; it speaks of a church governed by the "wisdom from below".'[1]

Like a volcano erupting from beneath the earth's surface, this poison spews forth from the evil passions in the heart.

Do they not originate from your evil pleasures that wage war in your members? (4:1)
What causes both the slow burn and the white-hot flashes of anger and rancor among them? 'Evil pleasures' or 'passions' translate *hēdonōn*. The Greek word usually refers to evil desires, but it should not be understood as sexual lusts only. The word includes any kind of lust for

1. Martin, 144.

power, position, or prestige that seeks to dominate. The
desire to 'have it my way or else' has caused much strife in
the body of Christ.

The battleground for these passions is in the 'members'
of the body. 'Members' (*melesin*) was used in 3:6 where
the tongue is set among the members of the physical body.
Here the members may refer to individuals in the body
of Christ or it may be consistent with 3:6 and mean those
members of the human body from which arise desire and
lust. Either way, these believers needed to understand
that their lusts and selfish desires amount to a campaign
('wage war' is from *strateuomenōn,*) against what is godly
and Spirit-filled. James graphically depicts members of
the spiritual body as walking 'civil wars.'

The graphic nature of this section leads one to inquire
about the audience of this epistle. How could these words
apply to a Christian community?

**You lust and you do not have. You kill and are jealous
and you are not able to get what you want (4:2)**
In verse 1 James chided the readers for their evil pleasures;
here he uses the more familiar word for lust, *epithumia*.
Literally, the word means 'to be hot (*thermal*) for a thing.'
Our desires arise from our innermost being and our bodies
carry out those lusts and desires. But had things become
so bad that Christians were actually guilty of killing? This
verse has generated long and complicated discussions by
many students of the Bible.

The Greek word for 'kill' is *phoneuete,* and it carries
a wide range of meanings that may help us in this
conundrum. The primary meaning is murder arising from
the motive of bloodthirstiness,[2] but it can also carry the
idea of 'destroy.' This metaphorical meaning seems to be
what James has in mind – 'you destroy and assassinate
the character and reputation of others because of your
jealous lusts.' Had James referred to literal murder the
perpetrators would have been hauled into civil courts and

---

2. R. C. Trench, *Synonyms of the Greek New Testament* (Eerdmans, 1953),
314.

executed. Though he probably did not have in mind an actual church situation where the members murdered one another,[3] James uses the strongest possible language to show how dangerous unchecked lusts and passions can be.

James has just written that moral murder and character assassination can be committed by those who give themselves over to their sinful desires. Why does this happen? Because 'you are jealous and not able to get what you want.' 'Jealous' in the Greek gives us our word *zeal*. It can carry negative or positive connotations. Here it means the ardent desire to obtain something. When one chooses pleasure instead of God, even murder can be the result.

With **you make war and fight (4:2)**
James returns to the point at which he began verse 1. Moo notes the inverse parallel structure crafted by the author:

A Fights and quarrels (v. 1a)
   B come from wrong desires (v. 1b)
   B Frustrated desire (v. 2a) leads to
A quarrels and fights (v. 2b)[4]

Closing this verse, James now takes a more pastoral slant:
You do not have because you do not ask (4:2)
'You seek to fulfill your desires in all the wrong places and ways,' James pleads. Christians so often battle with one another for that which they really do not need. The only way out of the mess is to go to God in humble, believing prayer, confident that God gives to His children what they most need (Matt. 6:33).

As I (Dale) write these words I think about a church in my community that is divided and full of contention because of differences over leadership and structure. The unbelieving community around us is well aware of the

---

3. Martin has a good section on how this may be taken quite literally: 'Murder was accepted as a 'religious' way to solve disagreements, as in Acts 9' (Martin, 143).
4. Moo (PNTC), 184.

dissension. Even the local newspaper did an article on the fight! I can just imagine what a laughing stock that church is to unbelievers around her who reason that Christians are no better than they are because they cannot even get along with one another. All the while the cause of Christ is hindered and the reputation of the local church is assassinated.

You ask and do not receive because you ask corruptly (4:3)
Self-centered believers pray, but they pray just like they live: corruptly. We can ask for the right things but with the wrong motives. James has already warned about asking with the wrong attitude, doubt (1:5); here he instructs us not to ask with the wrong motive. I may pray that my church would grow, that people will be saved, and that many will be baptized as disciples of the Lord. But if I pray for that with the motive that *I* will become known and that *I* will receive the accolades of man, I ask with evil motives.

A gentle nuance worth noting is that James writes in the active voice of ask (*aiteō*) in its first instance, but he switches to the middle voice the second time he uses it. Why would James change from 'you ask' to 'you ask *for yourselves*'? Some commentators do not think the shift is significant since it happens in numerous other places in the New Testament. Mayor thinks the emphasis serves to distinguish between prayers of the lips (active) and prayers from the heart (middle).[5] Adamson thinks it is a stylistic balance to make the active agree with the active verb 'receive.'[6]

Whatever the reason, the point is that they were praying selfishly, **in order that you might indulge your evil pleasures (4:3)**
The negative progression continues as the author expands on asking 'corruptly.' They do not receive because they wanted to indulge their evil pleasures (again, as in v. 1).

5. Mayor, 138.
6. Adamson, 169.

'Indulge' translates *dapanaō*, 'to spend.' It is a neutral word generally, but here it means the wasteful and selfish spending of what God graciously gives.

Jesus promised in Matthew 7:7 that we could ask and it will be given to us. But Jesus clearly had in mind that the focus of such praying is to further God's glory and His kingdom. He does not give us what we want so that we might spend it on our own selfish pleasures. F. J. A Hort comments, 'God gives not gifts only, but the enjoyment of them: but the enjoyment which contributes to nothing beyond itself is not what He gives in answer to prayer; and petitions to Him which have no better end in view are not prayers.'[7]

2. Conflict: Its Course (4:4-6)

Abruptly and harshly James exclaims: *moichalides* (adulterers)! He has already called them foolish in 2:20; now he indicts them as spiritually unfaithful people: **Adulterers and adulteresses! Do you not know that friendship with the world is hostility toward God? (4:4)** James now preaches in the style of the Old Testament prophets and uses a metaphor common to them. The term 'adulterers' was used by the prophets to speak of Israel as the covenant people who committed spiritual adultery in going after pagan gods (Hosea 9:1; Jer. 3; Isa. 54:5). Furthermore, the church is called the bride of Christ in Ephesians 5:24-25. So, the adultery James speaks of consists of loving the world and its pleasures more than the Lord. 'Adulteresses' is the plural form of adulterer, so referring to men as well as women.

The choice is clear – if one wishes to be a friend (*philia*) of the world he will be at hostility (*exthra*) with God. Spiritual adultery as synonymous with hostility or enmity (*echthros*) toward God certainly has its basis in Scripture (see further Ps. 110:1; Matt. 22:24; Mark 12:36; Luke 20:43; Acts 2:35; Heb. 1:13). James' words could not be more relevant for today. Instead of being faithfully wedded, we

---

7. F. J. A. Hort, *The Epistle of St. James* (London: Macmillan, 1909), 91.

can easily, by our evil ways, turn our backs on God and commit spiritual adultery. The modern term for marital unfaithfulness is 'affair,' but we prefer to call it what it is: adultery. John gives us a clear definition of the world (*kosmos*): 'the lust of the flesh, the lust of the eyes, and the pride of life' (1 John 2:16). It is the world system, the humanistic philosophy of life that does not follow God and His standards.

Does verse 4 serve as the clue to the meaning of the difficult and highly debated verse 5, or is its meaning dependent on verse 6? If verse 4 is the hinge, then the 'spirit' in our upcoming verse will be the human spirit with its downward tendency away from God. If verse 6 provides the clue, then God's Spirit is the One who is jealous for us. Verse 5 presents us with three major problems.

First, to what Scripture does James appeal when he writes: **Or do you think that the Scripture says to no avail? (4:5)** In keeping with most New Testament writers, James backs up his argument in verses 1-4 with an appeal to Scripture. 'To no avail' translates *kenōs*, 'empty' or 'in vain,' used in 2:20 of the empty-headed person and in Philippians 2 of the self-emptying of Christ.

This is problematic because we have no citation from the Old Testament that says exactly what follows. Some writers suggest that James is making an interpretive comment on Scripture in general, without reference to a specific passage. Others see James as referring to some text now lost to us, but well-known to his audience. Still other scholars, such as J. H. Ropes, think James is giving a rendering of Exodus 20:5.[8] It seems best to take Ropes' lead and understand James to be using his own paraphrased form of an Old Testament reference.

Second, should we join 'toward envy' or 'enviously' (*pros phthonon*) with the introductory formula or with the Scripture James is citing? In other words, do the Scriptures

8. James Hardy Ropes, *A Critical and Exegetical Commentary on the Epistle of St. James*, ed. Alfred Plummer and Francis Brown (Edinburgh: T & T Clark, 1916), 262.

argue 'with envy' or does 'with envy' belong with the spirit in the reference quoted by James? We have nothing close to a parallel with the Scriptures speaking 'with envy,' so it seems best to conclude that the words go with the scriptural reference itself.

The *third* difficulty is the subject of the quoted verse. How should it be translated? Moo gives us two possibilities:

1. James is referring to God's jealousy for His people, 'God yearns jealously for the spirit He has made to dwell in us' (NRSV).
2. James is referring to the human tendency to be envious, 'the spirit he caused to live in us envies intensely' (NIV).[9]

To these we may add one more:

3. The Holy Spirit is the subject of the main verb, 'The Spirit which He made to dwell within us yearns enviously.'[10]

The first option is grammatically possible, and while God does grieve when His people go astray, this translation is not the best. 'Envy' (*phthonon*) or 'jealousy' is never used in the New Testament in a positive sense and Scripture never says that God lusts (*epipothei*, 'to yearn after'). As for the third option, the Spirit imparted to us by God at salvation does, according to Galatians 5:17, lust against the flesh and He desires our complete loyalty to Himself. But the contrast stated by James in verse 6 leads this writer to conclude that it is option #2 above; it is the human spirit who is the subject.

We may now provide our translation of the problematic phrase: **the spirit which [God] made to dwell in us yearns enviously (4:5)**
The subject of the word 'dwell' (*katōkisen*) is God. He breathed into us the spirit of life, but that spirit imparted

---

9. Moo (PNTC), 188.
10. Hiebert makes a good case for this reading. D. Edmond Hiebert, *The Epistle of James: Tests of a Living Faith* (Chicago: Moody, 1979), 256.

at creation longs perversely for the enjoyment of worldly pleasures (v. 4). This, then, is a commentary on the depravity of mankind. We have suggested that verses 4 through 6 deal with the course of conflict, and this interpretation fits quite well within that scheme. Our depraved nature yearns enviously after what is antithetical to godliness, and such yearning results in conflicts among the body of Christ.

But He gives greater grace (4:6)

The antithesis of human envying is the grace God offers to us. Literally, the text states that 'He gives a greater gift (*charin*).' Due to the reference he quotes from Proverbs, it seems best to understand this gift to be the grace of God that enables us to overcome the natural tendency in verse 5 to lust and yearn for evil. The Scripture James was alluding to in verse 5 is indefinite, but in this verse the use of the Old Testament is straightforward and clear.

Wherefore it says, God opposes the proud but He gives grace to the humble (4:6)

This quotation from Proverbs 3:34 reinforces James' point about God providing great grace to overcome our self-centeredness. 'It says' is a bit vague because we do not know whether the subject is God or Scripture. Either way, the quotation warns against those who are proud but also clearly states the good news that God's grace is available to those who humble themselves. 'Opposes' is from *antitassetai*, a compound word composed of the familiar prefix *anti* and the verb *tassō*, 'to place or arrange.' The verb graphically depicts God placing Himself in battle array against those who are haughty. 'The proud' is without the definite article in the Greek, stressing the character rather than the identity of those whom God resists. The adjective (*huperēphanois*) refers to those who are arrogant, haughty, and proud. Hiebert describes this haughty individual well: 'Feeling himself conspicuously above others, he assumes an attitude of superiority and pride. Gripped with a false sense of self-sufficiency, he regards himself as the standard of excellence and disdains those who fall short of his standard.'[11] No wonder that war, conflict, and dissension stained the fellowship of this community!

3. Conflict: Its Cure (4:7-12)

True wisdom realizes that nothing short of a radical heart transplant will correct the problem presented in verses 1-6. But a heart transplant is just what God's grace provides. Second Corinthians 5:17 says that a person who is in Christ is a new creation. As such, our behavior must be brought in line with our new nature. The next four verses give the readers a spiritual exercise on how to repent and receive God's grace. The verses present a series of imperative verbs that stress repentance and have their culmination in purifying faith.

1. *Submit:* **Submit yourselves, therefore, to God (4:7)**

Repentance begins with the command to 'submit' to God. *hupotassō* (lit, 'to stand under') is the opposite of 'resist' in the previous verse. Richardson states, 'Like the call to humble oneself before the Lord in verse 10, the call is to stop resisting God.'[12] The middle/passive form should be understood in the sense of the middle voice, calling for their voluntary subordination to God. Too often we are like the little boy who was chided by his mother to stop standing up and squirming in church. She finally had to pinch him and demand that he sit down. His obstinate reply was, 'I'm sitting on the outside but I'm standing on the inside!' Submission to God means that we voluntarily align ourselves on the outside *and* the inside with God and His Word.

2. *Resist:* **Resist the devil and he will flee from you (4:7)**

The next command is to actively resist the adversary. 'Resist' is from *anthistēmi*, 'to oppose, withstand, set oneself against.' Verse 6 explained that God 'opposes' the proud, but the word here is different. The two ideas,

---

11. Hiebert, 259.
12. Richardson, 183.

however, are similar in intent – just as God sets himself in battle array against the arrogant, so we must do the same in our fight against the devil. Most Christians give little thought to the spiritual warfare in which we are engaged every day, but James' admonition is to take up the full armor of God and stand firm against the adversary (Eph. 6:10-20).

'The devil' is *diabolos*, the Greek equivalent to the Hebrew *haś-śātān*. Both mean 'the adversary, the accuser, the slanderer.' He has been referred to only indirectly in the epistle so far (2:19; 3:6). He is a living, personal being who has a mind, will, and emotions. Furthermore, he is *not* omniscient nor omnipotent nor omnipresent, but can only do what God allows him to do. He also has numberless minions called demons who do his bidding constantly throughout the earth. He is the embodiment of all that resists God, and he is at enmity with God.

James promises that if we will take a stand against the devil he will 'flee' (*pheugō*) from us. The word for 'flee' gives us our word 'fugitive.' We can send Satan on the run if we will deny him access to our heart and resist him. Jesus modeled this for us in the temptation experience on the mountain in Matthew 4. Using the Word of God, Jesus stood firm against him and he had to flee.

3. Draw near. **Draw near to God and He will draw near to you (4:8)**
This verse emphasizes the reciprocal nature of our relationship with the Father. When we take a step toward God (*eggisate*, 'to come near') we find that He already has taken a step toward us. He desires our fellowship and He desires that we love Him from a willing heart. The Psalmist said, 'The LORD is near to all who call upon Him, to all who call upon Him in truth' (Ps. 145:18). James may have had in mind the promise God made through Zechariah, 'Return to Me, and I will return to you' (Zech. 1:3). The place of safety for the Christian is at the throne of grace, and when we draw close to God we find His forgiveness, grace, and strength.

4. *Cleanse:* **Cleanse your hands, you sinners (4:8)**

This phrase speaks of the outward cleansing of the instruments of sin, referred to as our 'hands.' Here the hands stand for the entire outward life of a person. Martin observes that the two verbs in verse 8b and 8c, 'cleanse' and 'purify,' pertain to deeds in the first sense and to thoughts in the second.[13] Such outward sins needed a *chatharsis* (from the verb 'cleanse'), a thorough cleansing by God's grace (v. 6). 'Cleanse' also brings to mind the requirement for the ceremonial cleansing of the hands by the priests of the Old Testament as they approached God (see Exod. 30:19-21; Lev. 16:4).

The sharp address, 'you sinners,' is a vocative plural of the noun for sin, *hamartia*. Hiebert clarifies, 'While commonly used of the unsaved, the parallel with 'double-minded' makes it clear that James is applying the term to Christians.'[14] Their communion with God depended on a change in their worldly conduct because, as it stood, they were failing to maintain God's standards for His saints.

5. *Purify:* **and purify your hearts, you double-minded (4:8)**

'Purify your hearts' (*ēagnisate kardias*) again employs familiar Jewish ceremonial language (John 11:55). The same idea is found in 1 Peter 1:22 and 1 John 3:3, where a purification or sanctification of the heart is called for. As in 1:26 and 3:14, James uses the heart here to speak of the whole inner life. 'Double-minded' has the same connotation as in 1:8; they were 'two-souled,' divided between their commitment to Christ and yet wanting to be friends with the world. James sounds much like the Psalmist: 'Who shall ascend to the hill of the LORD? He who has clean hands and a pure heart' (Ps. 24:3-4a).

6. *Be Afflicted:* **Be afflicted (4:9)**

We do not hear much in today's world about genuine sorrow over sin. But that is what James calls for – a recognition of the shame and disgrace due to their sins. Satan has succeeded

---

13. Martin, 153.
14. Hiebert, 263.

in lulling today's church into a stupor when it comes to
seriousness about sin. The verb *talaipōrēsate*, used only
here in the New Testament, originally denoted hardship
and distressing circumstances, but came later to mean a
feeling of misery and wretchedness. Some commentators
think that James is commanding a voluntary abstinence
from certain comforts and luxuries.[15] Others hold that the
imperative is a call to ascetic practices such as prayer and
fasting in sackcloth to induce this feeling.[16] But James knew
that such activities were no substitute for inner mourning
and repentance. We first have to acknowledge our heart
condition before we can repent of it, and the writer demands
deep, penitent sorrow for his people's spiritual state.

7. *Grieve:* **mourn and weep (4:9)**
Inner affliction over sin will manifest itself in outward
expression. 'Mourn' (*penthēsate*) is the same word used
by Jesus in Matthew 5:4. It is a call to the godly sorrow
Paul spoke of in 2 Corinthians 7:10. 'Weep' translates the
familiar verb *klaiō*, 'to cry out.' The New Testament joins
the two words together often (e.g. Mark 16:10; Luke 6:25).
James is certainly not calling for an ostentatious show of
emotions; rather, a deep grief that cannot be concealed is
what he has in mind. The apostle may very well have had
Isaiah's call to repentance in mind, 'Let the wicked forsake
his way, and the unrighteous man his thoughts; let him
return to the LORD for he will have mercy on him, and to
our God, for he will abundantly pardon' (Isa. 55:7).

8. *Turn.* Genuinely penitent believers display a noticeable
contrast from their previous behavior. Raucous and
gleeful partying turns to repentant, quiet introspection.
**Turn your laughter into mourning, and your joy into
heaviness (4:9)**
'Turn' is a third-person imperative; literally, 'let it be
turned.' The command is from *metatrepein*, which means
'to turn into' and is found only here in the New Testament.

---

15. Mayor, 142.
16. Ropes, 270.

'Laughter' (from *gelōs*) may suggest two ideas. First, the 'joyful and festive' outlook of these sinners and double-minded people is quite out of order because, for them, there is no valid reason to laugh. Second, laughter sometimes reflected the attitude of a fool in the Old Testament (e.g. Prov. 10:23; Eccles. 7:6).[17] When the enormity of sin crashes down on a life, a reversal from superficial gaiety and levity ensues.

James is not suggesting that laughter is sinful. Certainly there is joy and gladness when we are rightly related to God through Christ. The Psalmist said in Psalm 126:2, 'Our mouths were filled with laughter, and our tongues with shouts of joy.' But true joy can never come until genuine repentance and cleansing are experienced. This spiritual cleansing is promised in 1 John 1:9: 'If we confess our sins, He is faithful and just to forgive us our sins and to cleanse us from all unrighteousness.'

9. *Humble:* **Humble yourselves in the sight of the Lord (4:10)**

The verb 'humble' is an imperative of *tapeinoiō* and is in the Greek tense that calls for a once-for-all action. The form is passive in voice, but the sense could be either middle, 'humble yourselves' or, since the middle voice was giving way to the passive,[18] the passive sense, 'let yourselves *be* humbled.' First Peter 5:6 has this same form and the same promise of exaltation. 'In the sight of' translates the Greek preposition *enōpion* and suggests the thought of being under the eye of the Lord. 'The Lord' is generally taken to mean God rather than Christ, but 'it seems more probable that James is thinking of the living God who has revealed Himself in Christ Jesus our Lord.'[19]

and He will exalt you (4:10)

Jesus juxtaposed the principles of humility and exaltation on several occasions: Matthew 23:12; Luke 14:11; 18:14.

---

17. Martin, 154.
18. Robertson, 53.
19. Hiebert, 265.

The way to true exaltation always passes through the valley of humility. Jewish readers of this epistle would be reminded of the same truth from Job 5:11; Psalm 113:7-8; and Ezekiel 21:26.

The Lord Himself will 'exalt' us. The verb is from *hupsos*, meaning 'height.' He will give us forgiveness and joy in our walk with Him. He will lift us up to levels of fellowship and service we never thought possible. There is a world of difference between the person who lifts himself up and the one whom the Lord lifts up. We must make sure that we are the latter.

Notice that the steps to true repentance end just where they began, with a call to humility. Conflict in the fellowship arises when the members seek to have their own selfish ways. Humble repentance is rare, but it is a cure for the woes of self-serving, egocentric desires.

As a final, general admonition toward clearing up the carnal conflicts in the body, James instructs them to refrain from speaking evil toward other members of the body. **Do not speak against one another, brothers (4:11).**
This verse recalls the truth that the tongue is a powerful and often misused agent in the Christian community (3:1-10), and is a primary source of conflict and contention. Martin notes the problem in linking this verse with what precedes it, but he rightly comments, 'Any attitude that shows disdain or contempt for others reflects pride on the part of the one with the scornful attitude. This is characteristic of the double-minded person (4:8), who needs to exercise humility (4:6, 10).'[20] So, despite first appearances, the flow of thought is quite cogent.

'Speak against' is a negative imperative, is in the present tense, and denotes 'stop' doing this. It is not only possible but probable that the conflicts James has addressed in the body were accompanied by these sins of the tongue. Some translations render *katalaleō* as 'speak evil.' It reflects the backbiting, faultfinding, harsh criticism that too often characterizes the body of Christ.

20. Martin, 163.

James gives two reasons to refrain from speaking evil against brothers and sisters.

First, **Anyone who speaks [evil] against a brother or judges a brother, speaks [evil] against the law and judges it (4:11)**
To disparage brothers and sisters in Christ is to disparage God's law. The 'royal law' (2:8) commands us to love one another. In 4:9 James called to repentance those who had a nonchalant attitude toward sin and toward God. In keeping with that idea, he insists that slandering and speaking evil of the brethren is tantamount to slandering the Lawgiver. Just as Moses shattered God's tablet of laws at Mount Sinai, so we break God's law when we judge and speak evil of our fellow believers.

One may ask how this judging and disdaining of fellow Christians may be equated with judging the law. This leads to the *second* reason James gives for refraining from speaking evil against fellow believers.

If you judge the law, you are not doers of it but judges (4:11)
The one who judges (*krineis*) the law is not a *doer* (from the common *poieō*) of it but sits in judgment against it, and, by implication, against the divine Lawgiver. We usurp God's place when we voice judgment against others. He alone has the right to enforce His decrees with life or death.

There is [only] one Lawgiver and Judge (4:12)
When we judge others and speak against them, we are in effect pushing God off His judgment seat and placing ourselves on it. This is an action of gross presumption because God's position is absolutely unique. *First,* He is the sole true 'Lawgiver' (*nomothetēs,* 'to establish' and 'law'). His laws alone are of permanent significance. *Second,* He is the one Judge (*kritēs*) of mankind (4:12). The One who gave the law also judges us according to it. And His judgments upon us are of eternal validity. He has the unique ability both to save and to destroy.

[He is] able to save and to destroy (4:12)

He says to us, 'There is no God besides me. I put to death and I bring to life, I have wounded and I will heal, and no one can deliver out of my hand' (Deut. 32:39). God alone is competent to judge justly (1 Cor. 4:4-5). For us to judge others, therefore, is to take upon ourselves a right which belongs to God. It is an infringement on God's prerogative. We do well to ask ourselves, 'Who am I to judge my neighbor?' or as Paul asks, 'Who are you to judge someone else's servant? To his own master he stands or falls' (Rom. 14:4). If we grasp the presumptuousness of our judging others we will tremble at the thought of engaging in it.

This section covers a lot of ground. James began by asking where wars and conflict arise, and the answer is from our own lusts and desires. Commands are then given for repentance and restoration to fellowship with God and with one another. James then reminds us that God alone has the right to judge others; when we speak evil of others we are trying to sit in God's judicial seat. Wisdom from God will help us to refrain from such judging and help us to avoid conflicts in the body of Christ.

Wisdom to Live By

- Consider the fights and quarrels that take place, sadly, among people who profess to be Christians. What desires are frequently behind them? What should our attitude be when others try to draw us into such conflicts?

- How should we define worldliness? Having crafted definitions, let's check it with John's definition in 1 John 2:15-16.

- Growing Christians continually repent. Are our lives filled with noisy, pretentious activity that masks the need for quiet reflection? Or do we maintain an attitude of self-examination and repentance?

11

Wisdom and Dependence on God
(James 4:13-17)

Elvis Presley and Frank Sinatra sang 'I Did It My Way.' Admittedly, the song is a beautiful one, but the life philosophy behind it is unwise and ungodly. In 4:1-12 James issued a warning against worldliness; here he challenges his readers against this type of proud, independent spirit. James 4 concludes with a denunciation of merchants for their presumption and arrogance (4:13-17). In his following paragraph, James castigates landlords for the same sins: presumption, arrogance, but especially for exploitation (5:1-6).

We have titled this section 'Wisdom and Dependence on God.' The opposite of such dependence is presumption, the insistence on 'doing it my way.' Three principles appear in these verses that help us avoid presumption and remember our dependence on God:

1. Presumption disregards our ignorance of the future.
2. Presumption disregards the brevity of our lives.
3. Presumption disregards the sovereign will of God.

1. Presumption Disregards Our Ignorance of the Future

As James moves on to another subject, the tongue is still part of it. The tongue can be used to express an unjustified confidence about the future that is in conflict with a genuine confidence in God.

Come now you who say (4:13)

The tongue can both boast and brag (4:16). It can boast by comparing us with others and making sure that we come off best. It can brag by expressing big ideas about us that exceed the bounds of reality. The beckon 'come now' (*age nun*) occurs only here and in 5:1 in the New Testament. It has the effect of saying 'listen up!' or 'give me your attention!' The identity of 'you who say' (a present participle, *hoi legontes*) is uncertain – is it members of the body or non-Christian businessmen? The lack of any reference to 'brethren' might suggest that the people were outsiders, but people in the Christian community were addressed as sinners and double-minded rather than as brothers and sisters (4:9). And the use of the tag 'the Lord wills' in 4:15 points to professed members of the congregation.[1]

Today or tomorrow we will go to this or that city, spend a year there, carry on business and make money (4:13)

James imagines businessmen sitting around their conference tables, making plans for future commercial enterprises. They were so sure of themselves that they spoke without restraint of what they would do, where they would go, and what profit they would make. They assumed that they could forecast what they were going to do on every day. But their boasting tongues led them to overlook the fact of God's providence.

The activity of planning is normal, even necessary, to any business endeavor. We should *not* interpret this verse as a denunciation of planning for the future – James reflects the teachings of Proverbs too often to suppose that (he even does so in the next verse!). No, the problem is not planning but the arrogance and presumption reflected in their words. The four verbs of the phrase are all future: 'we will go' (*poreusometha*), 'will spend a year' (*poiēsomen*), 'will do business' (*emporusometha*),[2] 'and make money'

---

1. Martin, 165.
2. A metaphorical usage. The term comes from two words: 'in' and 'to go.' It is an old word from *emporos*, a merchant or trader who 'goes in' and gets the business. It is a vivid picture of the Jewish merchants of the time. Robertson, 55.

(*kerdēsomen*), literally 'get gain.' The verse reveals five areas of arrogant certainty about their plans: certainty of future (we will go), certainty of place (into 'this or that' city, *tēnde*), certainty of time (spend a year), certainty of activity (carry on business), and certainty of result (make money). The error of these merchants is their confidence in the certainty of their plans.

We sometimes say, 'Man proposes, but God disposes.' It may sometimes appear that what men's tongues boast and brag about is justified when their plans all seem to work out smoothly. But, in fact, they do so only by God's permission. Recall the parable our Lord told about the rich man who presumptuously left God out of his planning (Luke 12:16-21). In the end, someone else would own all that the man amassed because he stored up treasure for himself and was not rich toward God.

2. Presumption Disregards the Brevity of Our Lives

In verse 14 James reminds us of just how brief our lives on earth are. In doing so he gives two important reasons for yielding to God in our plans.

First, we do not know what tomorrow will bring: **Whereas you do not know what *will be* tomorrow**.
MacArthur reminds, 'Life is far from simple. It is a complex matrix of forces, people, contingencies, and circumstances over which we have no control.... Despite that, some people foolishly imagine that they are in charge of their lives.'[3] 'Tomorrow' entails all that is planned by the merchants, but such planning is 'the height of foolishness'[4] because they have overlooked two fundamental facts: life is transitory and God is sovereign. James' Old Testament wisdom counterpart, the Proverbs, advises, 'Do not boast about tomorrow, for you do not know what a day may bring forth' (Prov. 27:1). This phrase is difficult to

---

3. MacArthur, 232.
4. Moo (PNTC), 155.

translate, but the idea is clear: life truly is short, and such cavalier exclusion of God from our planning should never characterize a believer's life.

A *second* reason why it is foolish to leave God out of our plans is because:
You are a mist that appears for a little while, *it is* there and then disappears.
Life is short. The older we get, the more we realize this truth that James recounts. The word translated 'mist' could either mean a vapor or smoke. Either meaning conveys a familiar figure of speech. James uses a play on two verbs with 'appears' and 'disappears'; the first is *phainomai* and the second is *aphanizō*. The idea of a mist, especially one that rolls in from the sea and then vanishes, would be especially relevant for sea merchants.[5] Elsewhere in the Bible similar pictures are used of the brevity of human life, such as the grass that withers (Isa. 40:6), the flower in the field that fades (Job 14:2), a leaf in the wind (Job 13:25), or a fleeting shadow (Job 14:2).

Instead of looking to God, who alone can sustain life, this person relies on what can be accomplished by his or her own efforts. Wiersbe's advice from this verse is worth heeding: 'We count our *years* at our birthday, but God tells us to number our *days* (Ps. 90:12). After all, we do live one day at a time, and those days rush by quickly the older we grow. Since life is so brief, we cannot afford merely to spend our lives, and we certainly do not want to waste our lives. We must *invest* our lives in what is eternal.'[6]

3. Presumption Disregards the Sovereign Will of God
How foolish we are to ignore the unchanging God and then proudly plan our future, a future that is as fleeting as the morning mist. If we align ourselves with God's will and live for Him, our lives will bear eternal fruit!

---

5. Adamson, 180.
6. Wiersbe, 132.

Instead, you ought to say (4:15)
Literally the phrase reads 'instead of your saying.' The expression goes back to verse 13 to 'you who say' and makes verse 14 something of a parenthesis that rebukes the 'practical atheism' they commit by leaving God out of their plans.[7] Quite contrary to the pride of verse 13, their attitude should be in keeping with James' words in this verse.

If the Lord wills we will both live and do this or that (4:15)
'If the Lord wills (from *thelō*)' expresses the attitude God blesses. James suggests that we develop a conscious awareness of God by speaking often of His will for our daily lives. To speak this way regularly will remind us of who is in control and of whom we should seek to please. But a danger arises in that the phrase can become just an empty, pious platitude. It can be trivialized by stating it glibly over inconsequential decisions, such as 'I'll have a hamburger for lunch, God willing' or 'If the Lord wills, I'll shoot par on the back nine.'

But uttered reverently and rightly it would not be a bad practice to take up. Manton argues that we should speak this way for two reasons. *First*, such explicit expression of God's providence is good for us. *Second*, we find frequent examples of it in Scripture (Acts 18:21; 1 Cor. 4:19, 16:7; Phil. 2:19, 24; Heb. 6:3).[8] It is the Christian's duty to refer everything to the will of God in light of life's uncertainties. We are not equal with God. We cannot see around the next curve or over the next hill. But God can, and if we 'acknowledge Him in all our ways He will direct our paths' (Prov. 3:6).

The error of 'you who say' in verse 13 is now stated plainly:
As it is, you boast in your arrogance (4:16)
(1) they boast, and (2) they are arrogant. 'As it is' is literally 'but now' (*nun de*). The idea is, 'as the matters stands at the moment.' The verb 'boast' (*kauchasthe*) was used in

---

7. Hiebert, 277.
8. Thomas Manton, *An Exposition of the Epistle of James* (Edinburgh: Banner of Truth, reprint, 1962), 392.

1:9 to denote a proper boasting or exaltation in response to God's perspective. Here, however, their glorying is presumptuous bragging about their plans rather than humble submission of those plans to God, who alone can determine what tomorrow holds.

As if their boastful attitudes were not enough, James adds that such attitudes are full of 'arrogance.' The noun (*alazoniais*) is plural, indicating that they repeatedly boasted this way. The KJV rendering 'vauntings' is a good one. The only other occurrence of the noun is in 1 John 2:9 where it denotes similar hollow pretensions in word and deed, 'an ostentatious display that goes beyond that which reality justifies.'[9] How foolish of frail mankind to think that we can dispose of our future any way we wish.

James' reproof here reminds me of the story I heard about a woodpecker that landed on a tree and began frenetically pecking away. Suddenly a storm came up and a bolt of lightning struck the tree, splitting it in half and knocking the woodpecker to the ground. Dazed momentarily, he picked himself up, flew away, and came back moments later with several friends in tow. 'There it is, boys,' he bragged, 'I did it all by myself.' People who think they can master their own ship and be captain of their own fate are just as wrongheaded as that bird!

Abruptly and tersely, James declares: **All such boasting is evil (4:16)**
This climactic ending suggests that James wants to emphasize that such behavior – presently exhibited by them – is inherently evil. The presence and providence of God has been left out, and their pride has ruled the day.[10] Presumptuous people are confident in the success of their self-made plans devised apart from consideration of Christ's Lordship. But this in no way negates the fact that God is still in control, and He can frustrate schemes among His children that are outside His will.

---

9. Hiebert, 279.
10. Martin, 168.

Whoever, therefore, knows the right thing to do and does not do it, to him it is sin (4:17)

I like the way J. B. Phillips translates the concluding verse of chapter 17, 'No doubt you agree with the above theory. Well, remember that if a man knows what is right and fails to do it, his failure is real sin.'[11] James ends this section with an admonition to these merchants to do good and stop disregarding God in their lives and businesses. His call is to acknowledge God in all our attitudes (v. 16) and actions (v. 13). Failure to do so is a sin of commission – not just omission – in neglecting to seek and follow God's desires for our lives. Sometimes we tend to think of sin as breaking a particular command, like one of the Ten Commandments. And that certainly is sin. But sin can also be the failure to do what God commands. Or it could be a matter of the heart or mind. James reminds these merchants of this because they likely were not thinking of themselves as sinful in their presumption. James also exhorts others in the Christian community through this summary sentence. The 'right' thing James speaks of here translates *kalos* and means 'morally good, noble, praiseworthy.' The word is found elsewhere in Matthew 5:16; Mark 14:6; John 10:32; Galatians 6:9; 1 Timothy 5:10.

Verses 13-17 reveal a preoccupation with this life and its values rather than eternity and the things of God. Once again James sounds much like his Master by echoing Jesus' parable in Luke 12:16-21. In that parable the land of a certain farmer was very productive and he began making plans much like the merchants in James 4. This parable illustrates the folly of leaving God out of our planning. How shortsighted it is to live for now when we could live for now *and* eternity.

Wisdom to Live By

- Read the parable in Luke 12:16-21. Do we find areas in our lives where we are guilty of the same kind of presumption?

11. Free Internet version accessed at http://www.ccel.org/bible/phillips/JBPhillips.htm

- Christians need to plan for the future, but they need to do so with faith and submission to God's will. What specific plans do we have? What is the difference between presumption in those plans and acknowledgement of the sovereignty of God?

- Believers need to remember the frailty and brevity of life. How can we remind ourselves to thank God for every day and to use each one for His glory?

12

Wisdom and the Judgment
(James 5:1-6)

James 5:1-6 stands out as perhaps the sternest warning in the New Testament about the sins of the rich. It really could be seen as an elaboration on Jesus' words in Matthew 19:24: 'It is easier for a camel to go through the eye of a needle than for a rich man to enter the kingdom of God.' Old Testament prophets such as Hosea, Amos, Micah, Joel, and Habakkuk similarly condemned the wealthy among God's people who trusted in and worshipped their wealth more than their Lord. We, however, seriously doubt that James is speaking to God's people here, but more on that later.

Any society that gravitates toward materialistic ideals needs to examine this section very carefully. Outward riches certainly do not guarantee righteousness; in fact, according to James, worldly riches can be one of the worst enemies of true righteousness. James' purpose in verses 1-6, carried over from Chapter 4, is to prevent Christians from placing their hope in earthly wealth. Ultimately, all earthly riches will perish, so it is pointless to build our lives around them. This section breaks quite naturally into three divisions:

1. The charges against the wealthy oppressors
2. The evidence against the wealthy oppressors
3. The verdict pronounced on the wealthy oppressors

1. The Charges Against the Wealthy Oppressors

Come now, you rich (5:1)

The tone of the epistle changes with the opening of
Chapter 5. Now James speaks with the thundering voice
of a prophet as he pronounces judgment on the rich.
This passage is meant to encourage James' readers who
are oppressed by the rich. They have little of this world's
goods and take comfort from knowledge of the future
demise of the rich. Future judgment is so certain that James
can already 'see' it.[1] 'Come now' has the same sense as in
4:13, 'attend to this; listen; give me your attention!' The
Greek word for 'rich' here consists of two words, *ploutos*,
meaning 'wealth,' and *krateia*, meaning 'rule' or 'control.'
Wealth and power are often linked.

weep and howl over the miseries coming upon you (5:1)

'Weep' (as in 4:9, *klausate*) is shown in the Old Testament
as a proper response to disaster (Lam. 1:1-2; Isa. 15:2, 5;
Jer. 9:1; 13:17), and that is precisely what they will soon
face. Their weeping should be characterized by 'howling,'
a word that sounds like what it expresses – *ololuzontes*.[2]
This is the only occurrence of this descriptive word in the
New Testament. Davids cites twenty-one references of the
word in the Greek Old Testament (the Septuagint), all of
them in the prophets and all associated with crying out
over divine judgment.[3]

Such a mournful reaction is justified because of the
'miseries' (*talaipōriais*) coming upon them. The only other
use of the term is in Romans 3:16 where Paul marshaled
forth Old Testament evidence to describe the woe and
misery of the human condition in sin. The plural form of
the word is used to show the weight of the gloom they
soon faced. Adamson relates the structure of verses 1-11 to
Psalm 58 where the unrighteous are condemned (58:1-9)
and the righteous are encouraged to remember that God
will indeed vindicate them in the end (58:10, 11).[4]

---

1. Note 'last days' in verse 6 and 'coming of the Lord' in verses 7 and 8.
2. A word that *sounds like* what it defines is called an 'onomatopoetic' word.
3. Davids, 175.

It is easy for Christians in this 'me-generation' to forget James' words. Jesus uttered a similar and equally sobering pronouncement: 'But woe to you that are rich, for you have received your consolation. Woe to you that are full now, for you shall hunger. Woe to you that laugh now, for you shall mourn and weep' (Luke 6:24-25).

The question may arise, 'What about believers who are blessed with much wealth in this life?' Is this passage directed necessarily at them? Is it inherently wrong to possess worldly riches that are gained honestly and used ethically? No, but such possessions must never be our priority or our god. Robertson eloquently writes:

> Christians cannot afford to make money by crushing the life out of others using the juggernaut principle. The Golden Rule ought to work in business. Christ claims control of money and the making of money. The Christian who acts on the... compartment principle of life and keeps his money in a separate bulkhead into which he does not allow Christ to enter is disloyal to Christ. Christ claims the right of a partner in our business, not a silent but an active partner. We are in business with Christ and for Christ, and the Christian has no right to rotten money.[5]

Your riches are corrupted and your clothes have become moth-eaten (5:2)

In this verse James presents the plain truth about greed and selfish hoarding of wealth. Three reasons are given for the bold, emphatic statement of verse 1.

First, the tenses change here to dramatic perfects – action that happened in the past and is now ongoing. The storehouses of their wealth are now useless; the fruit of their labors is rotting before their eyes. Three metaphors in this verse and the next demonstrate this.

(1) 'Your riches are corrupted.' Corrupted is from *sēpō*, 'to rot or destroy.' It occurs only here in the New Testament.

---

4. Adamson, 184.
5. Robertson, 169.

(2) 'Moths have eaten your clothes,' literally, 'have become moth-eaten.' Moth-eaten is a compound word from *sēs* (moth) and *brōtos* (to eat, as in John 6:13).

(3) **Your gold and your silver are rusted (5:3a).** Although James knew that these metals do not rust in the technical sense of the word, silver does corrode and gold will tarnish. Nevertheless, the word is appropriate because it parallels the loss of other forms of riches. 'Rust' is from *katioō*, a compound word found only here in the New Testament. It is another perfect tense verb that vividly shows the future as a present reality. The picture is a sad one: when the worldly wealthy open their wallet, they find rotted money; when they open their closets, they find moth-eaten clothes; when they open their treasure chest, they find rust.

A *second* reason for this judgment is that the riches are inappropriate and idolatrous: **Their corrosion will be a witness against you and will eat your flesh like fire (5:3)** 'Corrosion' is *ios*, translated 'poison' in 3:8. James prophesied that gold and silver will lose their value because what is impossible – their corrosion – will take place. God's judgment will make it a reality. And this corrosion will witness (*marturia*) against the wealthy who use their riches to oppress the poor and control the courts. The conjunction 'and' connects the revelation concerning the worthlessness of their gold and silver in the judgment with the personal doom of the rich. It points out closely how they link their lives and aspirations with their wealth.[6] Plummer aptly observes, 'In the ruin of their property their own ruin is portrayed.'[7]

The corrosive activity of the precious metals symbolically portrays the 'eating of their flesh' in the Day of Judgment. Rust consuming iron is a slow process, and James greatly intensifies the terror of the process by likening it to a fire, a familiar element in God's judgment scheme (Matt. 5:29-30; 10:28; 1 Cor. 3:13; Rev. 20:15).

---

6. Hiebert, 286.
7. Alfred Plummer, *The General Epistles of St. James and St. Jude* (Hartford: Scranton, 1903), 6:622.

Third, this judgment is at hand because James sees this Christian era as the final age of the world: **You have stored up your wealth in the last days (5:3)**
The verb translated 'stored up' means 'to gather, accumulate, save.' Here it is used in the literal sense, but the word is used in the Gospels in the figurative sense of storing up treasures in heaven (Matt. 6:20). 'Last days' indicates that James believed in the nearness of the coming of the Lord and the climax of history. Indeed, His coming could be very near, but we should not misinterpret His delay as a broken promise or an inability on His part to consummate the age.

The 'last days' refer throughout Scripture to the conviction that the end times have already broken in upon the world in Jesus (Hosea 3:5; Isa. 2:2; Jer. 23:20; Dan. 2:28; Acts 2:17; Heb. 1:2; 2 Tim 3:1). These people had left God out of their plans and treasured up riches as if they would last forever, but the end times, in which they have a chance to repent and put their wealth to righteous use, are already upon them. The kingdom is here *already* in Jesus, but still *not yet* finally and fully realized. That will happen at the grand finale of history.[8]

2. The Evidence Against the Wealthy Oppressors

James begins by calling attention to the rich who are tyrannizing these poor believers by marshaling evidence against them in the images that follow. He enumerates three specific sins of the rich.

First, they are guilty of fraud: **Behold, the wages of the laborers who mowed your fields, which you have withheld by fraud, cry out against you (5:4)**
We sometimes use the quip, 'money talks.'[9] This is certainly true in the case of those who wickedly defraud others – their sin will speak loudly at God's judgment. James uses 'behold' (*idou*) six times in his epistle (3:4, 5; 5:4, 7, 9, 11)

---

8. For more on the 'already-not yet' theme in Scripture, see C. Marvin Pate, *The End of the Age Has Come* (Grand Rapids: Zondervan, 1995).

for emphasis. Earlier, James spoke in general terms about impending judgment; here he is very specific.

The 'wages' (*misthos*, as in Matt. 20:8) of hired 'laborers' was being dishonestly withheld by rich landowners. 'Laborers' is *ergatōn*, anyone who works for hire, especially agricultural workers (as in Matt. 9:37). These day laborers mowed (*amaō*, only occurrence in the New Testament) and harvested the fields of absentee landlords. Such modestly paid workers were numerous in first-century Palestine. Their earnings were meager at best, and survival was a serious matter if they missed or could not find work. James is describing such modest, powerless employees who toiled under a blistering sun only to be bilked by powerful magnates who owned large estates. 'Fields' suggests extensive, large tracts of land.

The landowners systematically held back their wages. 'Held back' is from *aphusterēmenos* and means 'to hold in reserve dishonestly and thus defraud.' This is a pitiful picture of rich Jews abusing their own people. Motyer states that the practice of paying wages late or legally defrauding the worker of his wage is ancient, and a host of laws and prophetic threats demonstrate God's disapproval (Lev. 19:13; Deut. 24:14-15; Jer. 22:13; Mal. 3:5).[10] James dramatically portrays the withheld wages' shrieking cry (*krazei*, another onomatopoetic word as in 5:1). The idea is that the poor and starving workers are so weak that their wages have to cry out instead![11]

The brother of our Lord does not give the answer God provides as the poor cry out to Him but does use a significant name for the Almighty in this context: **The outcry of the harvesters has reached the ears of the Lord of Sabaoth (5:4)**
'Outcry' is *boai*, a different word from 'cry out' in the previous phrase that fills out the pitiful sounds of the oppressed. When God's people utter cries in the Bible they are usually

9. Wiersbe, 145-48.
10. Motyer, 177.
11. Joel Gregory, *James: Faith Works!* (Nashville: Convention Press, 1986), 101.

praying for deliverance from danger and for justice (for example see Exod. 2:23; 1 Sam 9:16; 2 Chron. 33:13).[12] 'Harvesters' (*therisantes*) complements 'mowers' in the previous clause.

Their cries have reached God. The Greek tense here is significant – it is a perfect tense, meaning the cries have reached God and will continue to be heard by Him. 'Sabaoth' is a transliteration of the Greek word that derives from the Hebrew *tsaba*, meaning 'armies' or hosts. The name points to the characteristics of God's might and power. Surely the Lord of all power, who has the authority to dispatch heavenly armies, will come to the aid of the suffering. Luke Timothy Johnson observes: 'Here James definitely evokes the experience of Israel in Egypt. At the burning bush Yahweh says to Moses, 'I have seen the affliction of My people in Egypt *and I have heard their shouts*' (Exod. 3:7).'[13]

The *second* sin James identifies is that of luxury: **You have lived on earth in luxury and self-indulgence (5:5)**
Such flamboyant living in itself is indeed sinful, but doing so with such little regard for the poor and suffering is unspeakable evil. 'Lived in luxury' (*truphan*) translates a verb that can have both a positive and a negative sense. Positively it means to take pleasure or delight in something. For example, Eden is called the Garden of Delight in Genesis 2:15; 3:24; Joel 2:3. Or, one can delight in goodness or good things (Neh. 9:25). Negatively, it means to live luxuriously and to be soft or wanton.[14] The latter is the meaning here.

'Self-indulgence' derives from a single Greek verb, *spatalaō*, used only here and in 1 Timothy 5:6. It carries the idea of giving oneself to the pursuit of pleasure or plunging into dissipation. In 1 Timothy 5:6, Paul used the word to speak of those who are dead even while they live. In Romans 1, Paul describes this kind of person whom God gives over to greater and greater depravity. Such ease and

---

12. Moo (PNTC), 54.
13. Luke Timothy Johnson, *The Letter of James*, The Anchor Bible (New York: Doubleday, 1995), 302. Emphasis in the original.
14. Ibid., 303.

luxury in the present highlights the contrast that awaits the ungodly rich, namely, the torment and misery that are being stored up for them (5:3b).[15]

We move forward now to verse 6, because it presents further evidence against the oppressors, even though the verdict against them is inserted into verse 5b. The exposition in this commentary has moved for the most part verse by verse, but here is a case where we think James adds one more bit of evidence after he has pronounced their doom.

You have condemned and killed the righteous; he is not resisting you (5:6)

Here is the *third* sin against them that James decries – injustice. Rather than supporting and vindicating the righteous, they 'condemn' (*katadikazō*) them. The verb means 'to pass sentence on' with the result of condemning. 'Killed' or 'put to death' is from *phoneuō*, translated murder in all its other New Testament uses (Matt. 5:21; 19:18; 23:31, 35; Mark 10:19; Luke 18:20; Rom. 13:9; James 2:11; 4:2). The implication is that the wicked rich are using the courts to judicially murder some of the abused poor.[16]

Commentators disagree over the identity of 'the righteous one' (*ho dikaios*). Some think it refers to Jesus and others think that James is referring to himself.[17] But the idea is more general – any laborer defrauded in this manner is the victim of such judicial abuse. Many in James' community of faith are victims of this injustice. Johnson points out the specific link that exists already in Scripture between idolatry, oppression, and murder (Deut. 12:30-31; Amos 5:4-6; Hab. 1:16; Jer. 2:27, 34; 22:3; Ezek. 16:49, 52; Isa. 1:21-23).[18] The mistreatment is even more egregious because the righteous do not defend themselves. The verb tense is present, which is a vivid way of portraying the real and ongoing tragedy occurring in James' day. Their actions of injustice are heinous in and of themselves, but even more

---

15. Martin, 180.
16. MacArthur, 249; Davids, 179.
17. Mayor, 160; Johnson, 304.
18. Johnson, 304.

so because they are committed against the defenseless and non-resistant. Wiersbe observes: 'Luxury has a way of ruining character. It is a form of self-indulgence. If you match character with wealth you can produce much good; but if you match self-indulgence with wealth, the result is sin. The rich man Jesus described in Luke 16:19-31 would have felt right at home with the rich men James wrote to!'[19]

3. The Verdict against the Wealthy Oppressors (5:5)

This wantonness, luxury, and injustice are an affront to God and to the needy, and James pronounces a terse and grim judgment on the perpetrators: **you have gorged yourselves in the day of slaughter (5:5)**.

The descriptive verb 'gorged' is *ethrepsate*, 'indulging or fattening oneself.' The idea is that of indulging one's passions and lusts. They are growing fatter and fatter, but not for the end that they expect.

'In the day of slaughter' is the key phrase in this verdict against the rich oppressors. In vivid language, James depicts the rich as cows – they have enjoyed their luxury, allowing themselves to get fat and not realizing that such a condition prepares them for the slaughterhouse of divine judgment.

The principal thrust of James' warning to rich oppressors is that there is to be a judgment. Those who abuse wealth are going to be punished at that judgment. Misery is going to come upon them (5:1). Being so sure of it, James bids them act now as they will then: 'Now listen, you rich people, weep and wail because of the misery that is coming upon you.'

The context shows that he is not writing to all who are rich, but to the rich who abuse their wealth. The judgment will be a time of wretchedness, distress, trouble and misery. The misery will be so immense that people will weep and wail. Weeping and tears can be of anguish rather than repentance, particularly when repentance has

---

19. Wiersbe, 148.

been resisted, and it will be too late for repentance then. 'Wail,' urges Isaiah in his prophecy against Babylon, 'for the day of the LORD is near; it will come like destruction from the Almighty. Because of this, all hands will go limp, every man's heart will melt. Terror will seize them, pain and anguish will grip them; they will writhe like a woman in labor' (Isa. 13:6-8). All that glitters is not gold, and God does not necessarily balance His books at the end of each day. But balance them He will, and James encourages the community of faith with this reminder.

This paragraph is a dismal one indeed. For now, sin seems to have dominion, and righteousness seems to be on the losing side. But take courage! The Lord of Hosts will be the equalizer. The meek really will inherit the earth (Matt. 5:3) and the perverse value system of this world will be turned on its end. Mary, the mother of Jesus, foresaw that her divine offspring would reverse the fortunes of all mankind: 'He has put down the mighty from their thrones, and exalted those of low degree' (Luke 1:52).[20]

Wisdom to Live By

- The way we earn, save, and spend money is one of the most telling barometers of our spiritual lives. As believers we need to develop and maintain a scriptural view of wealth. Money is the root of all kinds of evil if it is not yielded to the Lordship of Christ. Do we overestimate the value of money?

- Godless materialism will face God's sure and stern judgment. Earthly possessions can be deceptive gods that cannot sustain life and will be of no value when God's final verdict is rendered.

- God is attentive and concerned for the poor and oppressed, as Scripture consistently affirms. Do we give to and actively help the poor and oppressed?

---

20. Gregory, 103.

13

Wisdom and Patience
(James 5:7-12)

Runners know that the most grueling race is the 400-meter run. Longer races are run in track and field, but the 400-meter is the longest sprint. By the time racers reach the finish line their lungs are heaving and their hearts pounding. Knowing that relief is waiting at meter 401 helps the runner persevere. The previous section showed how James' readers were facing abuse and oppression for being followers of Christ, but in this section, and in the next and final one, James encourages them to keep running, for they will not have to sprint forever. God *will* intervene, but they need to know how to live until then.

The tone of the epistle changes again with this paragraph. In 5:1-6 the apostle spoke as a prophet and denounced the sin of the wicked oppressors; here he speaks with the voice of a pastor as he offers sympathy, support, and encouragement to the community of faith. The rest of the epistle is concerned with three essential exhortations on how to live 'until then': (1) live with patience and steadfast endurance (5:7-12); (2) live by praying knowledgeably and effectively in all circumstances (5:13-18); and (3) rescue those who lose patience and wander from the way. The last three chapters of this exposition will deal with these exhortations in order. In James 5:7-12, he focuses on living with patience.

1. The Command for Patience
2. Examples of Patience
3. The Incentive for Patience
4. A Postscript: Avoid Swearing and Idle Oaths While Maintaining Patience

1. The Command for Patience

This paragraph is the third time James discusses the matter of trials and tribulations that come upon the believer. His treatment of this subject is not as much circular as it is spiral in nature because each time he revisits the topic he lifts us to a higher plane. The first time we see the matter of trials and difficulties is in 1:2-8, where the apostle teaches us that such vicissitudes are helpful in the development of our faith. The second time the subject appears is in 1:13-18 where he helps us distinguish between trials and testings on the one hand and temptation to evil on the other. Now, as James deals with the trials of injustice and oppression that his readers were experiencing, he instructs them to endure it with patience, counting on God to rectify the wrong.

James commends his readers for not retaliating (5:6), but rather maintaining a spirit of gentleness and meekness.

Therefore be patient, brethren, until the coming of the Lord (5:7)

Three times in this section (vv. 7, 8, 9) James points out to the believers their great hope in the second coming of the Lord Jesus. The realization that things are not 'frozen in time' but that they are headed for heaven and God's vindication must have been tremendously comforting to this community of faith. 'Be patient' describes a person slow to anger, not a hot head, but one with a long fuse. It is different from the word 'endurance' in 1:3-4. J. H. Ropes notes that the word is found only rarely in secular Greek, 'for it is a virtue that does not flourish readily in the heart of natural man.'[1] The realization that believers are headed for 'a city whose builder and architect is God (Heb. 11:10)

---

1. Ropes, 293.

provides great hope for those who are being persecuted. For that reason, the more persecuted a church is the more eagerly it anticipates the Lord's return.'[2]

The 'coming' of the Lord is His *parousia*, an important New Testament eschatological term. It is commonly used for the second coming of Christ (see 1 Cor. 15:23; 1 Thess. 2:19; 3:13; 4:15; 5:23; 2 Thess. 2:1; 8:2; 2 Pet. 1:16; 3:4; 1 John 2:28). The reference is not just to the Lord's 'coming' but also to His very presence, the hope of the church (Titus 2:11-13). The glorious truth of our Lord's return and reign is mentioned in more than 500 verses in Scripture.[3] Patience is by all means a Christian virtue, and it is made possible by the confident assurance of Christ's return. James gives us three concrete examples of such long-suffering endurance: the patient farmer (v. 7), the persistent prophets (v. 10), and the patriarch Job (v. 11).

2. Examples of Patience

The *first* example James brings before us is *the patient farmer*. Knowing how difficult it is to be patient, he prefaces it with 'behold' (*idou*) to draw special attention to the illustrations that follow.

Behold, the farmer waits for the precious fruit of the earth (5:7)

Jesus refers to farmers frequently in the Gospels, as in Matthew 21 in the parable of the landowner and vineyard. The word here describes an independent landowner or tenant farmer rather than a day laborer. He plants his field and anticipates the yield, but he knows there must be an interval of time before his crops come to fruition.

'Waits for' translates *ekdechetai*, a compound word that means eager anticipation, as in Acts 17:16 and Philippians 3:20. 'Fruit' is from the common word *karpos*. It is 'precious' (*timion*, meaning honorable or valuable) because it requires hard work and because, in part, life is sustained by it. The farmer recognizes that the fruit is

---

2. MacArthur, 253.
3. Ibid.

not merely the result of his own labors, but that outside forces from God must contribute – sun, rain, fair weather. Likewise, the believer recognizes that the spiritual harvest we anticipate is also dependent upon the intervention of God in our affairs.[4]

being patient for it until it [he] receives the early and latter rains (5:7)

The subject of 'receives' is not stated – it could be the fruit or it may be the farmer who receives it since he is the subject of the illustration. I prefer the latter. The adjective 'early' (*proimon*) occurs only here in the New Testament. James refers to what is called in Palestine the 'early' rains that fall late October and early November. This rain is vital to the farmer to soften the soil and prepare it for planting. The 'latter' rains fall late April into May. These rains, accompanied by warmer weather, help to mature the crops. The more and longer the latter rains, the more the potential yield. Adamson comments, 'The farmer awaiting the harvest is a familiar Jewish picture of salvation and the Last Judgment. Like the farmer the Christian must be patient and depend on God to consummate his purpose.'[5]

James now applies the illustration with directness and power: **You also be patient; establish your hearts, for the coming of the Lord is at hand (5:8)**

He reiterates the same command with which he began verse 7, 'Just like the farmer, you also be patient.' Nature has taught the farmer this secret, and James wants his readers to realize it as well. 'Establish' is from *stērizō*, to support or make stable (as in Luke 22:32 and 1 Thess. 3:13). God strengthens us, but we are also active and responsible. God's intention is to produce in us the fruit of the Spirit (Gal. 5:22-23) and one key way that happens is through the crucible of trials and suffering. Instead of growing impatient with the Lord and others, we must yield to Him. We can stand this way only if our hearts are firmly established in the Word and prayer.

4. Hiebert, 297.
5. Adamson, 191.

The command to make our hearts stable is followed by an explanation: be stable in your faith *because* of the blessed hope of the Lord's near return. 'Is at hand' translates *eggizō* and it is in the perfect tense, which means literally 'the Lord's coming has drawn near and remains near.' Many years ago I (Dale) was with a youth group at a retreat on the coast of South Carolina. We were playing on a sandbar when suddenly the tide began coming in. The undertow was strong, and one boy was unable to swim. I told him to remain calm and keep his hands on my shoulders. I stayed with him as the waves kept crashing in and soon we were in water over our heads. As I treaded water for both of us, trying to keep us from sinking, panic gripped me because I was sure we would drown. Unexpectedly, a small motorboat appeared – from where I will never know. The man on the boat helped my friend into the little craft, explaining that he could not take both of us at the same time. 'You wait here,' he said, 'I'll be right back.' Calmly and at rest I floated in the ocean, secure in the fact that help was coming. And it did. When Jesus left this earth, He promised us, 'I'll be back.' This world is a sea full of sin, trials, and pain. But we can live in the sweet confidence that Jesus is coming again and He will calm all the storms of our lives. We have every reason to be stable because our confidence rests upon the unchanging God (1:17) who has given us His unchanging Word (1 Pet. 1:23), that 'He who is coming will come and will not delay' (Heb. 10:37).

James continues the application: **Do not grumble against each other, brothers, or you will be judged (5:9)**
Christian patience puts a restraint upon our grumbling against each other. Grumbling (*stenazō*, to sigh or groan due to unpleasant circumstances) is never more prevalent than when things are difficult in some way or other. Grumbling is a way of releasing some of our bad feelings. People may even argue that they feel better after a good grumble!

But, as we have seen earlier when dealing with slander (4:11, 12), grumbling is a form of judging. When we grumble, we are declaring that someone has either not done something that he ought to have done, or that he has done something wrong. When we grumble, therefore, we judge. If, however, we exercise patience and develop Christian stability – with our eyes on the Lord's return – we appreciate that His return will herald the Day of Judgment. We must, therefore, leave all judgment to Him.

He is well-equipped to judge, and He is ready to judge – in fact, He is **standing at the door! (5:9b)**
The emphasis with this use of 'at the door' is that of nearness, as in Mark 13:29 and Acts 5:9. But Richardson poses the question, 'Did James mean the doors of the local church, meaning He is eyewitness to everything that transpires within? Or did James mean the 'door' of the present into which the Judge is about to come for final judgment?'[6] Though either meaning is certainly possible, the latter option seems to fit the context better.

Sometimes God the Father is spoken of as the Judge (Heb. 12:23), and sometimes the Lord Jesus Christ is (Acts 10:42; 2 Tim. 4:1, 8), as in this case. The two truths are brought together in the fact that God the Father has fixed a day on which He will judge the whole world in justice by our Lord Jesus Christ, the Judge whom He has appointed (Acts 17:31). Part of the Father's honoring the Son is His appointment as the Judge of all men and women.

Few take grumbling seriously. But God does, and so does every Christian whose focus is on the Lord's coming. The manner in which we judge others in our grumbling against them is the way we shall find ourselves judged (Matt. 7:1-2).

A *second* example of patience used by the author to encourage his readers is the *persistent prophets*.

As an example of patience amid suffering, brothers, take the prophets who spoke in the name of the Lord (5:10)
Again the apostle addresses his Christian brothers and sisters affectionately, wanting to reinforce his plea to them

---

6. Richardson, 223.

to remember Christ's Lordship, His promise to judge evil, and their need to remain patient in the midst of suffering and oppression. He uses the prophets of old as an example of patience because the Old Testament prophets and these New Testament believers shared the common experience of being wronged and abused for their faith.

The prophets showed peerless patience and faithfulness despite the suffering they endured (see Heb. 11). Elijah was hounded and hated (1 Kings 18:10, 17). Jeremiah was thrown into a cistern with the threat of starving to death (Jer. 38:1-13). Amos was falsely accused of raising a conspiracy and was told to go back to where he had come from (Amos 7:10-13). Once more James reflects the Sermon on the Mount: 'Blessed are you when people insult you, persecute you and falsely say all kinds of evil against you because of me. Rejoice and be glad, because great is your reward in heaven, for in the same way they persecuted the prophets who were before you' (Matt. 5:11-12).

The prophets 'spoke in the name of the Lord.' Their words, reputations, and even their lives were directly related to God's redemptive purpose. Their situations were precarious for two reasons. *First*, they were *prophets*, and much of what they preached had not yet transpired, so they had to have great faith and hope in God. *Second*, they spoke publicly, affirming that God would indeed bring about His word through them. They died before they saw the fulfillment of their prophecies; nevertheless, they were revered for their endurance in difficult times. By drawing attention to these men of old, James encourages his readers to adopt the same kind of faith and long-suffering they exhibited.

Behold, we call them blessed who endured (5:11)

With this phrase James summarizes the general example of the prophets and prepares for the specific example of endurance provided by Job. This occurrence of 'behold' is the last in the epistle; the author once again calls special attention to these models of steadfast endurance. 'We call them blessed' (*makarizomen*, the verb form of the adjective

used in the Beatitudes) shows that James numbers himself
with his readers in expressing admiration for the virtue
found in the Old Testament heroes.

'Them ... who endured' (*tous hupomeinantes*) denotes
a class of sufferers who persevered and successfully completed their test of faith. They stood bravely 'under the siege
of trials without losing heart and so faithfully endured to
the end.'[7] The word here is different from 'patience' used
in verse 10; it is the term used in 1:3-4 for describing the
role of endurance in developing Christian character.

James now moves to present the patriarch Job as a specific
example of this steadfast endurance in the face of affliction:
**You have heard of the endurance of Job and you have
seen the final purpose of the Lord** (5:11)
The apostle assumes his readers knew Job's story quite
well. This is the only place in the New Testament where
the patriarch is mentioned directly. But the early Christian
community was familiar with him and, as W. E. Oesterley
shows, 'he occupied a high place of honor in post-biblical
Jewish literature.'[8] The endurance or patience of Job, though a
common colloquial expression, is not necessarily the picture
we derive of him when reading the Book. His 'impassioned
outbursts against the shallow platitudes of his so-called
comforters (Job 3:1, 11; 16:2) or his distressed protests to God
(7:11-16; 10:18; 23:2; 30:20-23) demonstrate that he was not a
model of Stoic impassibility.'[9] But the term James uses here,
once again, is not patience, as in verse 10, but 'endurance,
steadfastness.' In spite of all his unexplained sufferings, Job
is a stellar model of endurance under tremendous suffering,
and under it all he remained unswervingly devoted to the
Lord (1:21; 2:10; 16:9-21; 19:25-27).

A strong element of encouragement is given by 'the
final purpose (*telos*) of the Lord' in Job's case. In the end,
God revealed His purpose and showed that Romans 8:28
is true for the child of God. We cannot understand the

7. Ibid.

8. W. E. Oesterley, *The General Epistle of James*, The Expositor's Greek
Testament, ed. Robertson Nicoll (Grand Rapids: Eerdmans, 1967), 472.

9. Leslie Mitton, *The Epistle of James* (Grand Rapids: Eerdmans, 1966), 189.

purpose God has in mind until we come to the end. In the surprising conclusion to the Book, God restored Job's family, fortune, and friends. It reminds me (Dale) of the poem called *The Weaver*:

> My life is but a weaving,
> between my God and me,
> I do not choose the colors,
> He worketh steadily.
> Ofttimes he weaveth sorrow,
> and I in foolish pride
> Forget He sees the upper,
> and I the underside.
>
> Not till the loom is silent,
> and the shuttles cease to fly,
> Will God unroll the canvas,
> and explain the reasons why.
> The dark threads are as needful
> in the skillful weaver's hand
> As threads of gold and silver
> in the pattern He has planned.
>
> He knows, He loves, He cares,
> nothing this truth can dim.
> He gives His very best to those
> who leave the choice with Him.

3. The Incentive for Patience

We can remain patient and steadfast only by remembering that God has good purposes in mind for our lives, just as He did with Job. Jeremiah 29:11 likewise states, 'For I know the plans I have for you, says the LORD, plans for peace and not evil, to give you a future and a hope.'

because the Lord is very compassionate and merciful (5:11)
Job learned two things about God through the crucible of all he suffered. *First*, God is 'very compassionate.' This is a compound word found only here in the New Testament and coined by James. It consists of the adjective 'many or much' and 'compassion,' a noun used

in Matthew 9:36 where Jesus had 'compassion on the multitudes.'

But God is, *second*, 'merciful' toward us. This is the common word in the New Testament for God's benevolent dealing with His people (Luke 1:78; Rom. 9:16; 11:30, 32; 12:1; 15:9; 2 Cor. 1:3; Eph. 2:4; Heb. 2:17; 1 Pet. 1:3; 2:10). Any trial or suffering experienced by the child of God can be patiently endured by anticipating that He will indeed cause all things to work together for good (Rom. 8:28). The suffering of one of God's own elicits His mercy and compassion.

The patient farmer, the persistent prophets, and the patriarch Job all speak eloquently of the virtue of steadfast spiritual endurance. In today's culture, enormous value is placed on physical endurance, but does our generation place a similar premium on spiritual endurance? Hardly. James urges a spiritual 'ironman' kind of faith. 'The age calls for a Christian commitment that endures regardless of physical inconveniences, social ostracism, financial sacrifices, or vocational jeopardy.'[10]

4. A Postscript: Avoid Swearing and Idle Oaths While Maintaining Patience

How to divide the epistle at this point is unclear. Does verse 12 constitute a new thought with James or is it a postscript to his exhortation to patience amidst suffering? Commentators are divided, though the majority thinks that verse 12 is a separate and new subject.[11] Still, there are others who see a connection between it and the section on patience.[12] Indeed, Sadler offers the opinion that the vexing nature of this question has never been satisfactorily explained.[13] But this problem need not distract us, for Robertson is correct: 'The two exhortations [v. 12 and

---

10. Gregory, 111.

11. E.g., Martin, Davids, Oesterley, Adamson, Moo, Johnson.

12. E.g., Motyer, Richardson, Robertson, and Reicke; see Bo Reicke, *The Epistles of James, Peter, and Jude*, The Anchor Bible (Garden City, NY: Doubleday, 1964), 56.

13. M. F. Sadler, *The General Epistles of Saints James, Peter, John, and Jude* (London: Bell, 1899), 70.

vv. 7-11] need not have a close connection with each other. James has spoken of sins of the tongue more than any other sin, so it is quite natural that he should return to that now – whether or not it arises immediately out of what precedes.'[14]

But above all, my brethren (5:12)

What makes the contextual ambiguity even 'more maddening'[15] is the emphasis the author places on it. 'But' (*de*) is a strong connective and can denote either continuance of what precedes (with a translation of 'now' or 'for') or it may introduce a new idea ('but, on the other hand'). The command in this verse is the first of several that brings the epistle to a close (a common practice in New Testament books, as in 1 Thess. 5:11-27). 'Above all' (*pro pantōn*) sets this admonition apart as pre-eminent and pervasive. James is especially concerned about this particular fault perhaps because some recent incident has brought home to him how urgently the counsel is needed and he can be so insistent because of their common spiritual heritage ('my brethren').

The verse contains a prohibition, an instruction, and a reason.

First, the author gives us a *prohibition*: **do not swear, either by heaven or by earth or with any other oath (5:12)**
The Holy Spirit through James restricts the sin of swearing. This word (*omnuete*) does not refer (as it does so often in English) to cursing and illicit speech with the use of 'four-letter' words. Rather, it refers to taking oaths. The original purpose of an oath lay in guaranteeing a person's word. Calling upon God frequently provided a higher court of appeal. The formula of oaths originally had the character of conditionally cursing oneself if the statement proved to be false. Unfortunately, this sometimes led to using God's

---

14. Robertson, 183; Robert W. Wall, *Community of the Wise: The Letter of James*, The New Testament in Context (Valley Forge: Trinity Press International, 1977), 259-60. Herein cited as Wall, *Community*.

15. Wall, *Community*, 159.

name for the purpose of adding emphasis in the swearing of an oath.[16]

The fact that James introduces this section with the words 'above all' implies the importance of the restraint we ought to exercise in this matter of swearing and oath-taking. These words constitute James' final quotation from the Sermon on the Mount when our Lord said:

> 'Again, you have heard that it was said to the people long ago, "Do not break your oath, but keep the oaths you have made to the Lord." But I tell you, Do not swear at all: either by heaven, for it is God's throne; or by the earth, for it is his footstool; or by Jerusalem, for it is the city of the Great King. And do not swear by your head, for you cannot make even one hair white or black. Simply let your "Yes" be "Yes" and your "No" "No"; anything beyond this comes from the evil one' (Matt. 5:33-37).

Our Lord attacked the Jewish custom of oath-taking in its attempt to avoid the misuse of God's name, which explains the references to swearing by heaven, the earth, Jerusalem or even one's own head. Wall observes, 'Rather than invoking heaven's cooperation by swearing some oath, and thus trivializing God's sovereignty, we should follow the example of the prophets and Job and simply speak in the name of the Lord.'[17]

Second, we have *an instruction:* **But let your yes be yes and your no, no (5:12)**
Reiterating Jesus' words in Matthew 5:37, James calls for simple, straightforward, honest speech. 'People of integrity have no need to swear elaborate oaths to convince others of their truthfulness.'[18]

---

16. Does this verse forbid believers from taking oaths in court 'to tell the truth ... so help me God'? We do not believe the passage has that direct application. The fact that courts find it necessary to place a witness under oath is an acknowledgement that they recognize the problem James is addressing. Williams is on target: 'The use of oaths in court, to add reliability to what is said, is *just* what would be unnecessary if the words of James were obeyed.' R. R. Williams, 'The Letters of John and James,' in *The Cambridge Bible Commentary* (Cambridge: Cambridge University Press, 1965), 137.
17. Wall, *Community*, 260.
18. MacArthur, 271.

Then James gives us, *third*, the *reason* for this injunction: **so that you may not fall under judgment (5:12)**
Those who indiscreetly swear idle oaths will 'fall under judgment.' To say 'yes' and mean it or to say 'no' and equally mean it is a matter of integrity of heart rather than the mere formula of words. In this way James brings the argument full circle to remind us that we should be people without double minds, wholehearted with God and man. Motyer sums it up well: 'We practice a devotion to the truth with our lips because the truth dwells with us.'[19]

Wisdom to Live By

- In what areas of our lives do we most lack patience and endurance?
- What trials have we experienced? Has there been spiritual progress in our lives as a result?
- Are we persons whose words can be trusted?

19. Motyer, 185.

14

Wisdom and Prayer
(James 5:13-20)

That this final section of James' letter deals with four life problems and one primary solution is not at all surprising. The emphasis throughout has been on consistent living in the community of faith. This segment seems at first the most difficult part of the letter for which to give a title. But when we remember that James' major theme has been the relationship between faith and works, the title 'Wisdom and Prayer' fits because all four subjects are concerned with putting our faith to work in the most practical, down-to-earth, prayerful ways. Faith must be put to work in all of life's ups and downs. The four human experiences are:

1. Suffering (5:13)
2. Joy (5:13)
3. Sickness (5:14-18)
4. Wandering (5:19-20)

We noted in the introduction to the previous chapter that James' larger contextual concern is 'until then.' And his admonition here is: until then, be people of believing prayer. Our hymnals are treasure chests of great theology, and certainly an appropriate hymn for this passage is *Sweet Hour of Prayer*:

Sweet hour of prayer, sweet hour of prayer
That calls me from a world of care,
And bids me at my Father's throne
Make all my wants and wishes known.
In seasons of distress and grief
My soul has often found relief,
And oft escaped the tempter's snare
By thy return, sweet hour of prayer.

As we shall see, this passage has been a battleground for interpreters throughout the ages. Various groups have used it as a proof-text for their favorite theological soapbox, and many have been confused because certain faith healers have misapplied the verses. We need the help of the Holy Spirit to understand anything in the Word of God (1 Cor. 3), and especially so as we approach this paragraph. But, as the writer to the Hebrews confidently asserted, 'This we shall do as God enables us' (Heb. 6:3).

1. Suffering (5:13)

Before addressing the problem of illness, James referred to more general misfortunes in life. **Is anyone among you suffering, brethren? Then he must pray**.

Structurally, these sentences could be posed as declarations followed by imperatives, or as interrogatives followed by imperatives. Martin Dibelius regards them as declaratives followed by the commands: 'Someone among you is suffering; let him pray.'[1] Davids argues well that James intends interrogatives followed by imperatives, as in the NASB and NIV. Davids describes the result as 'the lively discourse of oral style.' It reflects James' desire to engage his readers personally, because he wants so much for them to put prayer into practice.[2]

The word 'suffering' emphasizes the internal distress caused by outward circumstances. It translates *kakopatheō*, 'to feel or experience bad or evil.' It is the verb form of the corresponding noun we saw in verse 10. It denotes the

---

1. Dibelius, 241, 252.
2. Davids, 191.

experience of misfortune or calamity. Paul used the same word for his 'suffering' when he was treated like a criminal and chained in prison (2 Tim. 2:9). James may have had in mind the persecution he had just discussed in verses 1-6. Or he may have been pointing to more general vicissitudes that afflict us all – problems, difficulties, hardships, and trials.

As an antidote, James instructs us to 'pray' and make it a constant practice to take our concerns to God. We should not grumble, seek to retaliate against wrongdoers, or even simply 'grin and bear it' like a Stoic. Rather, we should individually and collectively turn to God for relief and deliverance. The Psalms are full of testimonials concerning God's help when we pray (see Ps. 50:15 and Ps. 91:15 as examples). Another beloved hymn comes to mind in this context:

> Oh what peace we often forfeit,
> Oh what needless pain we bear.
> All because we do not carry
> Everything to God in prayer.
>
> Have we trials and temptations
> Is there trouble anywhere
> We should never be discouraged,
> Take it to the Lord in prayer.

2. Joy (5:13)

The second situation is one of joy. **Is anyone joyful? Let him sing praises**.

The Greek word for 'joyful' is *euthumeō* and describes one who is well in spirit and has a joyful attitude. Joy is a fruit of the Spirit (Gal. 5:22-23) and is much deeper than happiness, which is a fleeting emotion related to favorable circumstances. Stulac is right:

> Like James' original readers, we might allow times of happiness to make us complacent, and so we would pray less. The biblical instruction is again the opposite: pray more. Happiness is the very time to *sing songs of praise*.[3]

---

3. George M. Stulac, *James*, IVP New Testament Commentary (Downers Grove: InterVarsity, 1993), 180.

We also tend to forget about God in times of success and happiness, and we forget to be grateful when things are going our way. James instructs us, however, to develop a thankful attitude toward God when life is going favorably for us. We are to 'sing praises.' It is the Greek *psallō*, a descriptive term that gives us our word 'Psalms'. It is used in Acts 13:33; 1 Corinthians 14:26; and Ephesians 5:19. Psalms are the soul's expressions of joyful prayer, as the petitions of praise 'sing' their way to God.[4]

3. Sickness (5:14)

Times of sickness are the third human experience that should elicit prayer among God's people.

Is anyone among you sick?
No particular sickness is identified. The word for 'sick' is general, *astheneō*, meaning to be weak or sick. It is used thirty-two times in the New Testament to refer to both particular maladies as well as physical or emotional weakness caused by an illness. Like James' original readers, we easily feel defeated in times of sickness. Perhaps that is why James includes the elders here, whereas the first two experiences called simply for prayer on the part of the individual. Weakness makes us feel hopeless, as if there is nothing we can do. The biblical outlook is the opposite: there is something very significant to do, namely, to pray. Weakness is the very time for prayer. O. Hallesby, the great teacher on prayer, wrote, 'Your helplessness *is* your best prayer.'[5]

Let him call for the elders of the church, let them pray over him, anointing him with oil in the name of the Lord.
The praying process involves three elements that demand our attention. *First*, the suffering person 'calls for the elders of the church.' The sick one should 'call' for the spiritually mature, strong, wise men of the church. 'Call' is from

---

4. Richard R. Melick, Jr., 'Warnings and Instructions,' *Mid-America Theological Journal* 10:1 (Spring 1986): 69.
   5. Quoted by Stulac, 180.

proskaleō, to call alongside for help. It is the verb from which we get the title *Paraclete* for the Holy Spirit. He is the One called alongside to help us! Calling for the elders is an act of obedience and faith.

Scholars differ over whether the 'elders' (*presbuteroi*) are men holding a specific office in the church or whether it refers to a class of individuals who are spiritually mature. It is clear that the church chose elders early in its history, and James certainly reflects some of the earliest ecclesiology we know of. The elder is an alternate description of the pastor or pastors of local churches (see Acts 11:30; 15:2; 20:17).[6] The use of 'church' (*echchlēsia*) rather than synagogue, as in 2:2, is instructive. The early church certainly had its origins in the setting of the Jewish synagogue, and kinship in worship and structure are not surprising.

Elders, by definition in the biblical sense, are those who have the wisdom and the Christian maturity borne of many years in faithful service. The elders presumably have power in both prayer and discernment, and 'they are capable of exercising the faith necessary for the healing but also to discern the mind of the Spirit in such matters.'[7] When they are led to pray, therefore, they have sensed the purposes of God and will pray in accord with His will. As we shall see, they pray in faith, believing that what God reveals is what He desires to do.[8]

Second, they are to 'anoint him with oil.' It may appear that we have reversed the order here, but only so in the English versions. The tense of the participle 'anointing' is aorist and may mean that the action in the participle happens *prior to* that of the main verb. The Greek text reads, 'after anointing him in the name of the Lord let them pray over him.' 'Anointing' is from *aleiphō,* 'to anoint or rub down.' 'Oil' is *elaion,* 'olive oil' that was used in cooking, in lamps, and in treating injuries (see Mark 6:13; Luke 10:34).

---

6. A long treatise on church government and offices is not within our purview. I (Dale) agree with the opinion set forth by Gerald Cohen, *The Pastor as Elder* (Nashville: Broadman & Holman, 2004).

7. Melick, 70.

8. Ibid.

Throughout history the act commanded here by James has been interpreted in significantly different ways. This is because the text is quite abbreviated and ambiguous – no elaboration is provided at all. Also, there is no indication from Scripture that this anointing with oil had any sort of spiritual basis that would make it universally applicable or perpetually binding. If this was to be a requirement for the universal church for all time, we could reasonably expect that some foundation for the practice might have been supplied. We can summarize the interpretations of this passage into four groups.[9]

(1) Some scholars think that the 'anointing' referred to by James is simply a refreshing, encouraging act of friendship, much like when Mary anointed Jesus' feet (John 12:3; Luke 7:46). They argue that the Greek word *aleiphō* ('anoint') has to do with common rituals rather than a religious ceremony. In this sense James' admonition would be a call for the elders' prayers, accompanied by the cultural expression of that day which reflected love and friendship.

(2) Others suggest that oil was used as a daily item of toiletry in ancient times (much like cosmetics or perfumes are used today). In periods of sickness, distress, or fasting, this casual use of oil was suspended (cf. Ruth 3:3; 2 Sam. 12:20; 14:2; Dan. 10:2, 3; Micah 6:15; Matt. 6:16, 17). It is argued, therefore, that James may be exhorting the brethren to accompany their prayers with the 'anointing of oil,' i.e. the resumption of their *normal* activities. The oil would serve as a token of *confidence* in the power of their petition. While this concept may be possible, it does not readily commend itself to the ordinary expositor. Also, it does not explain why elders would be called to administer the oil.

(3) The most common interpretation holds that the use of oil was a *symbolic* act. In Bible times the practice of anointing with oil was frequently representative of God's

9. See Moo (PNTC), 238-40, for a similar breakdown with more discussion.

approval (see 1 Sam. 10:1; Ps. 89:20). Many biblical scholars are fairly confident, therefore, that the application of oil in James 5:14 is a symbolic act invoked in conjunction with *supernatural* healing. This idea may be correct, but there is one more view that I (Dale) believe offers the most merit.

(4) A number of writers contend that the oil of James 5:14 is merely a *medicinal* item which, together with the prayer, would be *providentially* efficacious in the healing process. Though view '3' may very well be the correct one, we need to develop the plausibility of this interpretation.

Robertson well notes, 'The vital question is whether the elders come in an official capacity to perform an ecclesiastical rite or whether they come as brothers in Christ and rub with olive oil as medicine.'[10] The Greek scholar agrees with the last position, as does MacArthur: '*Aleiphō* is not used in the New Testament to refer to a ceremonial rite.... It describes anointing one's head with oil (Matt. 6:17), the women's anointing of Jesus' body (Mark 16:1), Mary's anointing of the Lord's feet (John 11:2; 12:3) and anointing the sick with oil (Mark 6:13).'[11] Medicinally, this act was soothing as it provided relief from fevers when one was fanned after the rubbing down with oil. While commentators differ here, I (Dale) see this as the brothers in Christ doing all they can medically for the afflicted. With medicine in a primitive condition at the time, it may well be that they rubbed oil on the wounds of those who had been beaten as persecution for following Christ.

But even if one takes this to be a ceremonial rite, two observations are needed. First, it is not the oil that heals. See Mark 6:13 for a use of anointing with oil during the time of Jesus' public ministry. Most of the stories of healing by Jesus and His disciples have no mention of oil, and James' emphasis here is certainly on the power of the Lord rather than on any power in the oil. The promises of Jesus (John 14:13-14; 15:16; 16:23-24) give basis for expecting great power as we practice the principle of praying in His name.

---

10. Robertson, 189.
11. MacArthur, 277-78.

The second observation is that this has nothing to with the Roman Catholic Church's doctrine of extreme unction, which is a ritual performed when the priests expect one to die and as a preparation for death. What is in view in 5:14-15 is restoration to life and health.

Third, the elders are to pray. *Proseuchesthō* is one of several terms in the New Testament for prayer. It means 'to entreat, make intercession.' It marks the central ministry the elders perform for the sufferer, and by no means is the sick person precluded from joining in the prayers on his behalf. Richardson observes: 'Praying and touching as a group in the close proximity of the sick one intensifies and makes efficacious their faith for the healing.'[12]

A pastoral and practical observation is in order here. As a pastor of local churches for nearly twenty-five years, I (Dale) have been asked to provide this ministry a number of times and have asked myself, 'Should we anoint a sick person with oil when such a person calls for the elders?' My response has always been in the affirmative. I have made a practice of taking my ministerial staff and godly deacons from the church and going to the sick person after a time of spiritual inventory and preparation.[13] If the person insists on being anointed with oil I explain what I believe the passage describes. But knowing that I could be mistaken and appreciating the significance of a symbolic touching of the person's forehead with oil, we honor the request. Above all, I have sought to make clear that no power resides in the oil. All power belongs to God, and that power is appropriated through believing prayer. As for the outcome, we need first to examine verse 15.

In the immediate context in which James writes, we have three effects based on believing prayer.

First, The prayer offered in faith will restore the sick one (v. 15a)
Some years ago I (Dale) used George Stulac's quip on our church sign: 'A funny thing happens when you don't pray.'

---

12. Richardson, 232.
13. Churches that hold to a third office of elder, in addition to pastor and deacon, would certainly involve those men in this ministry.

Beneath this line was a word in small letters: 'Nothing.'[14] While a common word was used in verse 14 for prayer, here James switches to *euchē*, which occurs in only two other places in the New Testament (Acts 18:18; 21:23). It is a stronger term that denotes a fervent wish or petition. 'Will restore' translates *sōzō*, the New Testament word that means 'saved' and usually refers to spiritual salvation, but it can mean physical healing as well (see Matt. 9:21-22; Mark 6:56). Any view that defaults to a *spiritual* restoration here is not in keeping with the context. A physical restoration is the only responsible interpretation.

This unqualified statement that the prayer of faith will restore the sick person to physical wholeness is quite problematic for many. Is this an unconditional guarantee that every sick person will be healed when this process is applied? Biblical evidence and personal experience demand that we answer no. The crux is on the 'prayer of faith,' and it may well be that James and the elders know, from diligently seeking the heart of God, that He intends to heal this particular malady when the person exercises faith and calls for the elders. Motyer agrees, 'Prayer is by nature a commitment to the will of God, and all true prayer exercises its truest faith in patiently waiting to see what He has determined to do.'[15] We must always pray 'Thy will be done,' and apparently James and the church leaders had the sense that God's will *in this case* was to heal the affliction.

Second, **and the Lord will raise him up (5:15)**
Although this statement elaborates on the physical healing, a new dimension is added. To be 'raised up' (*egerei*) indicates the completeness of the physical restoration. The result will be a *real* healing. James' emphasis here is not on faith healers but on the power of God at work through the praying and believing Christian church.

The *third* effect is, **If he has sinned, he will be forgiven (5:15)**
James states the case conditionally ('if'), showing that sin *can* be an element in physical sickness, but not necessarily

---

14. Stulac, 183.
15. Motyer, 201.

so. Sophie Laws puts it well, 'James thinks of a possible, but not inevitable, association rather than a direct cause and effect relationship.'[16] James knows that some sickness needs confession of sin, but certainly not always. The point is that the Lord who heals is also the One who forgives. And, for those who need it, the healing does not stop with the body (the fruit) but extends also to the soul (the root).[17]

Before we leave these two crucial verses, we should summarize the teachings that are clearest. First, in this context the initiative rests on the person who is unwell: 'Is any one of you sick? He should call the elders of the church' (5:14). The individual who is unwell may not feel that it is appropriate, and his conviction should be respected. On the other hand, God may lay it upon a person's heart that this course of action is right for him.

Second, the elders – or the spiritual leaders of the local church – have a special responsibility to respond to this request. They are under-shepherds and men of Christian maturity and discernment. It is not for the members of the church to do this for one another; it is the responsibility of the spiritual overseers.

Third, we should not imagine anything magical about the anointing with oil. Although medicinal properties were attributed to olive oil, these are not emphasized. Rather, importance is attached to the believing prayer that accompanies the anointing. Our Lord Jesus did not need to touch the leper or the blind man's eyes as He healed them, but there was undoubted value in these actions for the persons concerned, and similarly with the anointing with oil. The anointing is in the name of the Lord, and that is the significant factor. It speaks of God's protection and blessing upon the individual.

Fourth, it is plausible that in his reference to the prayer offered in faith (5:15) James refers to the special gift of faith. All true prayer involves faith (Heb. 11:6), but James may have in mind the gift of faith the Spirit gives (1 Cor. 12:9).

16. Laws, 229.
17. Melick, 72.

As the elders gather around the person who is afflicted, having anointed him with oil in the name of the Lord, the Lord may give them special discernment to know exactly how to pray. Sometimes it may be that they should pray for grace to submit to God's will in the suffering (2 Cor. 12:9). But on other occasions the Lord may give the enlightenment and confidence to ask for very specific healing and it will be granted.

Fifth, there is special benefit for the sick person in this spiritual exercise even if physical healing proves not to be God's will. When we are unwell, it is extremely difficult to pray for ourselves with objectivity because we naturally want to be restored to health. Our spiritual under-shepherds are in a much better position to pray for us with discernment. In addition, when we are ailing we may find it almost impossible to pray at all. And here others may help us. As the elders pray with him, the sufferer is able to rest in the knowledge that through corporate prayer his circumstances are placed under God's control afresh, and if physical healing is not God's will, he may be sure of the spiritual healing he needs and the daily renewal of God's grace and peace.

This passage, then, does not provide a blanket guarantee that all physical sickness will be healed in this life. It assumes that God will disclose His will, and the prayer of faith asks in accordance with that purpose. Trouble, happiness, illness and sin – none of us knows when we may have to face these ordinary, everyday human experiences. But when we do, our faith must be put to work whether in prayer, praise, or confession of sin.

Therefore, confess your sins to one another and pray for one another, so that you may be healed (5:16)

'Therefore' (oun) shows that the exhortation to mutual prayer and confession in this verse is the conclusion the readers should draw from verses 14 and 15.[18] A spirit of openness should prevail in the church that encourages the confession of failures and faults. The author calls for

18. Moo (PNTC), 245.

a confession of specific sins, not just personal sinfulness. *Tas $amartias* points to definite acts of sins of which they are guilty. Confession of sin is the duty of every believer (1 John 1:9) and a powerful deterrent to sin. The sins that are confessed to the body seem 'naturally to relate to wrongdoings against other brethren that spoil the fellowship with one another and make it difficult to ... worship together as the people of God.'[19]

The same Spirit that encourages confession also promotes prayer – the kind of prayer that lays bare the heart and soul before the Lord. Mutual confession stimulates and gives direction to mutual intercession. 'So that you may be healed' is a very clear purpose clause with the verb *iaomai*. It is a versatile word used in the New Testament for spiritual restoration (John 12:40; Acts 28:27; Heb. 12:12-13), but we must acknowledge that it can point to physical healing as well (and this is the only sense that would be consistent with 'restore' and 'raise up' in verse 15). Some writers[20] wish to discard any possible meaning here for a literal and physical healing. But James seems too deliberate in emphasizing a physical restoration. Perhaps sin is the cause, and repentance on the part of the afflicted will bring relief; or maybe the spiritual leaders discern that *in this case* it is God's will to heal. However we wrestle with this text, we do not want to remove from it the clear and obvious intent.

The central principle of this passage is that God answers the prayers of His people when they are offered in faith and in accordance with His will: **The effectual prayer of a righteous man [has] much power (5:16)**
He reinforces his exhortation to pray with a reminder of the effective power of prayer. An interpretive question arises in this sentence. 'Effectual' translates *energoumenh* (we derive our word *energy* from it), a participle modifying 'prayer' that means 'having much energy, able to work.'

---

19. Tasker, 135. A rule of thumb might be that private sins should receive private confession and public sins public confession.
20. For example, MacArthur, 276-80.

It could function as an adjective (as our translation takes it) or it could be adverbial, meaning *'when* it works.'[21] We follow the adjectival use along with the KJV, 'the effectual, fervent prayer.'

'Righteous' signifies a person who is in right standing with God through Christ and who displays that through a life of faith. This is borne out in the example of Elijah (5:17), 'who had a nature like ours.' The energetic prayers of a righteous man are a potent force in calling down the power of God for physical healing and spiritual restoration. 'Typical of James, whenever someone is healed it is because it is God's will, and through prayers of faith believers may be involved in that process and in God's movements throughout our world.'[22]

This section on prayer ends with an example of the principle just stated, which James cites through two patriarchal heroes – Job models the patient endurance of present trials and Elijah models the prayerful attitude we should maintain in the face of trials.

Elijah was a man with a nature like ours; he prayed intensely for it not to rain, and it did not rain on the land for three and one-half years (5:17)
Knowing the stories of the mighty Elijah from 1 Kings in the Old Testament, we might put aside his example because he was such an exceptional servant of God. But James reminds us, he 'was a man with a nature like ours.' The Bible records that he suffered the same human weaknesses that we do: he became hungry (1 Kings 17:11), afraid (1 Kings 19:3), and depressed (1 Kings 19:9-14).

Two important parallels emerge with this illustration. *First,* Elijah was a normal human being. And, being every bit as human as we are, Elijah 'prayed earnestly.' Literally, the Greek text reads, 'he prayed with prayer.' *Second,* the situation resembles the one faced by James' readers. Just as the sick person is dry and lifeless, so the days in which Elijah ministered were just the same. The Old Testament

21. For a more technical treatment, see Ropes, 309; Adamson, 199.
22. Melick, 73.

never associates Elijah's prayer life with the incident reported here ('that it might not rain ... for three years and six months'). Likewise, the Old Testament does not tell us that the drought lasted for three and one-half years. We do know from 1 Kings 18:42 that he prayed for the drought to cease. Jewish tradition, however, includes ample evidence of these events, and James accepts them as correct.

Surely God worked a miracle when Elijah prayed again: **And again he prayed, and the heavens gave rain, and the earth produced her fruit (5:18)**
From Elijah we learn that half-hearted praying is an insult to God. If we truly believe that God is omnipotent, that He is the 'God of all flesh for whom nothing is too difficult,' then we should pray with absolute confidence in His ability to perform what we ask. And, if we have truly yielded our will to His in our requests, there is no room for half-hearted praying. Elijah prayed with fervent passion for a drought and he received it; he prayed for rain and God sent it.

4. Wandering

The epistle concludes with an admonition to rescue those who are straying from the truth: **My brothers, if anyone among you wanders from the truth and anyone among you turns him back (5:19)**.
James may have had specific individuals in mind. Commentators disagree concerning the identity of these who wander – are they fellow believers who have fallen by the wayside, or are they unregenerate and still in their sin? The wisest approach is to see these wanderers as a part of the church, though the genuineness of their salvation is yet to be proven.

Absent from James' conclusion are the customary greetings, benedictions, and personal remarks so common to most New Testament epistles. Martin notes that this may indicate James' intended use of the letter as more of a formal sermon.[23] First John ends with a similar pastoral

---

23. Martin, 218.

directive: 'Little children, keep yourselves from idols' (1 John 5:21). James appeals to them as 'my brothers' one last time.

'Wanders' or strays (*planaw*) may be passive or middle voice. If passive it suggests the individual is being led away from the truth; if middle the idea is that the person carelessly went off on his own. The indefinite pronoun 'anyone' (*tis*) emphasizes the danger that this could happen to any believer. The indefiniteness is compounded by the use of the pronoun again for the one who 'turns back' the straying brother or sister. Unlike the ministry of the elders to the sick in verse 14, this ministry of restoration applies to any and all members of the community.

'Turn back' is *epistrepsē*, a compound word with the preposition epi and the verb *strefw*, meaning to turn around. It is translated 'convert' in the KJV but it does not carry the theologically loaded idea of salvation. God does that work; we can convert no one in that sense but we can seek to turn others back to the God who saved them in the first place. And if we wonder about the connection between verses 19 and 20 and the immediately preceding verses, the answer seems to be either that nothing is more important in the restoration of a spiritual wanderer than prayer or that the discussion on the church is extended to another application. As one goes out to seek the wanderer, other Christians join together in prayer that the brethren who seek to turn him back may have success.

Let him know that he who turns back a sinner from his wandering ways (5:20)

'Let him know' (*gnwsketw*) can be understood as 'Brothers, be assured of this.' The pastoral heart of James continues to express itself in these final words to pray for and care for one another. 'Wandering ways' is the same adjective that we saw in verse 19 plus the noun $odos, a road or way. Here it is the ethical sense of one's way of life. The 'one who turns back' is a participle form of the verb in verse 19. Turning one back from such erring ways, notes Martin, 'has its roots in Ezekiel 33:11 where Jahweh is concerned to turn back His erring nation.'[24] Truth and error are mutually exclusive – one cannot walk in light and darkness at the same time. The ministry supplied here has been successful in turning a brother 'from' (or more literally, 'out of' because of the preposition ek) darkness and back into the way of truth.

Two results are promised for this ministry of restoration.

First, people will be saved from death: **will save him [his soul] from death and will cover many sins (5:20)**
'Will save' is the same grammatical form as in verse 15, but here it refers to the soul of the restored sinner. The text literally reads 'will save his soul.'[25] The soul is the inner life of the person in his/her relationship and responsibility toward God. That the person is saved 'from death' stresses the seriousness of the condition he was in. These are people in the community who stray from Christ and fall into sin.

Second, many sins will be covered. Cover (kalupsei) does not imply hiding or keeping sins secret. Rather, the sense is the same as the Old Testament concept of being forgiven and cleansed (Ps. 32:1; 85:2). Our love for the erring one must be like God's; once forgiven their sins should be remembered no more. Note that Galatians 6:1 establishes a principle for the one who would do the work of a spiritual restorer. He should himself be a spiritual person, and 'therefore the converter would scarcely be thought of as needing restoration or relief from the weight of unforgiven sin.'[26]

There is considerable debate over whose sins are covered – the erring one or the one who restores. Respected scholars (Mitton, Plummer, Ropes) hold that the one who converts a sinner secures for himself the forgiveness of his own sins. It is true that 'in ancient Judaism and some early church Fathers the belief was held that good deeds atone

---

24. Martin, 219.
25. A minor manuscript variance exists here. Some read 'a soul' and others 'his soul.' But either way, the context points to soul of the wanderer, not to the restorer.
26. R. J. Knowling, *The Epistle of St James* (London: Westminster Commentaries, 1904), 151.

for one's own sin,'[27] but such teaching was not inspired like Scripture is. And such a view runs contrary to many verses that clearly teach sin is covered *only* through repentance and God's grace. So, it is the sin of the returning prodigal that is covered. A compromise view given by Hiebert, however, holds some merit and may be James' intent: 'James means that there is a blessing for both the converted and the converter. There is no question that one who is instrumental in restoring an erring brother thereby gains a blessing for his own soul (Matt. 18:15).'[28]

With these pastoral words the epistle ends abruptly. That the ending was deemed undesirable in its suddenness explains why some later scribes added a concluding 'Amen.' But such an ending is in keeping with the nature and purpose of James' work. James, Jesus' half brother, denied the deity of Christ when He was on earth. But Jesus restored him, and this inspired letter is a fruit of that restoration. Little wonder that James closes with an appeal to restore others. Throughout the epistle James has called his readers to embrace true Christianity and to refuse mere false profession. In applying his tests for 'true religion' he has rebuked them for numerous inadequacies. In this fitting conclusion, however, James shows that his heart's desire is not to condemn but to restore unto repentance.

Wisdom to Live By

- Is our church fellowship one in which it is easy to share our troubles, happiness, and the spiritual burdens that we bear?
- What can we do as individuals to increase the warmth and reality of our Christian fellowship?
- What illustrations can we provide of the power and effectiveness of prayer, first, from the Bible, and second, from our own experiences?
- We should be concerned for the restoration of those who have wandered from the truth. Do we go out

27. Mitton, 214-15.
28. Hiebert, 337.

after them? What qualities are required of us if we are to be effective in doing so (see also 1 Cor. 10:12 and Gal. 6:1-5)?

15

Theology of James

In keeping with the purpose of the commentary, this chapter does not address many of the scholarly debates concerning James, though those familiar with such debates will likely spot my (Chris's) personal conclusions on many of the issues. Instead, this chapter seeks to set forth some primary themes of James so that the big picture of James' message can be more easily seen. It also strives to assess how James' teaching relates to and is informed by other biblical writers.

1. Themes in James

As mentioned in 'James in Context,' James moves from topic to topic quickly, in a way that leaves most readers who seek to uncover his primary structure scratching their heads. However, even from a casual reading, it is not too difficult to notice some of the primary themes in James – faith and works, suffering and testing, the poor and the rich, and words. Yet other themes are often missed and are observed only after multiple and more careful readings – wisdom for the community, consistency in the church and Christian life, love and mercy, and prayer. One reason for this is that these latter themes often function more as undercurrents and are frequently interspersed in passages designed to emphasize the more obvious themes.

In this section, I suggest the following as the major themes of James: (1) wisdom for the community, (2) consistency in the church and the Christian life, (3) suffering and testing, (4) the poor and rich, (5) words, (6) love and mercy, and (7) prayer. This list is by no means intended to be exhaustive. Some scholars suggest many more, including God, eschatology, law, and justification.[1] Further, James' themes are not easily packaged but can to some extent be helpfully distinguished. Wisdom for the community is linked to consistency in the church and Christian life. Suffering and testing are obviously connected to the poor and rich theme. Love and mercy interweave with several themes. Likewise, the theme of prayer is linked with wisdom, consistency, suffering, and love and mercy.

Since the specific interpretive issues of each passage in James have already been covered in the previous commentary section, I will typically highlight each theme and what James teaches about it and leave the reader to review the commentary section for most details. I will also focus on summarizing the teaching of the biblical texts and occasionally point out related scholarly works in footnotes. Some redundancy will be inevitable here and at times even helpful to understanding the themes and theology.[2]

1. Wisdom for the Community

As I argued in 'James in Context,' I believe that a primary theme of James is wisdom. I concur with R. W. Wall: 'wisdom is the orienting concern of this book by which all else is understood: after all, James refers to wisdom as the divine 'word of truth,' which is graciously provided to a faithful people to make sense of their trials and to guide

---

1. For more particulars about my understanding of the theology of James, please consult my next project: Christopher W. Morgan, *Wisdom for the Community: A Theology of James* in Explorations in Biblical Theology (Phillipsburg, NJ: Presbyterian and Reformed, c. 2010).

2. The wisdom for the community theme developed below was set forth previously in 'James in Context' to orient the reader to our perspective. It is repeated here.

them through those trials in order to insure their future destiny in the new creation.'[3] Yet I suggest that we go one step further. I believe that one of James' primary thematic concerns is *wisdom for the community*. What do I mean by this?

First, the letter of James has a background and focus that shows it to be an heir of Jewish wisdom literature. Martin maintains that James is a teacher in the Israelite-Jewish tradition and consciously reflects the wisdom traditions. Occasionally James uses language that seems to reflect the Old Testament wisdom traditions when he describes how rich people 'drag' the poor into court (2:6; Job 20:15 LXX), the 'withering' of riches (1:10-11; Job 15:30 LXX), and the call to perseverance (James 1 and 5; Job 15:31 LXX). James also uses pictures and metaphors that surely show his dependence on the Old Testament wisdom traditions. He compares the brevity of life to the fading flower (1:11; Prov. 27:1; Eccles. 12:6; Job 13:28) as well as citing the movement of the heavenly bodies (1:16-18; Job 38:33 LXX).[4] James also similarly links wisdom with themes such as the gift of God, peace, prayer, and faith. James is thus a Christian epistle with roots in the Old Testament wisdom tradition.[5]

Second, 'wisdom for the community' also means that James has a primary concern to dispense wisdom and its practical results. D. A. Hubbard puts it well: 'Wisdom takes insights gleaned from the knowledge of God's ways and applies them in the daily walk.'[6] This approach to wisdom is at the heart of James. James applies the truths about God

---

3. Wall, *DLNT*, 522.

4. Martin, lxxxvii-xc.

5. This is not meant to suggest that James is wisdom literature. It is not. James is thoroughly Christian, is not all that concerned with the intellectual search for wisdom, and does not fit many of the literary categories commonly associated with wisdom literature. James is a Christian epistle shaped by Old Testament wisdom literature. I am also not suggesting that its only background is Old Testament wisdom literature. James surely reflects the Old Testament prophetic tradition as is clear from its imperatives and passages like 5:1-6. And he quotes from the Pentateuch at least three times. For a careful approach to these matters, see also McCartney, 52-64.

6. Hubbard, 1650.

and His ways to such daily issues as trials, temptations, words, wealth, obedience, planning, brevity of life, etc. In doing so, James stresses that our response to these daily challenges must be consistent with God. James' frequent opposition to double-mindedness and his regular call for wholeness and integrity highlight his practical wisdom approach. Living in a unified and consistent manner is wisdom rightly applied.

Third, 'wisdom for the community' means that James addresses Christian living from a community/church perspective, not from an individualistic line of thinking. James is an ecclesiological document that speaks to real-life community concerns. In a sense, most New Testament epistles could be characterized this way. But the majority of sermons and commentaries on James neglect this. I must confess that the first two times I preached through the epistle of James, most of my sermons focused on the individual applications of the exhortations – facing trials and dealing with temptation at a personal level, individual obedience with reference to words, money, etc.[7] Regrettably, I did not notice James' intensely community-centered perspective until the last sermon in the 2001 series. Since that time, however, it has become increasingly clear to me that James writes with a community emphasis.

Though some of James' exhortations can correctly be interpreted from an individual standpoint, and though all of James' exhortations can be applied individually, a careful reading of James reveals this community emphasis. These Jewish Christians were a part of a local congregation ('synagogue' in 2:2) with teachers (3:1), elders (5:14), and members in need of the church leadership's prayers (5:14-16). These believers were experiencing significant trials (1:2f) and evidently serious oppression (2:6; 5:1-11). Some in their ranks were claiming they had faith but had little concern for personal holiness (1:22-25; 4:4) and failed

---

7. I am not saying that such sermons are necessarily incorrect. Preachers must give both individual and community applications in their messages. I am saying that I failed to notice the intensely community-centered teaching of James and therefore did not adequately apply his teachings at the church level.

to assist the poor or the marginalized (1:26-27; 2:1-13). The congregation also included others who were quarrelsome, bringing friction rather than peace (3:13-4:10). Therefore, James is writing to address community problems. His solution? James responds by giving 'wisdom for the community.'

To highlight how dominating this theme is in James, I restate some of the message of James using imperatives (as James loves to do) in the form of direct address to the church. In doing so, we can better sense the strong church community emphasis.

- church, when you are undergoing trials from the rich oppressing you, choose joy, trust God for wisdom, and endure (1:1-12).

- church, repent of your pride and anger. Instead, listen, be patient, and humbly receive the Word (1:19-21).

- church, do not just be religious, but obey the Word, control your words, take care of the oppressed, and be holy (1:22-27).

- church, do not show favoritism toward the rich who exploit you, but show love and respect to the poor (2:1-13).

- church, do not believe that you are saved by a faith that does not lead you to show love to the hurting. Show your true faith by works of love (2:14-26).

- church, do not let people be teachers or leaders who are divisive and destructive in their words (3:1-12).

- church, do not believe those who claim to be wise but are divisive. Their so-called 'wisdom' is not from God, but earthly, unspiritual, and demonic (3:13-18).

- church, why are you fighting? Stop wanting your own way. Stop wanting to be in the spotlight. Stop slandering and judging your fellow brothers and sisters. Instead, repent, be humble, and recognize there is only one Judge and Lawgiver (and you are not Him! [4:1-12]).

- church, persevere during this difficult time of oppression. God will judge the wicked, rich oppressors with severity. That time is coming (5:1-12).

- church, stop grumbling against each other. You will be judged, too (5:9).

- church, live in community with each other. Pray for each other when people are hurting. Praise the Lord together when others are happy. Pray for healing for each other when someone is sick. Confess your sins to one another. Do all you can to restore those who have wandered away from the truth (5:13-20).

So in the Old Testament wisdom tradition, James the Christian sage dispenses wisdom. But even more, James the pastor offers wisdom for the believing community who seem to be struggling with particular concerns. James' teachings about the church are outlined in the chart below.

The Church according to James

The Nature of the Church
- *Ekklesia*
- Primitive (met in synagogue)
- Family (use of 'brothers' throughout)

The Leadership of the Church
- Teachers (3:1)
- Elders (5:13-20)
- Covenant Members (3:6; 4:1)

The Characteristics of the Church
- Love (1:26-27; 2:1-26)
- Ministry (1:26-27; 2:14-18)
- Holiness (2:14-26; 4:1-12)

- Truth (3:1; see also Word/Law)
- Unity (3:2-4:10)
- Prayer (1:2-8; 4:1-4; 5:13-18)
- Restoration (5:16-20)
- Lives in the 'Already' and 'Not Yet'

2. Consistency in the Church and Christian Life

I consider consistency in the church and the Christian life to be the second most dominating theme in James. I tend to view it as an outgrowth of the wisdom for the community theme. Throughout his letter, James encourages and commands his readers to be consistent in their lives – individually and corporately. Do not be double-minded but complete, James asserts.[8] Moo calls this 'wholeness' and even maintains that this is James' primary theme.[9] Below I recount James' teaching related to consistency in the church and the Christian life. Notice how pervasive this theme is.

- When you endure trials, choose joy, have faith, and recognize God's work in maturing you (1:2-4).
- When you pray for wisdom, ask in faith; do not waver, be double-minded, or unstable (1:5-8).
- When you are tempted, do not blame God (He is good) but look at your heart (1:13-18).
- Do not only listen to the Word, obey it (1:22-25).[10]
- If you are genuine in religion, you will control your tongue, take care of the oppressed, and be holy (1:26-27).

---

8. Note how James uses 'double-mindedness' as the opposite of consistency in the church and in the Christian life. For an insightful look at double-mindedness, see Luke T. Johnson, 'Friendship with the World/Friendship with God: A Study of Discipleship in James,' in *Discipleship in the New Testament*, ed. Fernando F. Segovia (Philadelphia: Fortress, 1985), 166-83. Especially see 176-77. For a simpler but still helpful overview of James' call for consistency, see Laws, 29-30.

9. Moo, 46.

10. For a careful examination of this consistency theme in James 1:22–2:13, see T. B. Cargal, *Restoring the Diaspora: Discursive Structure and Purpose in the Epistle of James* (Atlanta: Scholars Press, 1993), 98-118.

- If you claim to keep the royal law of love, then treat the poor with respect and mercy (2:1-13).

- Do not only profess to have faith, demonstrate your faith by good works and love for others (2:14-26).

- Do not claim to praise God with the very tongue you curse others with, but control your words and use them to edify not to destroy (3:1-12).

- If you claim to be wise, then show it by a good life, filled with humility, considerateness, and love for peace (3:13-18).

- If you want to be exalted, do not exalt yourselves but submit yourselves humbly before God, repent of your sin, and live right (4:1-10).

- If you claim to care about the law, then do not slander and judge others; in so doing you break it (4:11-12).

- If you know to do what is good, then do it. Otherwise, it is sin (4:13-17).

- Do not grumble or swear, for you too will be judged (5:1-12).

In so many passages, James is exhorting, 'Be consistent!' Throughout the letter, James is commanding: 'Stop saying one thing and doing something else. Stop claiming to have faith and yet not trust God in your trials. Do not only listen to the Word, obey it. Do not presume you are religious (in a good sense), if you do not take care of the oppressed. Do not claim to keep the law of love while the whole time you treat the poor with disrespect. Do not claim to praise God with the very tongue you curse others with. Do not claim to revere the law while you slander others. Do not only claim to have faith, demonstrate it!' In other words, James opposes duplicity and 'double-mindedness' and calls for a holistic Christian living – people actually living out the gospel, not just claiming to embrace it. The particular sins in the church that James addresses are found in the chart below.

Sin and the Church in James

- Lack of faith (1:5-8)
- Pride (1:9-11; 4:6)
- Anger (1:20)
- Filthiness (1:21)
- Wickedness (1:21)
- Uncontrolled tongue (1:26; 3:1-12)
- Partiality (2:1-7)
- Judging (2:4; 4:11-12)
- Failure to show love (2:8-26)
- Cursing people (3:10)
- Jealousy (3:14)
- Selfish ambition (3:14)
- Boasting (3:14; 3:5; 4:13-17)
- Lying (3:14)
- Passions (4:1, 3)
- Quarreling in the church (4:1)
- Murder (4:2)
- Covetousness (4:2)
- Selfish motives (4:3)
- Friendship with the world (4:4)
- Slandering the family of God (4:11)
- Oppression and exploitation of the poor (5:1-6)
- Grumbling against the family of God (5:9)
- Swearing (5:12)
- Wandering from the truth (5:19-20)

3. Suffering and Testing

A third theme in James is that of suffering and testing (or trials). In a pastoral manner, James writes to a believing community (or believing communities) that had experienced much suffering and testing. It is not completely clear as to the context or the audience James addresses (see the 'James in Context' for more details related to the recipients of this letter). Audience analysis is tricky, but there are pieces of internal evidence that reveal that these believers were suffering. What types of suffering did they face? Some of the suffering indicated in the letter is vague; other aspects are quite specific. James begins his letter telling us these believers were experiencing 'various' trials – all types of unexpected tests (1:2). Some were 'suffering' (5:13). There was also widespread poverty, some of which was extreme – to the point of needing food and clothing (2:16). Many of these believers were persecuted, prosecuted (2:5-6), oppressed, and exploited by the wealthy (5:1-11). They had little political, social, or economic clout to address these concerns themselves. In addition, some of the believers were seriously ill (5:14-16). James addresses their difficulties in several passages: 1:2-12; 2:6-7; 2:15; 5:1-11; and 5:13-16. He responds to their suffering in two related but distinct ways. First, he encourages those who are suffering. Second, he exhorts the church how to respond properly to people's suffering.

In his encouragement of the suffering believers, James urges them to respond with joy, with the realization that perseverance is doing a divine work in them, with prayer to God for wisdom, with a recognition that the wicked rich will ultimately lose and the righteous poor will be vindicated, and with a promise that God will bless those who endure trials with faith and patience (1:2-12). He also warns them not to demean themselves by showing partiality to the rich oppressors (2:5-7). He later asks them to be patient in the midst of their suffering because the Lord knows of it, has not forgotten them, will return to judge, and in doing so He will ultimately vindicate the righteous and punish the wicked (5:1-11). James later urges those who are suffering to pray (5:13) and those who are sick to call for the elders of the church to pray over them and to confess their sins to fellow believers, if appropriate (5:14-16).

James also advises the church to respond appropriately to people's suffering. The church is not to show favoritism to the rich or exploiters but should stand with the poor and oppressed (2:5-7). The church must not allow mere religious platitudes to be a substitute for the important work of showing love to the hurting, feeding the hungry, and clothing the poor (2:15). The church also needs to remember to be patient in the midst of suffering. James reminds the church that the Lord sees the reality of her suffering and has not forgotten her, that the church is in the 'already' and 'not yet,' and that in the culmination of history the Judge will set the record straight. In the meantime, the church must persevere and not grumble at each other (5:1-11). Furthermore, the church leaders should pray for the sick and suffering (5:13-16).

4. The Poor and Rich

James does not really develop a new theology of wealth and poverty. Rather he assumes the Old Testament teaching and literary use of the 'poor' as oppressed and often righteous, as cared for by God (Deut. 10:18; Ps. 68:5), and as deserving the protection of God's people (Deut. 10:19).[11] James also stands in the same tradition as Jesus, who frequently denounced the rich and defended the poor (see the upcoming section *James and the Old Testament Wisdom Literature* for more details). The dark reality of poverty set the overall context of the letter, and therefore the theme of the rich and the poor receives much attention in James' letter. Many of the challenges facing the church community evidently relates to this poverty issue, such as trials, favoritism, faith and works, conflicts, presumption, oppression, and patience.

James addresses the issue of the rich and the poor in several passages with specific exhortations. He teaches that the poor should take pride in their exaltation, and the rich should take pride in their impending humiliation (1:9-11). He maintains that the rich will pass away like a withered flower. James also reminds the church that God demands that believers look after the widows and orphans

---

11. For a historical survey of the poverty theme in the Old Testament, Judaism, and the New Testament, see Dibelius, 39-47.

in their distress. True religion leads to taking care of the poor (among other things like holiness and self-control; 1:26-27). Further, the poor should be treated with dignity and respect by the church. There is no excuse for prejudice against the poor. Indeed, God has chosen many of the poor to be rich in faith and to inherit the kingdom of those who love Him (2:1-8). And when James instructs about the necessity of faith and good works, he chooses as his first example the need to help the poor (2:14-26). Part of the good works that evidence salvation is caring for (and not merely saying nice words to) the poor.

James addresses the moderately wealthy and warns that those in business should be careful to live in utter dependence on God and not presume they have the ability to succeed (including financially) on their own (4:13-17). Then James tells the rich exploiters of the poor to weep and wail because God's judgment on them will be severe. They will experience misery and suffering. The corrosion of their wealth will serve as a witness against them. The wages they failed to pay their workers will testify against them. By living in luxury and self-indulgence, they are increasing their punishment for the Judgment (5:1-11). In light of this Judgment, the persecuted believers (many of whom evidently were poor) are to persevere and not grumble against each other, knowing they too will be judged (5:7-11).

5. Words

As an extension of his wisdom for the community emphasis, James develops a theme centered on words and makes commands related to the use of words in every chapter (and in virtually every paragraph!). Wielding our words appropriately is central to our personal Christian growth, and especially for the edification of the body of Christ. Pastors know too well the significance of church members' use of words; all pastors have experienced the damage caused by those who misuse words. The believing communities addressed by James were clearly having problems in this area, so he tackles the issues head-on and exhorts them in their use of words.

In the first chapter, James urges the believers to be quick to listen and slow to speak (1:19). He maintains that they must repent of angry words (1:19-21). In his explanation of some distinctives of genuine religion, the control of the tongue is first on the list. True faith leads people to control their tongues. Those who fail to do so only deceive themselves (1:26).

In chapter two, James warns that we must speak and act in light of the coming judgment (2:8-13). In other words, we will be judged by our words (notice it is placed first again) and our works. This is reminiscent of Jesus' statement in Matthew 12:36-37: 'I tell you, on the day of judgment people will give account for every careless word they speak, for by your words you will be justified, and by your words you will be condemned.' James also emphasizes that mere words without corresponding deeds are empty and useless (2:14-26; especially 14, 16, 18).

Chapter three is well-known for its teaching on the tongue. The initial context is that of teachers. In Jewish life at that time, it was prestigious for a family to have a son training to be a rabbi.[12] It is only natural that in a Diaspora Jewish Christian community, a similar respect for pastors and teachers would result. Thus, James wants to emphasize that not everyone should strive to be a teacher. This role is reserved for the wise and mature. Because of their important position and their use of words to lead, teachers will be judged more strictly (3:1). James then acknowledges the universality of the sins of speech. He even uses the first person plural ('we'). He says that 'we all' stumble in many ways, and this includes the use of our words. No one has completely tamed the tongue (3:2; 3:8). If we can control our words, it shows we have thorough self-control (3:2). He also stresses that our words are powerful; the tongue's significance far exceeds its size (3:3-5). James teaches that the tongue is a fire (set on fire by hell) and a world of evil (3:5-6), that can corrupt the whole person and destroy one's life (3:6). He also urges consistency in the use of our

12. Walker, 43.

tongues – not praising God one minute and cursing others
the next (3:9-12). The inconsistency of words demonstrates
a double-minded person, since words reflect the heart
(3:10-12). Later in chapter three, James links good words
to true wisdom. True wisdom is shown in peaceable, kind,
and meek words (3:13-18). This emphasis seems to tie the
chapter together, showing the importance and qualities of
good teachers.

Chapter four continues this emphasis on the peaceable
results of wisdom by contrasting it with the reality of the
factions and battles in the believing communities. In a
style reminiscent of the Old Testament prophets, James
calls for repentance. He then demands that these believers
do not quarrel against, slander, or judge one another
(4:1-12). Later James suggests that people should verbally
acknowledge their dependence on God ('if it is the Lord's
will' in 4:13-17) and not boast (4:16; see also 3:14).

In his concluding chapter, James completes his theme
of words. He paints a dark picture of the future of the
wicked exploiters and asserts that the corroded wealth of
the rich and the wages they accumulated by defrauding
God's people will 'testify' and 'cry out against' them at
the Judgment (5:1-6).[13] He does this to encourage the
suffering believers and urge patience. James does not
let the Christians spend too much time rejoicing in the
punishment of the wicked oppressors, however. He
quickly turns the tables on the believers and commands
them not to grumble against one another (5:9). He then
warns them not to swear, but straightforwardly tell the
truth (5:12; see Matt. 5:33-37). Finally, at the close of his
letter, James points to the positive uses of words. Believers
should pray for those in trouble and the sick (5:13-16). They
should praise the Lord with those who are happy (5:13).
Furthermore, they are to confess their sins to each other as

---

13. Note here how the future judgment of the wicked oppressors of believers
is an encouragement to the suffering believers. Scripture is filled with passages
related to 'the comfort of Hell.' By this, I mean that the Scripture comforts the
suffering believers by stressing the reality of their persecutors' just and severe
future judgment (2 Thess. 1; Rev. 19-20).

they live life together (5:15-16). James concludes the letter encouraging the believers to restore those wandering from the truth (5:19-20).

Sins of Speech in James

- Blaming God for temptation (1:13-15)
- Being slow to listen and quick to speak (1:19)
- Angry, evil and filthy words (1:19-21)
- Uncontrolled tongue (1:26; 3:1-12)
- Judging (2:4; 4:11-12)
- Empty words devoid of action (2:8-26)
- Cursing people (3:10)
- Boasting (3:14; 3:5; 4:13-17)
- Lying (3:14)
- Quarreling in the church (4:1)
- Slandering one another in the family of God (4:11)
- Words of presumption (4:13-17)
- Grumbling against the family of God (5:9)
- Swearing (5:12)

6. Love and Mercy

Although love and mercy is another important theme in James, many commentators fail to highlight this theme. Maybe it is because James often addresses specific sins like partiality, mere religious platitudes, judging, pride, false claims of wisdom, slander, and oppression. Upon closer inspection, James' assault on these particular sins presupposes the importance of the righteous behavior James desires for these believers – wisdom, consistency, love, mercy, etc.

James emphasizes the importance of love and mercy in many ways. He asserts that true religion recognizes that God cares for the orphans and widows in their distress and so must His people (1:26-27). James demands that the people of God treat the poor with respect and love (2:1-7). He demonstrates the importance of keeping the royal law found in Scripture, 'Love your neighbor as yourself' (2:8). That believers must show mercy is evident in James' firm principles: God's judgment will be without mercy to those who have shown no mercy, and mercy triumphs over judgment (2:13). Even in James' famous faith/works passage, the works in view are acts of love for the hurting (2:14-17). Indeed true faith works. Or even better, true faith loves. True wisdom from God shows itself in peace, mercy, considerateness, and impartiality (3:13-18). James also teaches that the Lord Himself is full of compassion and mercy (5:11), which is the basis for our responsibility to be likewise. The church should display love and mercy to the hurting, sick, sinful, and wandering by praying for and restoring them (5:13-20).

7. Prayer

Another oft-neglected theme in James is prayer. James speaks of prayer frequently (every chapter but chapter three) and significantly. On many occasions James links prayer with other themes such as wisdom, consistency, suffering, community, church conflict, faith and works, love and mercy, and the nature of God. For our purposes, we will look at James' teaching on prayer in three ways: the prayer-hearing God, occasions for prayer, and believers' responsibilities in prayer.

Just as Jesus communicated many truths about God in His instructions concerning prayer in the Sermon on the Mount,[14] James likewise ties prayer to the person of God (for more on what James teaches about God, see the upcoming chart). God is a prayer-hearing God. God gives generously without finding fault (1:5; see also 1:16), and He gives in response to the prayers of His people (1:5-8; 4:2-3; 5:14-18). This makes it clear that He is also personal and relational, though unchanging in His nature (1:16-18). Further, James asserts that God is holy and demands proper motives from His people when they pray (4:1-10).

---

14. In the Lord's Prayer recorded in Matthew 6:9-13, we learn that God is Father, transcendent, holy, King, sovereign, providential, the forgiver of sins, and the one who guides His people.

James also assumes that God is able to answer prayer. He can heal the sick (5:13-16). He can forgive sin (5:13-16).

James records many occasions for prayer. Believers should pray when they are undergoing trials or suffering, as well as when they need wisdom (1:2-8). They should pray when they are troubled, happy, sick, or in need of forgiveness (5:13-16).

James also depicts believers' responsibilities in prayer. He urges them to 'ask' God, echoing Jesus in the Sermon on the Mount (Matt. 7:7). The present tense of the imperatives likely suggests the consistency of the asking. The people of God are responsible to ask God for wisdom (1:5), in faith (1:6; 5:15-16), without doubting (1:6), and with proper motives (4:1-10). Prayer must not be a substitute for action, however. The blessing or prayer offered for the hurting should be joined with loving deeds (2:15-16). Prayer offered in faith by the 'righteous' is effective and answered (5:15-16).[15] By righteous James is not merely referring to professed believers, but to those who are actually living in a manner that is consistent with Christianity (i.e. not the double-minded). Believers are also to pray in community – led by their church leaders, with each other, for each other, to praise God together when times are good, and to ask God to heal the sick and restore the wandering (5:13-20).

The Doctrine of God in James

1:1   God as Master ('James as bondservant of God')

1:5   God as generous Giver of wisdom

1:13   God as holy ('cannot be tempted nor tempts anyone')

1:17   God as transcendent ('from above')

1:17   God as Source of every good and perfect gift

1:17   God as Father of lights

---

15. Of course, James is not saying that every single time we pray in faith, God responds by giving us what we desire. The earlier commentary on these verses makes that clear. But we should not underestimate what James does say – God answers prayers offered by consistent, faith-filled Christians and churches.

1:17   God as unchangingly good ('no variation or shadow of turning')

1:18   God as Savior ('He brought us forth by the word of truth')

1:18   God as Creator ('of His creatures')

2:5   God as choosing poor to be rich in faith

2:5   God as promising kingdom to those who love Him

2:12   God as Judge

2:19   God as One (monotheism)

2:23   God as proper object of faith

2:23   God as Friend of Abraham and all true believers

3:9   God as worthy of blessing

3:9   God as Creator of humans in His image

4:4   God as jealous and wrathful

4:6   God as gracious

4:7   God as Lord ('submit therefore to God')

4:8   God as personal ('draw near to God and God will draw near to you')

4:8   God as demanding moral purity

4:12   God as Lawgiver

4:15   God as Sovereign King (controls history according to His will)

5:1   God as Avenger of His people

5:1   God as punishing the wicked

5:4   God as knowing our actions

5:4   God as Lord of armies

5:8   God as bringing final consummation of history

5:11   God as purposeful

5:11   God as merciful

5:11   God as compassionate

5:15   God as Healer of the sick

5:16   God as answering prayer

5:20   God as Forgiver of sins

2. James and Other Biblical Material

Having examined the historical and literary contexts of James (in 'James in Context'), and having considered the particular teachings of James in their immediate contexts (in the commentary), and having discovered major themes of James' letter, it is important for us to see how James' teaching relates to that of other biblical material.

A few things should be kept in mind as we seek to look at the various relationships. First, this section is intentionally selective. It focuses on the most significant relevant material: James and the Old Testament Law, Prophets, Wisdom, Teachings of Jesus, and Paul.[16] It does not strive to address particulars of James and the Synoptic Gospels, nor does it interact with the relationships of James with John or Peter. Second, this section does not address the related Jewish literature that James at times seems to echo. Third, this section does not attempt to address some of the thorny questions concerning the nature of the relationships between James and this biblical material. Instead, the focus here is to show how James' teachings and thought-world are rooted in the Old Testament Law, Prophets, Wisdom Literature, as well as the teachings of Jesus. In addition, this section compares the teachings of James to that of Paul, especially concerning the idea of justification.

1. James and the Old Testament Law

Even a quick reading of James demonstrates that his teachings and thought-world are deeply rooted in the Old Testament, including the Law. In fact, three of James' six Old Testament quotations are from the Law/Torah (all from ch. 2).

First, James 2:8 quotes from Leviticus 19:18, 'You shall love your neighbor as yourself.' James refers to this as the 'royal law according to Scripture.'[17] Luke Timothy Johnson

---

16. I (Chris) did not include a section on Old Testament historical books because the only clear references to this literature that I observed was James' teaching concerning Rahab (Josh. 6:25) and Elijah (1 Kings 17-18).

17. Obviously, James also echoes the teachings and emphases of Jesus here.

also observes a fascinating relationship with James and Leviticus 19: 'What is more striking is the way that he places this in the framework of partiality in judging, showing a clear allusion to Leviticus 19:15.'[18] James 5:4 seems to refer to Leviticus 19:13. Johnson suggests that James 4:11, 5:9, 5:12, and 5:20 also could be seen as thematic allusions to Leviticus 19:12-18.

Second, James 2:11 quotes from the Ten Commandments in Exodus 20:13-14 and/or Deuteronomy 5:17-18.[19] Consistent with his use of other quotations and allusions, James here lists the commandments in the same order as that of the Septuagint (rather than the Hebrew Old Testament): 'Do not commit adultery' then 'Do not commit murder.'

Third, James 2:23 quotes Genesis 15:6, 'Abraham believed God, and it was counted to him as righteousness.' This, of course, is a key verse in James' and Paul's understandings of justification and will be addressed later.

That James' teachings are rooted in the Old Testament Law is not only clear from his quotations, but is also observable from his allusions, echoes, references, and convictions. For example, James' command to hear and obey the Word (1:22-25) is strikingly reflective of the teaching of the Torah, especially Deuteronomy 6–7. James' emphasis on the unity of God (2:19) is obviously derived from the Shema found in Deuteronomy 6:4. James' assertion that humans are made in the image of God, and are therefore significant and worthy of respect, is linked to the teachings of Genesis 1:26-28. James' explanation of justification is based on the Abraham and Isaac narratives found in Genesis 15–22.[20] Further, James' convictions regarding God as Lawgiver and Judge echo the Old Testament Law. In sum, the teachings of James are firmly anchored in the Old Testament, including the Law,

18. Luke Timothy Johnson, 'The Use of Leviticus 19 in the Letter of James,' *Journal of Biblical Literature* 101:3 (1982): 393. James quotes here from the Septuagint rather than the Hebrew Old Testament.

19. Richard Longenecker, *Biblical Exegesis in the Apostolic Period* (Grand Rapids: Eerdmans, 1975), 200. See also Mahony, 173.

20. James again refers to the Septuagint, using the term *anenegkas* (the same term in Genesis 22:2, Septuagint).

which he considered trustworthy, unified, consistent, and authoritative for Christians.

2. James and the Old Testament Prophets

On occasion, James seems to mimic the tone and style of the Old Testament prophets. This even led A. M. Hunter to call James, 'the Amos of the new covenant.'[21] James' prophetic tone, style, and themes are especially clear in passages such as James 1:22-27; 4:1-10; and 5:1-6. In James 1:22-27, this approach can be seen in his command that the people of God not only hear the Word but also do it, mirroring prophetic teachings such as Ezekiel 33:32. James' assertion of God's demand for personal holiness in conjunction with the promotion of love and justice for the widows and orphans as reflective of true religion stands in continuity with Isaiah 1:10-20.

In James 4:1-10, James' indebtedness to the prophets can be seen in his rebuke of worldliness (4:4), reference to sin as spiritual adultery and as a violation of our covenant relationship with God (4:4; see Hosea; Isa. 54:5-6; 57:3; Jer. 3:20; Ezek. 16),[22] firm reminders of God's jealousy (4:5) for His people and for pure worship (4:5; see Zech. 8:2), and denunciation of the proud (4:6-7; see, Isa. 61:1; Zeph. 3:11-12). This approach is also clear in James' exhortation to 'draw near' or return back to God (4:8; Zech. 1:3; Hosea 12:6), his commands to wash and clean one's hands and hearts (4:8; Isa. 1:10-20; 66:17), as well as in his imagery of repentance as grieving, mourning, and wailing over sin (4:9; Isa. 15:2; Jer. 4:13; Hosea 10:5; Joel 1:9-10; 2:12; Micah 2:4).[23]

Nowhere does James more resemble an Old Testament prophet than in 5:1-6. In the manner of Amos, James bluntly rebukes the proud and wealthy landowners who were exploiting and oppressing the poor (e.g. Amos 8:4-6). James draws a picture of their impending doom and suf-

---

21. A. M. Hunter, *Introducing the New Testament* (Philadelphia: Westminster, 1948), 98.

22. Jesus also referred to 'a wicked and adulterous generation' in Matt. 12:39 and 16:4.

23. John W. Mahony, 173-83; idem, 'An Introduction to the Epistle of James.' *Mid America Theological Journal* 10:1 (Spring 1986): 1-10; Moo, 186-96.

fering. They will suffer affliction, their possessions will be ruined and even serve as witnesses against them, and their flesh will be consumed as by fire (e.g. Amos 1:12, 14; 5:6; 7:4; Isa. 30:27-28; 51:8; Jer. 5:14; Ezek. 15:7). The storehouses of their wealth will ultimately become storehouses of the coming wrath (e.g. Amos 3:10-11, 6:10-15; Micah 2:7). The rich will be judged, and they are pictured as animals headed to the slaughterhouse (Isa. 34:2-6; Jer. 12:3; 25:34-50). Furthermore, the wages they withheld from the poor day-laborers are keenly noticed by God Himself (e.g. Jer. 22:13). James even uses the terminology of Isaiah to describe God and His power to judge – the Lord of hosts (Isa. 5:9; see also 1:9; 2:12; 6:3; et al.).

Other strands of material in James also point to roots in the Old Testament prophetic tradition. For example, James' consideration of himself as a servant stands in continuity with both the Old Testament prophets and the teachings of Jesus. John Mahony observes: 'The servant-concept was a popular self-designation among the Old Testament prophets, e.g. Amos 3:7, Daniel 9:6, 10; Zechariah 1:6; Isaiah 34:23; 42:19; and Malachi 4:6.' James' teaching frequently alludes to or mirrors Old Testament prophetic material.[24]

James' use of a wave as a picture of the instability of the wicked (1:6) resembles Isaiah 57:20, 'But the wicked are like the tossing sea...' James' usage of the grass to illustrate the temporal nature of life (1:10-11) parallels Isaiah 40:6-8. James' reference to the scorching heat of the East wind (1:11) is reminiscent of the Old Testament prophets (Hosea 13:15; Jer. 18:17; Jonah 4:8; and Ezek. 17:10). James' emphasis on death as the consequence of sin stands in continuity with Ezekiel 18:4. James' concept of the people of God as a sort of 'firstfruits' (1:18) parallels the teaching of Jeremiah 2:3. James' command that the people of God not only hear the Word but also do it mirrors prophetic teachings like Ezekiel 33:32. In a manner similar to Isaiah 1:10-20, James asserts that God demands true religion, which is linked to personal holiness and to the promotion of justice for

---

24. For a more careful treatment of these and more, see Mahony, 173-83.

and love shown to the widows and orphans. James' imperative 'listen' (2:5) and address 'come now' are also in keeping with the prophetic style and tone (e.g. Isa. 51:4, 7). Moreover, his use of the prophets as examples of those who persevere also illustrates this.

In sum, while James is not a prophetic work *per se* (it is an epistle), James often writes in the tone, style, and themes of the Old Testament prophets. This approach is particularly prominent in his calls for hearing and doing, genuine religion, protection of the oppressed, heartfelt repentance, and judgment on the rich exploiters.

3. James and the Old Testament Wisdom Literature

The letter of James not only reflects the Old Testament Law and Prophets but also has a background and focus that shows it to be an heir of Old Testament wisdom literature. On occasion James uses language that seems to reflect the Old Testament wisdom traditions when he describes how rich people 'drag' the poor into court (2:6; Job 20:15 LXX), the 'withering' of riches (1:10-11; Job 15:30 LXX), and the call to perseverance (James chs. 1 and 5; Job 15:31 LXX). James also writes with pictures and metaphors that show his dependence on the Old Testament wisdom traditions. He discusses the brevity of life with the fading flower (1:11; Prov. 27:1; Eccles. 12:6; Job 13:28) and refers to the movement of the heavenly bodies (1:16-18; Job 38:33 LXX).[25]

Other examples abound. The truth that 'God opposes the proud but gives grace to the humble' in James 4:6 is a quotation from Proverbs 3:34 (LXX). James' analogy of the tongue as a fire (3:6) resembles the teachings of Proverbs 16:27 and 26:21. His reference to the tongue as a poison is similar to that of Psalm 140:36. James' linking of wisdom and peace (3:13-18) is in keeping with Proverbs 3:17. James' call for mourning rather than laughing is similar to Ecclesiastes 7:2-7. James' castigation of the all-too-frequent presumptuousness (which he equates with boasting) in human planning (4:13-17)

---

25. Martin, lxxxvii-xc.

seems to be an application of Proverbs 27:1: 'Do not boast about tomorrow, for you do not know what a day may bring.' The temporal nature of life is also depicted in the same text as a vapor or mist, which is similar to Job 7:7 and Psalm 102:3. Plus, James' overall idea in 4:13-17 – namely, that human plans are contingent and God's will is sovereign – resembles Proverbs 19:21: 'Many are the plans in the mind of a man, but it is the purpose of the Lord that will stand.'[26] James' use of Job as a model of endurance also shows his dependence on the Old Testament wisdom tradition. James similarly links wisdom with themes such as the gift of God, words, suffering, peace, the transitory nature of life, prayer, and faith. James, then, has deep roots in the Old Testament wisdom tradition.

In addition to having foundations in the Old Testament wisdom tradition, James also has a primary concern to teach about wisdom and its practical results. James applies the truths about God and his ways to such daily issues as trials, temptations, words, wealth, obedience, planning, brevity of life, etc. In doing so, James stresses that we find wisdom solely in God and that our response to daily challenges must be consistent with God's person and ways. James' frequent opposition to being double-minded and his regular call for a wholeness and integrity fit well with and serve to highlight his practical wisdom approach. Living in a unified and consistent manner is wisdom rightly applied.

4. James and the Teachings of Jesus

As we have seen, James' teachings and thought-world are deeply rooted in the Old Testament. And though the epistle of James says very little about the person of Jesus, its message is thoroughly Christian. Douglas Moo states it well: 'No New Testament document is more influenced by the teaching of Jesus than James.'[27] The teaching of

---

26. I owe several of these references to Mahony, 173-83. See also Richardson, 32.

27. Moo, *James* (PNTC), 27.

Jesus can be seen in almost every section and almost every theme of James.[28]

In what way does James reflect the teachings of Jesus? Although it is beyond the goals of this commentary to interact significantly with related scholarly issues,[29] it is suggested that if the traditional view of the authorship of James is correct, then he would likely have heard some of Jesus' teaching and was aware of many of the oral traditions surrounding it. The frequency of thought parallels between James and the teachings of Jesus combined with the lack of precise verbal parallels point to James' awareness of the unwritten traditions of Jesus' teaching, but also seems to indicate that James did not possess any written copies of the Gospels.[30]

James displays similarities to the teachings of Jesus in many of his general words/phrases, in his style, and in his convictions.[31] James also stresses many of the same themes as Jesus: wisdom, consistency, persecution and suffering, faith and works, love and mercy, prayer, etc.

More specifically, James' message often comes across as an extension of the teachings of Jesus in the Sermon on the Mount/Sermon on the Plain (Matt. 5-7; Luke 6). Bruce Metzger believes, 'Luther was right in applying the criterion 'whatever promotes Christ is apostolic,' but wrong in not recognizing that the epistle of James also 'promotes Christ' by its practical application of the Sermon on the Mount.'[32]

---

28. Massey H. Shepherd, 'The Epistle of James and the Gospel of Matthew,' *Journal of Biblical Literature* 75 (Winter 1956): 40-51. Shepherd even makes this claim concerning the teachings of Jesus in Matthew alone (p. 47).

29. Examples of such debates include James and its relationship to the Synoptic Problem, James and its relationship to Matthew, Luke, various traditions of Jesus' teaching, etc. Those interested in such issues should consult James B. Adamson, *James: The Man and His Message* (Grand Rapids: Eerdmans, 1989), 169-94; Peter H. Davids, 'James and Jesus,' in *Gospel Perspectives: The Jesus Tradition Outside the Gospels*, ed. David Wenham (Sheffield: JSOT, 1985), 63-84; P. J. Hartin, *James and the Sayings of Jesus*, JSNT 47 (Sheffield: JSOT, 1991); Shepherd, 40-51.

30. Davids, 49. This seems to support an early date.

31. Dibelius, 28.

32. Bruce M. Metzger, *The Canon of the New Testament* (Oxford: Clarendon, 1987), 244.

In order to communicate the historical order (that James received his material from Jesus) and to show how often James' teaching seems to echo the Sermon on the Mount, I will outline the parallel teaching according to the order of the Sermon on the Mount (Matt. 5-7). I will also make reference to Matthew first and James second (I will also reference Luke if his account is closer).[33]

- The poor as recipients of the kingdom (Matt. 5:3; Luke 6:20; James 2:5)
- Call for mourning (Matt. 5:4; Luke 6:25; James 4:9)
- Praise of meekness (Matt. 5:5; James 3:13-18)
- Mercy given to the merciful (Matt. 5:7; James 2:13)
- Purity of heart (Matt. 5:8; James 4:8)
- Peacemaking (Matt. 5:9; James 3:18)
- Joy in trials and persecution (Matt. 5:10-12; James 1:2)
- Prophets as examples of perseverance through trials (Matt. 5:12; James 5:10-11)
- God as Father (Matt. 5:16 et al.; James 1:17)
- Perfection and unity of the Law (Matt. 5:17-19; James 1:25; 2:8-11)
- Seriousness of a seemingly small infraction of the Law (Matt. 5:19; James 2:10)
- Unrighteousness of anger (Matt. 5:22; James 1:20)
- Lust and the course of sin (Matt. 5:27-30; James 1:13-15)
- Prohibition of oaths (Matt. 5:34-37; James 5:12)
- Expectation of non-resistance (Matt. 5:39; James 5:1-6)
- Demand for perfection (Matt. 5:48; James 1:4; 3:2)
- Condemnation of religious hypocrisy (Matt. 6:1-18; James 1:26-27; 2:14-26; a central theme throughout both)
- Decay (by moths and rust/corrosion) of stored-up wealth (Matt. 6:19-20; James 5:2-4)

---

33. Especially helpful for the two lists were Davids, 47-48; Mahony, 233-44; and Richardson, 34-35.

- Rejection of dual eyes/masters/double-mindedness (Matt. 6:22-24; James 1:8; 4:8)

- Transitory nature of life (Matt. 6:34; James 4:13-16)

- Command against judging (Matt. 7:1; James 4:11-12)

- Our judging of others affects how God judges us (Matt. 7:1-2; James 2:13)

- Asking God and receiving/overall theology of prayer (Matt. 7:7-8; James 1:5; 4:2-3)

- God as good and giver of good gifts (Matt. 7:9-11; James 1:17)

- Character depicted as fruit (Matt. 7:16-20; James 3:10-18)

- Fruit (figs and grapes) as consistent with type of tree/root (Matt. 7:16-19; James 3:12)

- Severe future judgment of wicked (Matt. 7:16-27; James 5:1-6)

- Danger of mere profession of faith (Matt. 7:21-23; James 1:26-27; 2:14-26)

- True follower of Christ hears and does (Matt. 7:24-27; James 1:22-25; 2:14-26; a central theme throughout both)

- True follower of Christ perseveres through trials (Matt. 7:24-27; James 1:2-8; 5:7-11)

The list above demonstrates not only that James' teaching is significantly related to Jesus' but also that teachings from *every* major section of Jesus' Sermon on the Mount are found echoed in James.

But James' teaching reflects more than the teachings of Jesus in the Sermon on the Mount. So in order to show how frequently James' teaching resembles the overall teachings of Jesus, I will outline the echoes according to the order of material in James. Although the material here is similar to that above, it is not merely repetitious because it is not confined to the Sermon on the Mount and incorporates all potential echoes of the teachings of Jesus found in James. Some of what follows are actual parallels, some may be echoes, and others may result from a shared cultural and religious context.

- Joy in trials and persecution (James 1:2; Matt. 5:10-12)
- True followers of Christ persevere through trials (James 1:2-8; Matt. 7:24-27)
- Demand for perfection (James 1:4; Matt. 5:48)
- Command to ask God and it shall be given to you (James 1:5; Matt. 7:7-8)
- Asking in faith without doubting (James 1:6; Matt. 21:21)
- Rejection of dual eyes/double-mindedness (James 1:8; Matt. 6:22-24)
- Blessing of the poor, warning to the rich (James 1:9-10; Luke 6:20-24)
- Blessing upon those who persevere through trials (James 1:12; Matt. 10:22)
- Lust and the course of sin (James 1:13-15; Matt. 5:27-30)
- God as Father (James 1:17; Matt. 5:16 et al.)
- God as good and giver of good gifts (James 1:17; Matt. 7:9-11)
- Salvation as new birth from God (James 1:18; John 3:1-8)
- Unrighteousness of anger (James 1:20; Matt. 5:22)
- The Word as implanted as a seed (James 1:21; Matt. 13:1-13; 18-23)
- True follower of Christ hears and does (James 1:22-25; Matt. 7:24-27)
- Perfection and unity of the Law (James 1:25; Matt. 5:17-19)
- Obedient will be blessed in their doing (James 1:25; John 13:17)
- Condemnation of religious hypocrisy (James 1:26-27; Matt. 6:1-18)
- Danger of mere profession (James 1:26-27; Matt. 7:21-23)

- The poor as recipients of the kingdom (James 2:5; Matt. 5:3; Luke 6:20)

- Analogy of rich in faith toward God (James 2:5; Luke 12:21)

- Emphasis on love command in Leviticus 19:18 (James 2:8; Matt. 22:34-40)

- Perfection and unity of the Law (James 2:8-11; Matt. 5:17-19)

- Commandments against murder and adultery given in same order and in judgment context (James 2:8-11; Matt. 5:21-30)

- Seriousness of a seemingly small infraction of the Law (James 2:10; Matt. 5:19)

- A person's judging of others affects how God judges us (James 2:13; Matt. 7:1-2)

- Mercy shown to the merciful (James 2:13; Matt. 5:7; 18:21-35)

- Final salvation evidenced in feeding, clothing, and ministry to fellow believers (James 2:14-17; Matt. 25:34-46)

- Condemnation of religious hypocrisy (James 2:14-26; Matt. 6:1-18)

- Danger of mere profession (James 2:14-26; Matt. 7:21-23)

- True follower of Christ hears and does (James 2:14-26; Matt. 7:24-27)

- Judgment according to works (James 2:14-26; Matt. 16:27)

- Character depicted as fruit (James 3:10-18; Matt. 7:16-20)

- Fruit (figs and grapes) as consistent with type of tree/root (James 3:12; Matt. 7:16-19)

- Command to show good works (James 3:13; Matt. 5:16)

- Praise of meekness (James 3:13-18; Matt. 5:5)

- Praise of peacemaking (James 3:18; Matt. 5:9)

- Asking God in prayer and receiving (James 4:2-3; Matt. 7:7-8)

- Imagery of 'world' as evil sphere (James 4:4; John 15, et al.)

- Rejection of dual eyes/two masters/double-minded-ness (James 4:4-8; Matt. 6:22-24)
- Purity of heart (James 4:8; Matt. 5:8)
- Call for mourning (James 4:9; Matt. 5:4)
- Warning to those who laugh and call to 'mourn and weep' (James 4:9; Luke 6:25)
- Paradox of humility and exaltation (James 4:10; Matt. 23:12; Luke 14:11)
- Command against judging (James 4:11-12; Matt. 7:1)
- Transitory nature of life (James 4:13-16; Matt. 6:34)
- Judgment coming on the rich (James 5:1-6; Luke 6:24-25)
- Severe future judgment of wicked (James 5:1-6; Matt. 7:16-27)
- Decay (by moths and rust/corrosion) of stored-up wealth (James 5:2-4; Matt. 6:19-20)
- Expectation of non-resistance (James 5:1-6; Matt. 5:39)
- True follower of Christ perseveres through trials (James 5:7-11; Matt. 7:24-27)
- Expectation of the 'Parousia' or coming of the Lord (James 5:7-8; Matt. 24:3, 27, 37, 39)
- The coming of the Lord 'draws near' (same verb; James 5:8; Luke 21:28)
- Nearness of Jesus' coming as standing at the 'door' (James 5:9; Matt. 24:33)
- Prophets as examples of perseverance through trials (James 5:10-11; Matt. 5:12)
- Prohibition of oaths (James 5:12; Matt. 5:34-37)
- Elijah narrative and the three-and-one-half year drought (James 5:17; Luke 4:25)

In sum, it is hard to overestimate the influence of the teachings of Jesus on James' thought.

5. James and Paul

Discussion of the relationship between the teachings of James and Paul is normally dominated by the debates

surrounding the interpretation of James 2:14-26. These
debates typically center on what James meant by asserting
the centrality of faith and works in justification and
whether or not his views are compatible with those of the
apostle Paul. Indeed, upon initial glance a contradiction
seems inevitable. James 2:24 says, 'You see that a man is
justified by works and not by faith alone.' But Romans 3:28
says, 'For we hold that one is justified by faith apart from
the works of the law.' Is this a contradiction in Scripture?
Does James refute Paul's teaching on justification? What
are we to think about this apparent problem?

It is important to begin by recognizing that this issue
actually turns on three related but distinct questions.
First is the historical question: To what teaching is James
responding? In other words, is James addressing the
claims of Paul, a misunderstanding of Paul, or something
else altogether? Second is the theological question: What is
James actually teaching concerning justification, faith, and
works?[34] Third is the 'canonical question:' Are the teachings
of James and Paul compatible or inconsistent?[35] Too often
people begin by asking the canonical question. However,
New Testament theologian Adolf Schlatter appropriately
warns, 'It does not make any sense to compare James
to Paul before at least James has been understood.'[36] He
is right. Careful interpretive and theological method
requires that we explore the historical question first, then
the theological question, and only upon that foundation
are we capable of answering the canonical question. So we
will consider each question in order.

Three types of answers have been given to the historical
question. One view is that James is responding to Paul's
teaching concerning justification. We might call it the
'James vs. Paul' view. The great reformer Martin Luther is
the most well-known defender of this view. Focused so
intently on refuting the Roman Catholic Church's teaching
on salvation as connected to the church, sacraments, and

---

34. I owe some of this framework to Richard Bauckham, *James: Wisdom of
James, Disciple of Jesus the Sage* (London: Routledge, 1999), 119.

35. Bauckham, 119.

36. I here quote Bauckham, 119.

good works, Luther embraced Paul's teaching on justification but rejected that of James. Luther concluded that while John, Romans, Galatians, Ephesians, and 1 Peter '... show you Christ and teach you all that is necessary and salvatory for you to know.... St. James' epistle really is an epistle of straw, compared to these others, for it has nothing of the nature of the gospel about it.'[37] Luther even maintained that James 'is flatly against St. Paul and all the rest of Scripture in ascribing justification to works [2:24]. It says that Abraham was justified by his works... [2:21]; though in Romans 4 [:2-22] St. Paul teaches to the contrary that Abraham was justified apart from works, by his faith alone, before he had offered his son....'[38] The critical scholar F. C. Baur also represents this conflict view. Baur believed that James, a proponent of Jewish Christianity, stood opposed to Paul, the apostle to the Gentiles. According to this view, James' and Paul's teaching are contradictory and intentionally so. Thus, any attempt to harmonize them would be misguided.[39]

A second common response to the historical question is that James addresses people who have misunderstood Paul's view of justification by faith and have fallen into some sort of antinomianism, possibly over-emphasizing a believer's freedom in Christ to the point that obedience to Christ is not mandatory. This might be called the 'James vs. Paulinism' view. According to this view, there is no need to see a conflict between James and Paul because James does not have Paul's theology in mind. James is critiquing some who have taken Paul's idea and distorted it to the point

37. See *Martin Luther's Basic Theological Writings*, ed. Timothy F. Lull (Minneapolis: Fortress, 1989), 117. See also Timothy George, "A Right Strawy Epistle': Reformation Perspectives on James,' *The Southern Baptist Journal of Theology* 4:3 (Fall 2000): 20-31.

38. *Luther's Works: Word and Sacrament* (Philadelphia: Muhlenberg, 1960), 35:396.

39. Ibid. More recent scholars who follow this 'conflict' view include G. Lüdemann, M. Goulder, and M. Hengel. See G. Lüdemann, *Opposition to Paul in Jewish Christianity*, trans. M. E. Boring (Minneapolis: Fortress, 1989); M. Goulder, *A Tale of Two Missions* (London: SCM Press, 1994); M. Hengel, *The 'Hellenization' of Judaea in the First Century after Christ*, trans. J. Bowden (Philadelphia: Trinity Press International, 1989).

that good works are unnecessary in following Christ. Most holding to the 'James vs. Paulinism' view would seem to suggest a late date (enough time for followers of Paul to distort his teaching) and therefore a different author than James, the brother of Jesus.[40] John Piper, however, holds this position but maintains the traditional view of authorship and date. He suggests, 'James is not contradicting Paul here but teaching something compatible with Paul's teaching and correcting a misuse of Paul's teaching. Paul was very aware that his teaching of justification by faith alone was being distorted and misused....'[41] Piper refers to Romans 3:8; 5:20; 6:1; and Galatians 5:13 as examples of Paul's responses to such distortions. Paul had to regularly maintain that his understanding of grace leads to obedience and does not provide a license to sin.

The third major answer given to the historical question is that James speaks to an issue unrelated to Paul. We might call this the *'James without reference to Paul'* view. According to this view, James is addressing an issue from a different context than Paul. James' focus centers on the nature of genuine faith. People with genuine faith overcome trials, are doers of the Word, take care of the oppressed, control their speech, exemplify holy lives, are deeply interested in the poor, etc. James 2:14-26 follows this train of thought and shows that true faith not only offers verbal platitudes to the poor but actively expresses itself in works of love. This genuine faith is vindicated by corresponding works. Whereas James seeks to explain the nature of genuine faith, Paul addresses the salvation of the Gentiles. Paul seeks to protect the doctrine of grace and the truth that Gentiles can become Christians through faith in Christ and

40. See 'James in Context' for more on the issues related to date and authorship. Scholars who hold to this view include Leonard Goppelt, *Theology of the New Testament* (Grand Rapids: Eerdmans, 1982), 2:209; W. Marxsen, *Introduction to the New Testament* (Philadelphia: Fortress, 1970), 230-31; C. Leslie Mitton, *The Epistle of James* (Grand Rapids: Eerdmans, 1966), 8. I noticed these quotes first in Robert H. Stein, 'Saved by Faith [Alone]' in Paul Versus 'Not Saved by Faith Alone' in James,' *The Southern Baptist Journal of Theology* 4:3 (Fall 2000), 4-19.

41. John Piper, 'Does James Contradict Paul?' sermon delivered August 8, 1999. See www.desiringgod.org/library/sermons/99/080899.html.

not through good deeds or Jewish identity markers like circumcision, Sabbath-keeping, and food laws. Therefore, proponents of this view argue that apart from the verbal similarity between Paul and James (words like justified, faith, and works), there is actually very little contextual resemblance.[42]

Personally, I find the 'James vs. Paul' view too quick to suppose conflict. The historical acceptance of James as canonical, the theological importance of the unity of Scripture, and a hermeneutical rejection of the canon within the canon together preclude the 'James vs. Paul' view.[43] Furthermore, Luke recounts that Paul and James were in agreement on the issue of justification by faith, the full inclusion of the Gentile Christians, and the usage of Jewish regulations (Acts 15). In addition, if James was seeking to set Paul and his theology straight in terms of the Law and its requirements, then James surely failed to do so. He simply does not raise key issues that would be at the heart of such a dispute with Paul – the nature of circumcision, Sabbath-keeping, food laws, and other ceremonial laws. A careful reading of James and Paul shows that they are addressing different subjects and different false teachings.

The 'James vs. Paulinism' view is a potentially fruitful viewpoint. Acts 21:17-26 does indicate that James warned Paul that many misunderstood his view of the Law. It would not be hard to see how some would have extended that to Paul's teaching on justification. As Piper observed, Paul himself seems to recognize this possibility. Most teachers know the frustration of having a student or group of students who misinterpret, misquote, or distort their teachings. Sometimes their claims are assumed to be that of their teachers when in reality they are errors that need

---

42. Recent scholars who hold to a version of this view include Robert Stein, 4-19; Ronald Y. K. Fung, 'Justification' in the Epistle of James,' in *Right with God: Justification in the Bible and the World*, ed. D. A. Carson (Grand Rapids: Baker, 1992), 146-62; see also the commentaries by Davids, Johnson, and Adamson.

43. Attempts to employ a 'canon within the canon' are ultimately unhelpful. Though there may be a tendency for all interpreters to do this in some sense, it is important that other biblical writings be interpreted on their own account and not be understood primarily in light of Paul.

to be addressed. This view makes sense of the issues. Yet, as mentioned previously, if James was addressing even a distortion of Paul's doctrine of justification, then he did not address key issues like circumcision, Sabbath-keeping, and food laws which seem to be at the center of the tensions in Acts 15 and 21. This omission is conceivable if the distortions of Paul's view did not address such concerns.

So then the question must be raised: Is it necessary to suppose that James is responding to Paul or a distortion of his teachings? The two primary reasons some suppose this connection include the tradition set by Luther and the striking similarity in terminology. Concerning the tradition, Richard Bauckham laments that both the 'James vs. Paul' and the 'James vs. Paulinism' views require James to be interpreted 'in a historical position relative to Paul and Paulinism.'[44] He follows Luke Timothy Johnson who likewise complains that scholars continue to read what is different from Paul with primary reference given to Paul, rather than letting James and other such material stand as simply different in emphases.[45]

I would add that rather than having in view Paul or a distortion of Pauline theology, it would be more natural for James to be echoing the emphases of the Law, prophets, wisdom literature, and especially the teachings of Jesus. That would make more sense of the indicators that point to an early date of James' writing, as well as be more consistent with the other material found in James. Although the emphasis on faith and the necessity of corresponding obedience can be found in the Old Testament Law, prophets, and wisdom literature, for the sake of ease, just a quick glance at the teachings of Jesus shows how James likely is following his trajectory. The obedient will be blessed in their doing (James 1:25; John 13:17); true religion involves not only external observances but also a matter of full obedience, which includes the heart (James 1:26-27; Matt. 6:1-18); love of God and others is central to Christianity – believing the facts

44. Bauckham, 119.
45. Ibid. See also Johnson's commentary, 191.

are not enough (James 2:8; Matt. 22:34-40). Note especially how James 2:14-26 resembles the teaching of Jesus in that final salvation is evidenced in showing works of love for fellow believers (Matt. 25:34-46). It condemns religious hypocrisy (Matt. 6:1-18). It warns of a mere profession of faith that will not result in justification at the judgment (Matt. 7:21-23). It reminds readers that a true follower of Christ hears and obeys (Matt. 7:24-27). It envisions that judgment will be according to works (Matt. 16:27). It also displays Jesus' teaching that fruit will evidence one's faith (Matt. 7:16-20).

What about the remarkable similarity in terminology between James and Paul? Further, what about the reference to Abraham in both of their arguments? New Testament scholar Robert Stein has most helpfully addressed the differences in terminology.[46] He looks at how James and Paul use 'faith/believe' as well as 'works.' He notes that James employs the noun 'faith' sixteen times – five outside this passage (1:3, 6; 2:1, 5; 5:15) and the rest in 2:14-26. The verb form 'believe' is only used three times in James – all three times in 2:14-26. It is interesting to note that, with the exceptions of its usage in 2:14-26, faith in James always has a positive meaning: faith during trials (1:3), praying in faith (1:6; 5:15), faith in Christ (2:1), and the poor as rich in faith (2:5). Genuine faith is being assumed in these passages. Faith is more than intellectual assent to doctrinal truths but includes an element of personal trust and commitment to God.[47] When James treats 'faith' in 2:14-26, however, he is engaging a real or imaginary opponent (this argumentation is called a 'diatribe') over the nature of faith. That James differs over the nature of faith with this opponent is clear when each reference to faith in the passage is noted, as Stein helpfully lists:

2:14a It is a faith that possesses no works;

2:14b It is a faith that cannot save;

46. Stein, 5-8.
47. Ibid.

2:17   It is a faith without works that is dead;

2:18a It is a faith that is distinct and separate from works;

2:18b It is a faith that is contrasted with works;

2:18c It is contrasted with a faith shown by works;

2:20   It is a faith without works that is useless;

2:22a It is contrasted with a faith that works along with works;

2:22b It is contrasted with a faith perfected as a result of works;

2:24   It is a faith that is alone; and

2:26   It is a faith without works that is dead.[48]

This can also be seen in James' usage of 'believe' (a cognate of faith):

2:19a It is assent to the biblical proposition that God is one;

2:19b It is a kind of faith that even demons possess; and

2:23   It is contrasted with the kind of faith Abraham possessed.[49]

It is clear that we must distinguish between 'faith' as understood by James and the kind of 'faith' envisioned by James' opponent. James considers this opposing view of faith as bogus. True faith includes intellectual assent to truths, but also includes personal trust and manifests itself in obedience to God as well as acts of mercy toward others.

This view of genuine faith in James actually resembles Paul's view very closely. For Paul, faith is a wholehearted trust in Christ for salvation.[50] Faith in Christ is not merely believing truths about Christ, but is relational and includes personal commitment to Jesus and His ways. Justification is by faith and leads to a life of obedience. Those claiming

---

48. Ibid.
49. Ibid.
50. Ibid.

faith in Jesus while remaining in a life of sin are vehemently attacked by Paul (Rom. 6:1). In fact, Paul asserts the 'obedience of faith' (Rom. 1:5) and the necessity of 'faith working through love' (Gal. 5:6).

Not only does a careful examination of the use of 'faith' in James show that James is not responding to a truly Pauline understanding of faith, but a look at the usage of 'works' enables us to interpret this matter better as well. James mentions 'works' fifteen times – twelve times in 2:14-26 and three other times (1:4 – linked with endurance; 1:25 – linked with doing and not only hearing the word; and 3:13 – linked with good behavior characteristic of wisdom).[51] Stein concludes: 'It should be noted that in 2:14-26, and in the rest of James, 'works' are always seen positively and, when described, involve acts of loving mercy, kindness, and obedience to God.... They have nothing to do with ritualistic or ceremonial actions.'[52]

The apostle Paul normally does not use 'works' in this way. When Paul uses some form of 'works' in conjunction with his teachings related to justification, he contrasts them with faith and grace. For Paul in that context, 'works' typically refer to trying to gain a right standing before God. Used in this way, these 'works' are not justifying (Rom. 3:20), seek to make God a debtor in giving salvation (Rom. 4:2), and undermine the gracious nature of salvation (Rom. 11:6).[53] Sometimes Paul also refers to the 'works of the law' and in doing so often refers to circumcision, Sabbath-keeping, food laws, and other ritualistic/ceremonial laws. Opposing the Judaizers, Paul maintains that Gentiles can become Christians apart from performing these Jewish ceremonies and regulations. Thus, Paul critiques 'works' when he argues that salvation is based on the grace of God and the atoning death and resurrection of Christ. We receive salvation as a gift from God, through faith, not because of works.

---

51. Ibid.
52. Ibid., 7.
53. Ibid.

But Paul also clearly teaches that salvation issues in good works. It is helpful to note Paul's understanding of works in Ephesians 2:8-10: 'For by grace you have been saved through faith. And this is not your own doing; it is the gift of God, not a result of works, so that no one may boast. For we are his workmanship, created in Christ Jesus for good works, which God prepared beforehand, that we should walk in them.' Notice the two ways 'works' is used in this passage. First, it is not the way of receiving salvation. Salvation is by grace through faith. It is not based on our efforts and is not a result of our works. Yet, salvation issues in 'good works,' which are indicative of Christian living and eternally planned by God. So for Paul are good works necessary in salvation? Yes and no. They are not the means of receiving salvation. God graciously gives salvation through faith. But true faith issues in good works, love, fruit, and obedience to Christ.

Using similar evidence, Peter Davids maintains that James and Paul are addressing completely different subjects:

> Paul is justifying the reception of Gentiles into the church without circumcision whereas James is discussing the problem of the failure of works of charity within the church (which may be totally Jewish). If James intends to contradict Paul, he has so misunderstood him that his use of biblical citations and the meanings of similar expressions are totally different. This would hardly indicate he had read Romans.[54]

Because the verbal similarity between Paul and James does not also display itself in similar uses of the terms themselves, it appears unnecessary to posit that James was responding to Paul or to a distortion of his teaching. But the careful reader may ask: what about the appeal to Abraham in both accounts? Does that not point to James as responding to Paul or a distortion of him? Richard Bauckham helpfully addresses this question at length. He suggests, 'That James uses the example of Abraham to prove his point is not surprising but virtually predictable, since for Second Temple Judaism Abraham was *par excellence*

---

54. Davids (NIGNT), 131.

the exemplar of faith in God.'[55] Bauckham continues, 'God had already declared Abraham righteous on account of his faith in Genesis 15:6, but this verdict was confirmed when his faith is tested and proves itself in Genesis 22.'[56] Bauckham concludes:

> James' account of Abraham's faith and works would close-ly follow established Jewish interpretation, adopting key terminology already used in that discussion, which James only needs to apply to the particular issue he addresses. Paul would be dependent on the same Jewish exegetical tradition with reference to Abraham, but more creatively adopts the terminology to make a different point: that Abraham was already justified by faith in the promise before he obeyed the commandment of circumcision and became the forerunner of specifically Jewish works. This hypothesis, that James and Paul are both continuing, in their different ways, a Jewish exegetical discussion of Abraham's faith, ac-counts for the parallels and differences between them more satisfactorily than postulating a direct relationship between them.[57]

Bauckham's case is persuasive. It seems then that the 'James without reference to Paul' view is the most compelling response to the historical question. The question then follows: to what is James responding?

One promising answer to this question might be that James expands on the thought begun in 2:1-13. Thus, James would be warning the believers not to court the wealthy or give such credibility to the faith of the rich who participate in their community. James would be giving a caution: the rich (and others) who offer empty words to the oppressed Christians without also meeting their tangible needs are displaying a lack of love, and therefore a lack of faith. True faith issues itself in good works – which James especially characterizes as deeds of mercy. This would also make sense of the heroes of Abraham and Rahab, depicted as people who are generous.[58]

---

55. Bauckham, 122.
56. Ibid., 123.
57. Ibid., 131.

Another strong possibility is that James simply continues his overall call for consistency in the church and the Christian life. He would be addressing a practical heresy. Bauckham posits the following scenario:

> [W]e need only suppose that James was aware of the danger that some of his readers, complacently priding themselves on their monotheistic belief, neglected practical works of charity. They need not have professed the doctrinal view that their faith was sufficient to justify them, but they behaved as though this were the case. So James voices for them the theological claim that could express their attitude and behavior in order to show them that these cannot be defended.[59]

Thus, the context would be understood more broadly and as essentially the same as that of the rest of James. Such a practical heresy is perennial – people often fail to live out what they claim to believe. The Old Testament Law, History, Prophets, and Wisdom Literature all frequently address this common concern. Jesus targeted this recurrent problem as well (e.g. Matt. 25:35-46).

Addressing the historical question is important but we still need to consider the theological question: What is James actually teaching in 2:14-26? Since the commentary section has addressed this at length, I will offer a summary. James teaches that true faith includes intellectual assent to truths, but also includes personal trust and manifests itself in obedience to God as well as acts of mercy toward others. Orthodox theology is important but insufficient. Genuine followers of Christ not only hear the Word, they do it; they not only claim to have faith, their lives reflect it in their walk with God and with their deeds of love for the oppressed.

With that in mind, the canonical question can be appropriately addressed: are the teachings of James and Paul compatible or contradictory? The answer to this question falls into place now that the historical and theological questions have been appropriately addressed. James

58. Davids maintains that Abraham and Rahab are both depicted by Jewish tradition as examples of charity. See Davids (NIGNT), 132-33.
59. Bauckham, 125-26.

and Paul are not inconsistent. They are not contradictory but complementary. James and Paul speak to different church problems in different church contexts. Both messages need to be heard today. When we are tempted to assume we are Christians but consistently fail to follow Christ's commands, James reminds us that true faith leads to obeying God and loving others. When we are tempted to suppose that we can contribute to our salvation, Paul reminds us that salvation is through the atoning death of Christ, is by grace alone, and is received by faith alone (i.e. a personal trust in and commitment to) in Jesus Christ. Thus, Paul cautions us to remember that we are saved by God's grace and not because of anything we contribute, and James urges that true Christians follow Christ's teachings and love others.

Bibliography

Adamson, James B. *James: The Man and His Message*. Grand Rapids: Eerdmans, 1989.

_____. *The Epistle of James*. New International Commentary on the New Testament. Grand Rapids: Eerdmans, 1976.

Baker, William R. "Above All Else': Contexts of the Call for Verbal Integrity in James 5:12.' *Journal for the Study of the New Testament* 54 (1994): 165-94.

_____. *Personal Speech-Ethics in the Epistle of James*. Tubingen: Mohr, 1995.

Bauckham, Richard. *James: Wisdom of James, Disciple of Jesus the Sage*. London: Routledge, 1999.

Burns, John A. 'James, the Wisdom of Jesus.' *Criswell Theological Review* 1:1 (Fall 1986): 113-36.

Cargal, T. B. *Restoring the Diaspora: Discursive Structure and Purpose in the Epistle of James*. Atlanta: Scholars Press, 1993.

Chester, Andrew, and Ralph P. Martin, *The Theology of the Letters of James, Peter, and Jude*. New Testament Theology. Cambridge: Cambridge University Press, 1994.

Cheung, Luke L. *The Genre, Composition, and Hermeneutics of James*. Waynesboro, GA: Paternoster, 2003.

Church, C. L. 'A Forschungsgeschichte on the Literary Character of the Epistle of James.' Ph.D. diss., The Southern Baptist Theological Seminary, 1990.

Davids, Peter H. 'James and Jesus.' In *Gospel Perspectives: The Jesus Tradition Outside the Gospels*. Edited by David Wenham. Sheffield: JSOT, 1985, 63-84.

_____. *The Epistle of James*. New International Greek New Testament Commentary. Grand Rapids: Eerdmans, 1982.

_____. 'The Tradition and Citation in the Epistle of James.' In *Scripture, Tradition, and Interpretation*. Edited by W. Ward Gasque and William Sanford LaSor. Grand Rapids: Eerdmans, 1978, 113-26.

Dibelius, Martin. *A Commentary on the Epistle of James.* Hermeneia. Revised by Heinrich Greeven. Philadelphia: Fortress, 1976.

Dockery, David S. 'True Piety in James: Ethical Admonitions and Theological Implications.' *Criswell Theological Review* 1:1 (Fall 1986): 51-70.

Francis, Fred. O. 'The Form and Function of the Opening and Closing Paragraphs of James and 1 John.' *Zeitschrift für die neutestamentliche Wissenschaft* 61 (1970): 110-26.

Fung, Ronald Y. K. 'Justification' in the Epistle of James.' In *Right with God: Justification in the Bible and the World.* Edited by D. A. Carson. Grand Rapids: Baker, 1992, 146-62.

George, Timothy. "A Right Strawy Epistle': Reformation Perspectives on James.' *The Southern Baptist Journal of Theology* 4:3 (Fall 2000): 20-31.

Halson, B. R. 'The Epistle of James: Christian Wisdom?' *Studia Evangelica* 4 (1968): 308-14.

Hartin, P. J. *James and the Sayings of Jesus.* JSNT 47. Sheffield: JSOT, 1991.

Hiebert, D. Edmond. *The Epistle of James: Tests of a Living Faith.* Chicago: Moody, 1979.

Hort, F. J. A. *The Epistle of St. James.* London: Macmillan, 1909.

Howard, Tracy L. 'Suffering in James 1:2-12.' *Criswell Theological Review* 1:1 (Fall 1986): 71-84.

Hubbard, David A. 'Wisdom,' in *The Illustrated Bible Dictionary,* ed. J. D. Douglas (Downers Grove, IL: InterVarsity, 1980), 1650.

Johnson, Luke Timothy. 'Friendship with the World/Friendship with God: A Study of Discipleship in James.' In *Discipleship in the New Testament.* Edited by Fernando F. Segovia. Philadelphia: Fortress, 1985, 166-83.

_____. *The Letter of James.* The Anchor Bible. New York: Doubleday, 1995.

_____. 'The Use of Leviticus 19 in the Letter of James.' *Journal of Biblical Literature* 101:3 (1982): 391-401.

Keener, Craig. *The IVP Bible Background Commentary.* Downers Grove, IL: InterVarsity, 1993.

Kirk, J. A. 'The Meaning of Wisdom in James: Examination of a Hypothesis.' *New Testament Studies* 16 (1969): 24-38.

Knowling, R. J. *The Epistle of St. James.* London: Westminster Commentaries, 1904.

Laws, Sophie. *A Commentary on the Epistle of James*. New York: Harper & Row, 1980.

Lea, Thomas D. *Hebrews and James*. Holman New Testament Commentary. Nashville: Broadman & Holman, 1999.

Loh, I-Jin, and Howard A. Hatton, *A Handbook on the Letter from James*. UBS Handbook Series. New York: United Bible Societies, 1997.

MacArthur, Jr., John. *James*. Chicago: Moody, 1998.

Mahony, John W. 'An Introduction to the Epistle of James.' *Mid-America Theological Journal* 10:1 (Spring 1986): 1-10.

_____. 'The Origin of Jacobean Thought.' Ph.D. diss., Mid-America Baptist Theological Seminary, 1982.

Manton, Thomas. *An Exposition of the Epistle of James*. Edinburgh: Banner of Truth, reprint, 1962.

Martin, Ralph P. *James*. Word Biblical Commentary. Waco: Word, 1988.

Mayor, J. B. *The Epistle of St. James*. 2d ed. London: Macmillan, 1913.

McCartney, Dan G. 'The Wisdom of James the Just.' *The Southern Baptist Journal of Theology* 4 (Fall 2000): 52-64.

Melick, Jr., Richard R. 'Warnings and Instructions.' *Mid-America Theological Journal* 10:1 (Spring 1986): 51-76.

Millikin, Jimmy A. 'Trials and Temptations.' *Mid-America Theological Journal* 10:1 (Spring 1986): 11-30.

Mitton, Leslie. *The Epistle of James*. Grand Rapids: Eerdmans, 1966.

Moo, Douglas J. *James*. Tyndale New Testament Commentaries. Grand Rapids: Eerdmans, 1985.

_____. *The Letter of James*. Pillar New Testament Commentary. Grand Rapids: Eerdmans, 2000.

Morris, Leon, and Donald W. Burdick. *Hebrews, James*. Expositor's Bible Commentary. Grand Rapids: Zondervan, 1996.

Motyer, J. Alec. *The Message of James*. The Bible Speaks Today. Edited by J. Alec Motyer and John R. W. Stott. Downers Grove: InterVarsity, 1985.

Nystrom, David P. *James*. The NIV Application Commentary. Grand Rapids: Zondervan, 1997.

Oesterley, W. E. *The General Epistle of James*. The Expositor's Greek Testament. Edited by Robertson Nicoll. Grand Rapids: Eerdmans, 1967.

Penner, Todd C. *The Epistle of James and Eschatology: Rereading an Ancient Christian Letter*. JSNTS. Sheffield: Sheffield Academic Press, 1996.

Plummer, Alfred. *The General Epistles of St. James and St. Jude*. Hartford: Scranton, 1903.

Rakestraw, Robert V. 'James 2:14-26: Does James Contradict the Pauline Soteriology?' *Criswell Theological Review* 1:1 (Fall 1986): 31-50.

Reicke, Bo. *The Epistles of James, Peter, and Jude*. The Anchor Bible. Garden City, NY: Doubleday, 1964.

Richardson, Kurt A. *James*. New American Commentary. Broadman & Holman, 1997.

Robertson, A. T. *Studies in the Epistle of James*. Nashville: Broadman & Holman, n.d.

_____. *Word Pictures*. Vol. 6, *General Epistles and Revelation*. Grand Rapids: Baker, 1933.

Ropes, James Hardy. *A Critical and Exegetical Commentary on the Epistle of St. James*. Edited by Alfred Plummer and Francis Brown. Edinburgh: T & T Clark, 1916.

Sadler, M. F. *The General Epistles of Saints James, Peter, John, and Jude*. London: Bell, 1899.

Scaer, David P. *James, The Apostle of Faith: A Primary Christological Epistle for the Persecuted Church*. St. Louis: Concordia, 1994.

Scott, R. B. Y. *The Way of Wisdom*. New York: Macmillan, 1971.

Seifrid, Mark A. 'The Waiting Church and Its Duty: James 5:13-18.' *The Southern Baptist Journal of Theology* 4:3 (Fall 2000): 32-39.

Shepherd, Massey H. 'The Epistle of James and the Gospel of Matthew.' *Journal of Biblical Literature* 75 (Winter 1956): 40-51.

Sloan, Robert B. 'The Christology of James.' *Criswell Theological Review* 1:1 (Fall 1986): 3-30.

Stein, Robert H. ''Saved by Faith [Alone]' in Paul Versus 'Not Saved by Faith Alone' in James.' *The Southern Baptist Journal of Theology* 4:3 (Fall 2000): 4-19.

Storms, Sam. *Pleasures Evermore: The Life-Changing Power of Enjoying God* (Colorado Springs, CO: NavPress, 2000), 247.

Stott, John R. W. *Men with a Message: An Introduction to the New Testament and Its Writers*. Revised by Stephen Motyer. Grand Rapids: Eerdmans, 1994.

Stulac, George M. *James*. IVP New Testament Commentary. Downers Grove: InterVarsity, 1993.

Tasker, R. V. G. *The General Epistle of James.* Tyndale New Testament Commentary. Grand Rapids: Eerdmans, 1957.

Taylor, Mark E., and George H. Guthrie, 'The Structure of James,' *Catholic Biblical Quarterly* 68 (2006): 681-705.

Taylor, Mark E. 'Recent Scholarship on the Structure of James.' *Currents in Biblical Research* 3 (2004): 86-115.

_____. *A Text-linguistic Investigation into the Discourse Structure of James.* London: T & T Clark, 2006.

Tidball, Derek. *Wisdom from Heaven: The Message of the Letter of James for Today.* Fearn, Scotland: Christian Focus, 2003.

Walker, Larry L. 'Speech and Wisdom (James 3).' *Mid-America Theological Journal* 10:1 (Spring 1986): 43-50.

Wall, Robert W. *Community of the Wise: The Letter of James.* The New Testament in Context. Valley Forge: Trinity Press International, 1997.

_____. 'James, Letter of.' In *Dictionary of Later New Testament and Its Developments.* Edited by Ralph P. Martin and Peter H. Davids. Downers Grove: InterVarsity, 1997.

Wells, C. Richard. 'The Theology of Prayer in James.' *Criswell Theological Review* 1:1 (Fall 1986): 85-112.

Wiersbe, Warren. *Be Mature: An Expository Study of the Epistle of James* (Wheaton, IL: Victor, 1982), 35.

Williams, R. R. 'The Letters of John and James.' *The Cambridge Bible Commentary.* Cambridge: Cambridge University Press, 1965.

Subject Index

Scripture Index

Acts(cont.)

10:38.....................95
10:42....................182
11:19f......................38
11:28.......................23
11:30....................195
12:1-2.....................21
12:17.......................17
13:33....................194
15 ....17–18, 135,
.................242, 243
15:2 195
15:13-21 19
15:23-29 19
17:16....................179
17:31....................182
18:18....................199
18:21....................163
20:17....................195
21 243
21:17-26...............18, 242
21:18-25...................135
21:20....................133
21:23....................199
26:5.......................84
27:37.................119, 120
28:27....................202

Romans

1:5 246
2:11 91
3:8 241
3:16 168
3:20 246
3:24 103
3:28 ....109, 239
4:2 246
4:2-22 240
4:3 111
4:11 110
5:1-5 ....43, 46
5:20 241
6:1 ....241, 246
6:23 ....67, 71
8:2 100
8:28 ......44, 46, 184, 186
9:16 186
11:6 246
11:30....................186
11:32....................186
12:1 186
12:9 137
13:9 174
14:4 157
15:9 186

1 Corinthians

2:14 134
3 192
3:3 133
3:13 170
4:4-5 157
4:19 163
6:6 137
8:6 127
12 120
12:9 200
13:6 122
14:26.....................194
15:3-8 16
15:23....................179
15:36....................109
15:44....................134
15:46....................134
16:7 163

2 Corinthians

1:3 ....64, 186
1:3-7 47
5:9 98
5:10 101
5:17 ....72, 150
7:10 153
12:9 201
12:20....................133

Galatians

1:13 132
1:18-19 17
2:1-16 18
2:9 17
2:16-18 103
3:6 111
3:10 98
3:11 103
5:6 246
5:13 241
5:17 148
5:20 133
5:22-23 ....180, 193
6:1 206
6:9 165

Ephesians

1:3 49
1:7 94
1:13 72
1:17 64
2:1-3 67
2:4 186

2:6 94
2:8-9 94
2:8-10 247
4:11 117
4:26 78
4:30 95
5:8 ....71n13
5:19 194
5:24-25 146
6:9 91
6:10-20 151

Philippians

2:3 136
2:15 87
2:19 163
2:24 163
3:20 179

Colossians

1:15 72
2:3 137
2:18 84
3:25 91

1 Thessalonians

2:19 179
3:13 ....179, 180
4:15 179
5:11-27 187
5:23 179

2 Thessalonians

2:1 179
2:10 122
2:14 94
8:2 179

1 Timothy

3:3 136
5:6 173
5:10 165
6:9-10 89

2 Timothy

2:9 193
3:1 171
3:12 47
4:1 182
4:8 182

Titus

2:11-13 179
3:2 136

1 KINGS

THE WISDOM AND THE FOLLY

DALE RALPH DAVIS

1 Kings
The Wisdom and the Folly

Dale Ralph Davis

'...this exposition enables the contemporary reader to breathe the air of 1 Kings, re-live its challenges, and above all, to encounter the personally the God who speaks and acts throughout its pages. This is a book to unsettle spiritual complacency and challenge us to a deep integrity in our relationship with the living God.'

David Jackman

'Robust – that's the word ...a robust understanding, defence, explanation and application of 1 Kings as the Word of God. Here is no "1 Kings in my own words" – the boring, fruitless fate of most commentaries on Bible History – but a delicious feast of truth, proof that the ancients were right to call the historians "prophets".'

Alec Motyer

'The range of scholarship is extraordinary (is there any learned book or paper on 1 Kings that this writer has not winkled out?), His humour and humanity, plus a priceless American-style turn of phrase, add relish to the dish. Here is a safe and strong pair of hands to guide new, and older, readers through the treasure – and the uninspiring bits – of 1 Kings.'

Dick Lucas

Dale Ralph Davis is pastor of Woodland Presbyterian Church, Hattiesburg, Mississippi. Previously he was Professor of Old Testament at Reformed Theological Seminary.

ISBN 978-1-84550-251-5

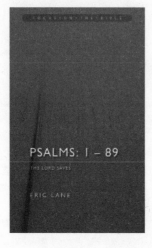

Christian Focus Publications

publishes books for all ages

Our mission statement –

STAYING FAITHFUL
In dependence upon God we seek to help make His infallible Word, the Bible, relevant. Our aim is to ensure that the Lord Jesus Christ is presented as the only hope to obtain forgiveness of sin, live a useful life and look forward to heaven with Him.

REACHING OUT
Christ's last command requires us to reach out to our world with His gospel. We seek to help fulfil that by publishing books that point people towards Jesus and help them develop a Christ-like maturity. We aim to equip all levels of readers for life, work, ministry and mission.

Books in our adult range are published in three imprints.

Christian Focus contains popular works including biographies, commentaries, basic doctrine and Christian living. Our children's books are also published in this imprint.

Mentor focuses on books written at a level suitable for Bible College and seminary students, pastors, and other serious readers. The imprint includes commentaries, doctrinal studies, examination of current issues and church history.

Christian Heritage contains classic writings from the past.

Christian Focus Publications Ltd
Geanies House, Fearn,
Ross-shire, IV20 1TW, Scotland, United Kingdom
info@christianfocus.com

Our titles are available from quality bookstores and
www.christianfocus.com